OUT OF BONDAGE

OUT OF BONDAGE

THE STORY OF

ELIZABETH BENTLEY

THE DEVIN-ADAIR COMPANY
NEW YORK : 1951

OUT OF BONDAGE

CHAPTER I

As the S.S. *Vulcania* sailed into New York Harbor that July day in 1934, I leaned on the deck rail and looked at the skyline wistfully. It was good to be back in my own country after a year's study in Italy, I thought, and yet what, really, was I coming back to? I had no home, no family. Nor was there much prospect of finding a teaching position. From all that I had heard abroad, the economic situation in the United States had not greatly improved. True, I still had some money left from my father's estate but that would not last too long. Somehow I must find a way to earn my living. Standing there on the deck, I felt alone and frightened.

By September, the future looked even gloomier. After days of wearing out shoe leather and nights of writing letters of application, I realized that the possibility of my getting back into the teaching field was remote. Nor did there seem to be any other positions for which I was qualified. All those years of academic study have been wasted, I thought bitterly. There doesn't seem to be any place in the world for young professionals like myself. Then I grimly determined to make the best of a bad situation. I enrolled in the Columbia University business school, took a cheap furnished room in the neighborhood, and settled down to learn shorthand and typing. After six months of this, I would be in line for a secretarial job.

Yet I was haunted by the problem of our maladjusted economic system. Although I was only in my mid-twenties, I had already seen two depressions, the second worse than the first. Each had left in its wake suffering, starvation, and broken lives. What lay ahead of us now, I wondered. Complete chaos? That was possible but not for long. Chaos would undoubtedly be succeeded by a Fascist state. I shivered at the prospect. A year of living under Mussolini's regime had left me with no great love for Fascism. There must be some other way out, I thought, some plan that would insure a just world where men could live and work like human beings. But what? I didn't know.

At this critical juncture I became friendly with a girl who had a room down the hall from me. Her name was Lee Fuhr. She was a nurse taking courses at Teachers' College of Columbia University in order to get an academic degree. Shorter than I, square and solid, with yellow hair and blue eyes that betrayed her Dutch ancestry, she gave the impression of being very sturdy and independent. I felt that Lee had a definite goal in life and was heading toward it, unswervingly.

Her life, it seemed, had not been an easy one. Coming from quite a poor family, she had spent her teens working long hours at very little pay in the cotton mills of New Jersey. That, I realized, must have been very hard and unpleasant work. I remembered vividly the time that a group of Gastonia strikers had come to solicit funds at Vassar and their horrible description of conditions then prevalent in the textile industry. Compared to her I had been very fortunate, I thought. True, my parents had never been very well off, but at least I hadn't had to work during my high-school days—except, of course, to earn spending money.

Lee, it turned out, had always been determined to be a nurse. By working hard and saving her money, she had finally managed to go to nursing school and get her R.N. degree. She married soon after, but her husband had died while she was carrying her first child. Undismayed, she had gone back to nursing, managing not only to support herself and Mary Lee but also to put aside enough to tide her over a year at Teachers' College. It had always been the dream of her life, she said, to have a college degree. With that behind her, she could get into public health work.

Lee's glowing enthusiasm made me feel as if, in a way, I were reliving my own past. As far back as I could remember, I had passionately wanted a good college education so that I could one day become a school teacher, as my mother had been before her marriage. To that end, I had studied very hard—even given up many of my outside activities—in order to qualify for the necessary scholarship at Vassar College. Yet, in my case, had it been worth it? I hoped desperately that Lee wouldn't be disappointed, as I had been. After all her struggles it would be a pity if the prized diploma were just one more piece of paper to hang on the wall.

As I got to know Lee better, I began to realize she was one of the most unselfish people I had ever known. Her own difficult life, instead of making her callous, seemed on the contrary to have heightened her innate sympathy for other human beings. To everyone in trouble she gave unstintingly of her time, money, and understanding. She reminds me of my mother, I thought. She, too, had been uninhibitedly friendly and ready to help others in time of need. I remembered that when anyone on our block had been ill, Mother had been the first one there to cook dinner and clean the house. Our house, too, had always been cluttered up with lonely people whom she, despite our meager budget, had invited in for a "home" meal.

I often wondered just why it was that Lee, in spite of her unhappy experiences in the textile mills, was not more cynical. Yet she would always say that although people were suffering and starving today, all this would be different in the future. How this was to be done, she didn't at first tell me—indeed she gave very evasive answers to my direct questions—yet from some of her vague remarks I knew she was spending a great deal of her time working with groups that were helping to relieve poverty. Once or twice she even took me to large benefit parties given by groups whose names I have now forgotten but which at the time sounded like highly humanitarian organizations.

As time went on, I told her about my experiences in Italy and she was very much interested. My first-hand impressions had, she said, only confirmed her belief that Fascism was an ugly and dangerous thing. Moreover, she, too, seemed to be worried about the possibility of the United States becoming Fascist. Human misery was bad enough now, she agreed, but under that sort of regime it would be ten times worse. In fact, she said, she then belonged to an organization which was trying to enlighten the American people about the evils of Fascism and Nazism. The name of it was the American League Against War and Fascism. Why didn't I come over to one of their meetings at Teachers' College and listen to the proceedings? Not only would I be interested myself to learn what Americans were doing in a practical way to prevent Fascism from coming to this country, but I could contribute to the work of the group by telling them what I personally had seen over there.

[6]

I had never heard of the American League Against War and Fascism, but its title, its program, and the list of people sponsoring it were impressive. Certainly, I thought, every decent person ought to hate both these evils and be willing to do something to prevent their coming to pass. One man alone, or even a handful of them, could do nothing; an organization of this size, however, especially when it included well-known molders of public opinion, such as religious leaders, writers, and professors, could probably exert a considerable influence. I felt suddenly that Lee had given me a breath of new hope. Here, evidently, was a group of people who not only thought as I did but were willing to do something about the situation. Enthusiastically I told her I would be glad to go to a meeting.

The Teachers' College branch of the League seemed to be composed mainly of graduate students and professors, with a scattering of people from the neighborhood.

When the meeting began, I listened intently as they animatedly discussed the work they had done and their plans for the future. I was impressed by their single-mindedness of purpose and their intense energy—they look like the sort of people who would really get things accomplished, I thought. Some of my own discouragement began to ebb away as their optimism and fervor communicated itself to me. I decided suddenly that I would join the organization and do what I could to help the anti-Fascist cause.

Surprisingly enough, from then on my life took on a new zest. I seemed to have cast off the old feeling of listlessness and despair. As I threw myself ardently into the work of fighting Fascism, I found that my own personal problems faded further and further into the background. Sometimes, indeed, I even forgot to think about them.

[7]

When I did remember, they no longer seemed to have cosmic importance. Perhaps you don't have too much of a personal future, I would say to myself, but at least, with your small efforts, you are contributing to a worthwhile cause.

Then, too, in the small group of League members in Teachers' College I found a circle of friends, warm and hospitable. They welcomed me casually and easily, as if they had known me all their lives, and soon I found myself dropping into their homes in the evening for a chat, or shopping or going to the movies with them. I felt no embarrassment at not being well-off financially. There were, I discovered, others in the same predicament, only instead of being ashamed of their pennilessness, they accepted it as a fact and made no pretenses. Even those who were well-off lived simply and unpretentiously. Money, to them, seemed to be something that was nice to have but didn't have much importance either in their way of life or in their judgments of people.

As I came to know them better, I realized that they, too, like Lee were generous and genuinely kind under all circumstances. They seemed to have a heartfelt concern for the welfare of other human beings. At first I attributed this to the fact that many of them came from small towns where neighborliness is taken for granted; then I discovered that it rose more from their profound belief in the essential brotherhood of man. This explained, too, their curious lack of the usual prejudices against people of another religion, race, or color. They seemed to have no interest in whether a man was Protestant or Catholic, Jew or Gentile, Negro or White.

Often I couldn't quite figure out what made them tick,

and close as I was to them I sometimes felt there was a wall between us. What was it, I wondered. Was it because, for no reason that I could put my finger on, they had achieved an inner sureness that I lacked? They seemed to have found a philosophy of life that left them with no doubts and no torments; they were moving steadily and unswervingly, yet with unflagging ardor, toward some final goal which I didn't quite understand. Struggling as I was in confusion, I found myself alternately irritated and envious. What had they found that I hadn't—and how had they been able to do it?

This same outlook on life, I discovered, seemed to prevail in other parts of the League. Certainly it was general in the New York City office, where I was now spending a good share of my time. I had gone down there originally when Lee Fuhr suggested that I might be able to help them in research work on Italian Fascism. They were terribly short-handed, she said, and besides they had no person who was an authority on Italy.

My first sight of the office, located in the third-floor loft of a building on Fourth Avenue, had been a distinct shock. It's certainly a fire trap, I said to myself, as I climbed the rickety wooden stairs and, panting for breath, stood in the doorway. The interior was even less prepossessing—dirty and dusty—and what few windows there were looked as though they could stand a good washing. A small part of the front section had been partitioned off to make two offices, each containing a battered desk and two or three chairs. The remainder, with the exception of a very crude mimeograph office in the rear, stretched emptily back— broken only by two long plank tables, flanked by wooden benches, and vast stacks of literature strewn about the floor.

[9]

There seemed to be no provision for proper lighting; two or three light bulbs, unshaded, hung from the ceiling on long cords.

I had been half inclined to walk out again, but a short, stocky man with brown hair and a turned-up nose had looked up from tying a bundle of papers and had bustled over.

"Come on in," he said cheerily, "and don't mind the mess. We don't have the money to spend on fancy fronts."

I soon found myself forgetting the shabbiness of the office and getting interested in the work to be done. I was introduced to a lean, dark, determined-looking woman who emerged from one of the offices. She was, it turned out, Pauline Rogers, executive secretary of the city office of the League.

"This is Harold Patch," she said, waving to the short, stocky man, "one of the editors of our publication *Fight*. He'll take you under his wing and see that you find yourself at home."

Patch impressed me as a rather odd character but a thoroughly likable one. He was dressed shabbily and rarely seemed to have enough money to buy proper food, but it never seemed to affect his good spirits nor did it hamper his enthusiastic capacity for doing immense quantities of work. This attitude, strangely enough, was shared by all the other staff members; they never seemed to be upset about living on the ragged edge of poverty—indeed, they joked about it continually.

Patch was a voluble soul; as he worked, he chattered incessantly. Before long I had found out that, despite his mere twenty-five years, he had drifted in and out of quite a number of assorted political organizations, including the Anarchists and the Socialists and a few odd ones like the American Association for the Advancement of Atheism.

Unaware of what I was putting my foot into, I said jokingly one day, "Haven't you ever tried the Communist Party?"

A dead quiet fell over the group at the table. Across the way, Sol put down his pencil and stared at me.

Patch hesitated. "No, not yet." Then he looked at me appraisingly. "What do you know about it?"

"Not a thing, except that there is one," I answered cheerfully. "Just thought that, since you seem to have been in so many other peculiar organizations, that one might have been on your list."

No one made any comment and we returned to our work. It was only later that the full import of this conversation dawned on me. Meanwhile, I was seeing Lee Fuhr more often; many nights we would cook supper together and discuss the affairs of the League. By then I was beginning to feel a little more optimistic about the immediate future of the United States. Certainly if the League continued to grow, to expand as it was then doing and to educate the American people, there was a chance that we could avoid the evils of Fascism. The only thing that bothered me was its essentially negative aspect—the organization's program stated very definitely that it was *against* war and Fascism but it was rather vague in what it stood *for*.

"Yes, I suppose that's true," Lee agreed. "But in holding back the forces of Fascism we are protecting the democracy that we have in this country."

"What democracy?" I asked, sardonically. "If my ancestors knew how the ideals they fought and died for had been mangled, they would turn in their graves!"

She stared at me for a moment and then lit a cigarette slowly.

"I know," she said, crumpling the empty package of matches in her hand. "There's no use trying to kid ourselves that conditions in this country are good. Our economic set-up is rotten clear through and completely belies our professed belief in basic Christian principles. But I don't need to tell you that. You seem to know already."

Of course I knew—in fact, it had been brought to my attention forcibly when, at the impressionable age of twelve, my parents and I had moved to a steel town in western Pennsylvania. That had been in the summer of 1920, right in the middle of a depression that had struck after World War I. Poverty and starvation hung like a pall over McKeesport. Wages had been slashed mercilessly, good workers were thrown out on the streets, and families just barely managed to survive—or died of hunger. A year previously, a then-still-small steel union had in desperation gone out on strike and had been quite literally starved out, since they had no more funds to continue. There had been no relief agencies, except for one small private one that operated on a shoe string and had finally had to fold up for lack of money.

Lee frowned thoughtfully.

"It's not a hopeless situation, you know," she said slowly. "If we can maintain our constitutional guarantees in this country and ward off the dangers of Fascism, we may be able gradually to evolve to a good society that will really guarantee a human being the essentials for a decent life."

Could we, I wondered. What had built the McKeesports of this country but the callous greed of human beings? I remembered vividly the day Mother had returned, white faced and grim, from the relief agency where she worked as a volunteer. She had, she said, been investigating the ownership of a filthy tenement whose rickety stairs had collapsed, injuring one of her clients. That afternoon she had discovered the owner was not only one of the wealthiest men in the town and a leading citizen but was on the executive board of her relief agency! She had turned to me bewilderedly, but with an undercurrent of anger.

"Elizabeth, how could anyone be so greedy for money that they'd make it that way?" she asked.

I had thought then that perhaps McKeesport was not typical of the average American industrial city, but as time went on I was to find the same pattern of misery and suffering repeated in other towns. And always it stemmed back to some man's hunger for money. Yet now Lee was saying that there was hope that someday things would be different. I turned to her impulsively.

"Your idea sounds like a good one," I said wistfully, "and yet I wonder if it would work out in practice. After all, as long as men are greedy there will be social injustice."

"Greed isn't essentially a part of human nature," she replied firmly. "It's only a by-product of the profit motive. That's the trouble with our present civilization. People have been taught to work only to accumulate money for themselves, without regard to the welfare of their neighbor. If, however, we could eliminate the profit motive—produce for use and not for profit—we would have the beginnings of a good social set-up."

That was true, I thought. In fact, I remembered that that had been the idea of the League for Industrial Democracy I had belonged to briefly while I was in Vassar—"production for use and not for profit." I had heartily agreed with

[13]

that point of view at the time. Surely man's greed, symbolized by his grabbing for profits, was at the base of much of the suffering of the world.

Why had I drifted into the League for Industrial Democracy? Probably because I had finally realized that, whether or not I liked it, this new industrial civilization was here to stay and somehow it must be reconciled with the Christian ethics on which I had been reared. Then, too, I had come to feel that if anything constructive were to be done about social injustice, it would have to be the result of collective action. Mother, single-handedly, had tried to alleviate suffering in McKeesport and had been able to accomplish very little. Here, I had thought, was a nationwide organization that had behind it the strength of many people.

Yet I had not continued my affiliation with the L.I.D. for any great length of time. Somehow, in spite of my agreement with their point of view, I had felt that they were impractical dreamers who spent a great deal of time discussing social evils but not accomplishing much. It was, I had felt, not enough to have a good goal; you must also have a definite plan on how to reach it.

"But since nobody's ever really tried to build that kind of a society," I objected, "how do you know that it could be accomplished?"

"They're doing it right now in the U.S.S.R.," she answered enthusiastically. "There the means of production are in the hands of the people instead of being owned by private interests. And it's working out very well. When a man feels that he has a stake in the enterprise he's working in, and besides is sure that he and his family will be guaranteed a decent livelihood, he does a much better job."

Russia! Yes, I remembered that Hallie Flanagan, my dramatics teacher in Vassar College, had studied over there not long before and had told us all about the new social experiment that was being carried on. Interested as I was in Russian literature, I had listened fascinatedly. It seemed from her descriptions that at long last that country had emerged from the semibarbarism of the Czarist regime and was building up a new society that might well be envied by many of the more advanced nations. Indeed, her enthusiasm had been so contagious that I had wanted to go over there and see for myself.

Yet this new social order had only been set up at the price of a violent and bloody revolution. The Russians, therefore, had been able to wipe the slate clean and start from scratch.

"You aren't suggesting that we have a revolution over here, are you?" I asked apprehensively.

"Good heavens, no!" she laughed. "The historical conditions in the U.S.S.R. were entirely different from what they are here. Over there, in view of the savage repression of the former regime, a bloody revolution was inevitable. But in the United States it's another story. We can arrive at the same goal but by using peaceful means—legislation, collective bargaining, and so on. Little by little, the workers in this country can come to have more participation, financial and executive, in the affairs of production, until at last all the enterprises will become somewhat like cooperatives, with the former owners either selling out or becoming managers. From then on, the path to a new social order will be very smooth."

As she continued to talk, I found myself more and more impressed by what she said. Certainly, I thought, ever since my college days I had been convinced that the only decent future society would be based on the principles she had outlined. There was no going back to the old-fashioned, small-town world in which I had been brought up. All this had been replaced by a vast impersonal industrial civilization which somehow, if life was to have any meaning, must be reconciled with the basic Christian ideals that my parents had taught me. As far as I could see, the only way to do this was to set up a society that did away with the old motives of selfishness and greed and stressed the necessity of working for the welfare of mankind. Indubitably, doing away with the profit motive and substituting the goal of social service was the only way to achieve the brotherhood of man that we hoped for.

In retrospect, I wonder just why it was that Lee's explanation of how we could build a better society impressed me so profoundly. Basically, I suppose, it was because I wanted passionately to believe that someday, no matter how far distant in the future, there would be a decent world where a man could work and live like a human being. Yet, actually, similar programs had been presented to me in the past and I had not felt that they were either sensible or practical.

Was it perhaps because my experience with the American League Against War and Fascism had given me new hope? Certainly, if large numbers of decent Americans could be rallied together to fight against war and Fascism, those same people could be interested in building a new society. The average person, it seemed, was not so much uninterested as unaware of what was going on; once awakened, he could be a tremendous force for good. If all the little people, like myself, stood together and worked toward a common goal, there might indeed be hope for a better world.

Or was it possibly because in my fear that we might be

dragged backward into the physical and intellectual slavery of Fascism, I was willing to accept any constructive plan that seemed halfway workable? After all, there was no guarantee that Lee's ideas were not half-baked ones, as illusory as the others, but now was the time for action, I felt, and not for philosophizing.

Yet, over and above this, there were probably other reasons for my mounting enthusiasm. Wasn't it perhaps because I looked on Lee as a solid, practical person with her feet squarely on the ground—the sort of woman who would never indulge in idle daydreaming? Or, even more important, wasn't it because her fervor and obvious sincerity had communicated themselves to me? Probably I shall never know the answer, yet the fact remains that after I had left her that night, I was beginning to be convinced she was right.

During the next few days I thought over what Lee had said, and when I again ran into her I was quite ready to continue the discussion. By then I was interested in how this program was going to be put into effect. After all, no movement could succeed without an adequate organization.

"I suppose that when the League finishes fighting war and Fascism it will become the center of a movement to work toward this new society," I said tentatively.

"Perhaps," Lee smiled, "but actually it's a very large and unwieldy organization and it needs a smaller group of well-trained and well-disciplined people to give it a driving force. You know how the average person is. He tends to slump and grow uninterested unless he is urged to go on."

"But where are you going to find such a group?" I demanded.

"You don't have to find them," she answered amusedly.

"They already exist. In fact, they are the ones who hold the American League together and give it cohesiveness and driving force. Without them, the organization would muddle around and accomplish nothing. Well meaning as the average member is, he needs direction."

I found myself puzzled by her cryptic remarks. "Who are these people?"

She looked at me appraisingly. "The Communists. They will be the ones who will rally around them all the progressive forces in this country and will lead them to a new society."

I stared at her in amazement. "Then you're . . . a *Communist?*"

"Yes, I'm a member of the American Communist Party," she said quietly and waited for my reaction.

I can't remember whether or not I was shocked, but I was most certainly surprised. She didn't look anything like my preconceived idea of a Communist. I had, to my knowledge, never met one before. Yet in the back of my mind I probably had tucked away a definite mental picture of what I had expected a Communist to look like. I struggled to bring that image into focus, but I found suddenly that I was having difficulties. Come to think of it, just what *had* I expected a Communist to look like? Certainly not the conventional portrait of a bearded terrorist with a bomb in either pocket. Perhaps, then, like the characters in the German play *Man and the Masses* which we had produced at Vassar—hungry, ill-clad revolutionaries, driven by desperation. No, not in the United States—more probably like the down-and-outers I saw around Union Square, the queer ones that argued with each other interminably in phraseology that I couldn't understand. I found confusedly that I didn't have a very clear picture in mind at all. I only knew I hadn't expected that a Communist would look like Lee— well fed, nicely dressed, well balanced, and healthy. I suddenly became aware that I was staring at her intently, as if she were a strange animal in the zoo, and I flushed with embarrassment.

"You're horrified, aren't you?" she said with amusement.

"No," I replied truthfully, "I'm not. It's just that you're not the type."

"There isn't any type," she said scornfully. "We have all sorts of people in our ranks, all the way from poor workers up to middle-class people, like doctors, professors, lawyers. Why, in Teachers' College you'd be surprised to find . . ." She stopped abruptly and looked at me warily: "I shouldn't have said that; just forget it. And please don't mention to anyone that I'm a Communist Party member. I told you that in confidence."

"I certainly won't give you away," I promised; then, puzzled: "But why make such a secret about it?"

"Personally, I don't care," she answered proudly. "I'd be willing to tell anyone. But you know as well as I do that Communists aren't in good standing in this country; people seem to have the cockeyed idea that we're terrorists carrying bombs. Actually, of course, we're very normal people, except that we have a more highly developed social conscience than most. But to return to your question. With the current prejudice about Communists, it might be very difficult for some of our comrades to get jobs if their affiliation were known. Therefore, unless we are in an environment where we can be accepted for what we are, we keep our

[19]

membership secret. Even those of us who would be willing to come out in our true colors keep quiet in order to protect the other comrades."

As I continued to look dubious, she went on: "I know what that New England mind of yours is thinking. It's hypocrisy and you don't approve of it. Well, it isn't. If you were a lone Democrat in a strongly Republican community, and you found you would be ostracized if your political affiliations were known, wouldn't you keep quiet?"

Yes, I supposed she was right. As I had discovered by sad experience, especially in Italy, you could get yourself into a lot of hot water by defending unpopular views. And besides, nothing constructive was achieved anyway.

As the days went by, I asked Lee more and more questions about the Communist Party, all of which she answered cheerfully and patiently. It was, so she told me, a political party, like the Republicans and the Democrats, only much smaller; it differed from them, also, in that its structure was much more closely knit and its membership much better disciplined. The basic group in the organization was the "unit" and it consisted of two types: the "shop" unit (comprising all the Communists in a given factory, office, or plant) and the "street" unit (organized according to a geographical area and including all those who had no unit in their place of work). The units pyramided up to a "section," the "sections" to a "district" and the "districts" up to the Central Committee—the ruling body of the American Communist Party. Moreover, the American Party had international affiliations—it was part of a worldwide federation (somewhat like the League of Nations) which was composed of the Communist parties from many different countries. This body was called the Communist International (the Comintern, for short) and its headquarters was located in Moscow, mainly because Russia was the only country that had set up Communism.

Communists, so I gathered, were very hard-working people; no one was accepted for membership who was not willing to live up to the rigid obligations he assumed.

Had I had any previous knowledge of the Communist Party, I would doubtless have been skeptical about its program, instead of accepting it, as I did, at face value. Unfortunately for me, however, my first acquaintance with the Party came during the famous "united front" period when the Communists had, to all intents and purposes, abandoned their former revolutionary aims and represented themselves as being the leaders of a coalition of all progressive forces to beat back the tide of war and Fascism and to work peacefully toward a new world. I was, of course, not the only one who was taken in by this clever propaganda. A good share of the "liberals," at least on the Columbia campus, hung around the outskirts of the Communist Party. Many of them became members, as I eventually did. Those who escaped did so not because of their intelligence or good intentions but, ironically enough, because they felt unable to make the sacrifices involved. And even many of these never tore themselves completely free; they remained around the fringes of the movement, helping the Communists in small ways.

Lee, evidently assured that I was interested in Communism and a trustworthy person, began gradually to introduce me to other Party members. I was surprised to learn that many members of the Teachers' College branch of the League belonged to the movement. Hastily I revised my previous ideas. Communists, obviously, were not hungry, ill-clad revolutionaries nor queer bums from the Union Square area. They were intelligent, respectable people, well thought of in the community—they dressed and lived just like any other normal American. Indeed, if anything, they were far better people than the average citizen; where others were out for themselves, they thought about the welfare of their neighbor. They seemed to be continually engaged, at the sacrifice of a considerable amount of time and energy, in humanitarian projects, such as better housing for the poor, more relief for the underprivileged, and higher wages for the workers. It is they, I thought, who are the modern Good Samaritans. It is they who are putting into practice the old Christian ideals that I was brought up on. Why, I said to myself, they're acting just as my mother taught me good Christians should.

By now Lee had begun to suggest that if I agreed with the Communist program, I should join the Party. Each time she brought the subject up, however, I found myself becoming very evasive. I would tell her I wanted more time to think the matter over. Actually, I think, I was convinced that Communism was the only solution to the world's ills but I hesitated to take the final plunge. Lee got more and more exasperated.

"Either you believe in Communism or you don't," she said finally, "and if you do, you have to join us and do something about making it come to pass."

"I *do* believe in it—at least I think I do," I replied feebly, "but I'm not sure that I should join the Party. After all, there are so many considerations involved . . ." my voice trailed off into uncertainty.

"You're just ducking the issue," she said accusingly. "If

you really believe in something you combine action with theory. How many times have you complained to me about the so-called religious people who go to church nobly on Sunday and then spend the rest of the week cheating their fellow men! Well, you're no better than they are. You haven't the courage of your convictions."

I winced at her words. Yes, I had said that and I had meant it. Long before, I had given up any belief in organized religion because I had felt that it was a travesty on the real ideals of Christianity. The well-fed parishioners who came to worship only to show off their clothes, the sleek missionaries who returned periodically to collect funds and talk condescendingly about the "poor, benighted heathen," the suave ministers who carefully edited their sermons so that they wouldn't offend the wealthy members of the congregation. That had no relation to the basic Christian concept of the brotherhood of man, I had thought; it was, in fact, sheer hypocrisy.

Yet now I realized, starkly, that I, too, was a hypocrite. I was giving lip service to a belief and not living up to it in actual practice. Stunned at this discovery, I looked over at Lee to find that she was eyeing me hotly.

"I thought you said that you had a 'New England conscience,'" she said contemptuously. "Well, if you have, it ought to be bothering you pretty badly right now. How, feeling as you do, can you go to sleep in your comfortable bed each night and eat three good meals a day, knowing that less fortunate people are homeless, starving and living like animals. They're your brothers, but *you* don't care."

She slammed out the door and I sat down weakly on the bed, thinking she was perfectly right. I *do* believe in Communism, I said to myself firmly; it's the only salvation for humanity. If I join the Communist Party, I can help to bring about a new social order in America. Why, then, am I hesitating?

If I did join, what would it mean to me personally? I would, of course, be embarking on a strange new life—leaving behind me all my past friends and associations and, in effect, closing the door on all that had gone before. That would be extremely difficult but it wasn't the worst problem. Becoming a Communist would mean that I would have to give all my time and energy to the Party, giving up personal comforts and, such as it was, my social life. Could I make that sacrifice? And even if I could, was I willing to join a group that, in the eyes of the people I had grown up with, were social "outcasts"? I felt myself wavering. I wasn't a martyr and I didn't want to be one. Yet how could I believe something and not live up to it?

Back and forth I vacillated during the next few weeks, struggling to decide what I should do, while the Communists watched from the sidelines. Sometimes they were very friendly and welcomed discussions with me; sometimes they gave me the "silent" treatment and left me severely to myself. Lee had moved out and taken a cheap walk-up apartment on West 124th Street, just off Amsterdam Avenue. Drawn by an irresistible magnet, I used to visit her there quite frequently, yet I was never sure of my reception. Sometimes she would be very cordial; we would discuss Communism animatedly and she would tell me what the Party was doing. Sometimes she would act as if she had no desire to see me, would retire into a corner with a book and ignore me pointedly. Occasionally, she would get very annoyed.

"Look," she would say, "don't try to get me to solve your problems. I've got enough on my hands already. I told you that you will never be happy until you coordinate your beliefs and what you do about them. After all, your ancestors had the courage to come all the way to this country to find freedom of thought. They fought in the American Revolutionary War, sometimes at the cost of their lives, in order to build up a decent civilization. We, the Communists, are the pioneers of a new world order, just as your forebears were pioneers for humanity in their days. They wouldn't have hesitated to fight for their beliefs, so why do you?"

After one of these sessions, I would crawl back home, feeling that I was indeed lower than the ugly things one found under a rock. Meanwhile, down in the city office of the League, Patch had attached himself to me, helping me with my work, eating lunch with me, and always the discussions seemed to drift around to Communism. Patch, it seemed, had been thinking about joining the Party. He had, he said, decided to do so. Forlornly I looked at him. It seemed as though I was the only person who couldn't make up her mind. You're a coward, I said to myself, a miserable coward; you haven't got the guts to fight for what you believe in. Patch was eyeing me sympathetically, as if he understood what I was going through.

"I'll wait for you to make up your mind," he said, "and we can join together. That will give you the courage to take the plunge."

I wasn't aware that this was one more clever psychological trick: unbeknownst to me, Patch had been a member for some time. Yet, though I felt very badly about refusing, I still hesitated.

"No, Patch," I said finally. "You make your decision and I'll make mine."

For some time I continued in this state of vacillation, tortured by my inability to make a decision, until I think the Communists, persistent as they were, began to give up hope. Evidently they considered that I might continue indefinitely in this impasse and that I wasn't worth wasting time on. When I asked them questions, they gave grudging answers and sometimes they would even look at me with contempt. One day I asked Lee whether a person joined the Communist Party under his own name. She looked at me with annoyance.

"No, he doesn't," she said. "I told you that once before. He takes another name. But what do you care? You're not going to join."

Night after night, I would walk the floor, trying to decide what I should do; somehow I knew that, unless I could make up my mind, I would never find peace. But I wouldn't be joining a social club, I said to myself desperately. If it were something casual like that, I wouldn't hesitate—after all, if I didn't like what I found, I could always resign. But the Communist Party, I knew, was different. Once you decided to join, it was for keeps. It meant that once and for all I would have to take a definite stand—and stick by it. Could I do it? I didn't know. It was so much easier to drift along and not commit myself to anything definite.

Time went by, and late one gray March afternoon in 1935 I found myself sitting wearily in a chair, staring at the bare trees on Riverside Drive. I had just come back from another fruitless job search, and the bleak weather matched my mood. There just doesn't seem to be any personal future for me, I thought despondently. I can't get back into teaching, and with the business field overcrowded as it is it will probably be impossible to get a secretarial position, especially with my lack of experience. Loneliness and despair crowded in on me; I craved companionship desperately. I thought of Lee. Her house was warm and friendly and there I could forget my troubles. Then I remembered that it was Tuesday, the day when all over the city the Communists had their weekly unit meetings. Well, hers wouldn't be until eight o'clock and perhaps I could have a brief visit with her before then.

Would she be glad to see me, I wondered. Probably not; she regarded me as a spineless individual who didn't have the courage to stand up for her convictions. Why, I thought to myself, couldn't I stop this mental seesawing and make a decision? After all, there was no doubt but that I believed in the Communist program. It was a simple, clean-cut, practical explanation of the suffering and evil in the world; moreover, it offered a concrete way in which these evils could be remedied. And since I believed it, I would, as Lee had said, never be completely happy until I combined action with theory. True, it meant sacrifices, but nothing really important was achieved painlessly and besides the goal Communism offered was worthwhile giving up many things for. After all, I thought to myself, I am part of the "lost" depression generation. There will never be any great personal future for me—if I can manage to keep my head above water, I'll be doing well. But at least I can see to it that the generations of the future don't have to go through what we did. I could help build a new world where such conditions were a thing of the past.

I stopped pacing the floor, finding suddenly that I had

made up my mind. In that moment it seemed as though all my doubts and hesitations had been wiped away: I knew I belonged with the Communists and was going to join them. Hurriedly I put on my hat and coat and walked over to Lee's house, where I found her curled up with the *Daily Worker* while the dinner simmered on the stove. She looked up at me with a frown, putting the paper aside.

"You can't stay long," she said. "The unit bureau is meeting here in half an hour."

I still wasn't too well acquainted with the set-up of the Communist Party, but I did know what she meant. Each unit had a governing body which was called the "bureau"; it was composed of the leader (the "organizer"), the educational director (the "agit-prop"—a shortening of the longer phrase "agitation-propaganda"), and the financial secretary (the "finance sec"). It was this group that, in addition to their specific duties, met weekly, usually just before the unit meeting; discussed the affairs of the cell, and drew up an agenda of things to be taken up by the comrades.

"I won't be a moment, Lee," I said. "I just want to sign an application to join the Party."

She stared at me a moment without speaking. Then she got up from her seat on the window sill and came slowly toward me. "Are you quite serious about it?"

"Yes," I said quietly. "It has taken me some time to decide but at last I'm completely sure I know what I'm doing."

She smiled at me then. "I'm very glad. You'll never regret your decision." She moved over to the desk and began rumaging through it as she talked. "I don't believe I have any application forms here. No! I think I used the last one just the other day."

It was an anticlimax. Here I had finally found the courage to join the Communist Party and there were no application blanks. Lee laughed at the downcast expression on my face.

"Don't worry," she said. "I'll get one from the organizer when he comes this evening and then I'll fill it in and submit it to the bureau. Two sponsors are needed. Comrade Leonard and I can sign because we know you the best. I'm quite sure the unit will accept you as a member. A lot of people, unbeknownst to you, know you and will vote to take you on." She picked up a pencil and made notes on a piece of paper. "I know most of the essential data about you. Let's see, you're still unemployed, aren't you? Good. Now, what name do you want to take?"

I hadn't thought about the matter up till then, yet there seemed to be only one possible name. I was a New Englander of old American stock; I was the pioneer who was carrying on the traditions of human liberty that my ancestors had fought for.

"I'll take the name 'Elizabeth Sherman,' " I said. "I am a descendant of Roger Sherman—the man who signed the Declaration of Independence for the state of Connecticut. His sister's name was Elizabeth."

"That's a good idea," she said, writing the name down. "Now here's the address where our meeting is being held tonight. We meet in different comrades' homes. We change every week to insure that no outsiders get in."

I looked at the slip of paper she handed me. It gave the number of an apartment on the sixth floor of a building that stretched from West 123rd Street to West 124th Street, just off Broadway.

"Come at eight o'clock," she added.

"What do I do when I get there?" I asked helplessly.

She laughed. "Just knock on the door and someone will let you in. We'll be expecting you." Then she crossed the room and held out her hand warmly to me: "Welcome to our ranks—comrade!"

As I went down the worn stairs to the street, I felt suddenly very much at peace with the world. Now at last I was where I had always belonged—with the people who were fighting for a decent society. As I walked toward Amsterdam Avenue, I forgot that it was a gray, dismal day and that piles of dirty snow lay in heaps on the pavement. For me it was a beautiful world, full of hope. Mingled with a sense of profound peace was a strange exaltation. Somehow I felt released from all the bonds that had tied me down.

We will build a new world, I thought to myself, a world in which there will be no suffering, no poverty, no pain!

CHAPTER II

At eight that night I stood in front of the apartment; I could hear the sound of voices inside. I knocked and there was silence; then the door opened and a short, stocky man with close-cropped dark hair stuck his head out.

"Yes?" he said, uncertainly.

Just what do I say now, I wondered. I was reminded of prohibition days, when you knocked on the doors of speakeasies and said that "Charlie" had sent you.

"Lee told me to come here," I said tentatively.

"Oh," he smiled. "Come on in."

Inside, the small living room was warm and homelike but utterly inadequate for the twenty-five or so people who overflowed onto windows sills, arms of chairs, and on the floor. A number of familiar faces smiled greetings. Good heavens, I thought to myself, I didn't know *they* all were Communists. A comrade occupying a chair at the other end of the room got up and motioned for me to take it, so I climbed carefully over several people squatting on the floor and sat down, feeling unduly conspicuous.

The meeting, it seemed, was just starting. Interestedly I sat back and listened to the proceedings. It was a long and evidently well-prepared agenda, and under the expert direction of the chairman item after item went through smoothly. The organizer read the directives from the section—books to be read, tasks to be accomplished; the agitprop gave a lecture on the current problems facing the Party; various comrades reported on work they had done in campus organizations. I was impressed by the serious way in which these people behaved. Although by then more than two hours had passed, they didn't seem restless—they neither fidgeted nor looked at their watches. They seemed utterly engrossed in what was going on. In the brief intermission when the comrades got up to stretch their legs, the finance sec collected dues and the literature agent sold publications. I found myself next to two old friends.

"How do you like the Party?" one of them asked.

"It's amazing," I said. "I've never seen such an earnest and well-disciplined group of people."

The first one smiled. "That's the strength of the Party; it's composed of men and women who care enough about their principles to subordinate everything else to them."

The chairman, who was also the organizer, was calling the meeting to order again. Hastily I asked who he was.

"Oh, that's Comrade X," said the second comrade. "He's a food worker over in the cafeteria. This is a shop unit that takes in all the graduate school—professors and students, and also the maintenance men."

A food worker! Out of all the intellectuals available, the unit had chosen a plain, ordinary worker for their organizer. This, I thought to myself as I went back to my seat, is really democracy. In the Communist Party it doesn't matter what your background is, it's your ability that counts.

As the meeting continued, I found myself increasingly impressed by the discipline of the members. They even seemed to have reached that stage of impersonality where they could view their own actions with complete detachment—knowing and admitting when they had been wrong, without trying to rationalize or excuse themselves. This, I later learned, was a basic concept of Communism and was called "Bolshevik self-criticism." How many people, I wondered, would be able to admit their shortcomings to themselves, let alone stand up before a group as large as this and analyze their conduct so dispassionately. I came out of my reverie to realize that a small comrade on the other side of the room was being chided by the finance sec for being behind in his dues.

"I know," he said quietly, "I should have paid them on time and there's no excuse for my being in arrears. I'll bring all the money next time."

If that had been me, I thought, I would have tried to give some good excuse, but this man is grown up enough to accept criticism when it is justified. What a really mature group of people they are. In pursuit of an ideal they have been able to divest themselves of all their petty personal emotions. Suddenly I felt very humble in their midst. Never, I thought desperately, will I be able to live up to their standards.

The meeting broke up quite late. On my way home I went with a group of comrades to a nearby cafeteria for a cup of coffee. I sat and listened while they continued to discuss current problems, now and then stopping to explain some point to me. More and more I found myself impressed with their intelligent grasp of world affairs. I hoped wistfully that someday I, too, would have developed such a keen brain.

And I wished I had their energy. Already it was well past midnight, yet, although undoubtedly most of them had to get up early and go to work, none of them showed the slightest inclination to leave. Struggling to keep my eyes open, I wondered drowsily whether this was a special occasion or whether they did this every week. Later, I was to discover that these long-drawn-out post-unit meeting discussions over a cup of coffee were almost a ritual in those semiopen days of the Party. You could walk into any cheap cafeteria late on a Tuesday night and find a similar group huddled together, talking animatedly.

For the next month or so I continued to be attached to the Columbia unit, attending its weekly meetings, paying my dues (mine were, as I recall, ten cents a week because I was unemployed), and working in the Teachers' College branch of the American League. Automatically, too, I became a member of the Communist "fraction" (or caucus) in the League, which meant an extra meeting since we always got together once a week to decide what policies should be presented to the organization.

I finally found a job. I was hired as a case worker for New York City's Emergency Home Relief Bureau.

This new status meant that I had to be shifted to a new Communist unit operating in my place of work. Carefully I filled out a form in triplicate—one copy to remain with the Columbia unit; another to go to the Harlem section, and the third, together with my newly acquired Communist Party membership book, was to be presented by me to the organizer of my new cell. I was given her name and told to look her up but, until we made connections, I was to continue to report to my old unit.

Making contact with Comrade H. proved to be extremely difficult. The Relief office was so set up that it was almost impossible to locate anyone who didn't work on the same floor with one, and when I was able to find out her lunch time and to arrange to meet her "accidentally" in the hall, even then she was with two other people. I took my courage into my hands. It was now or never.

"Could I speak to you a moment?" I asked hesitantly.

She looked at me searchingly (as I discovered later, she had been told that a new comrade was to report to her but, not knowing my real name, she had been unable to contact me) and I felt somehow terrified at her steady gaze. Suppose she wasn't the right person?

Aware that she was eyeing me impatiently, I managed to find words. "The section told me to look you up."

Her glance didn't shift; if anything, it became sharper. "Yes? Well, in that case, meet me up there tomorrow night."

She turned on her heel and walked down the stairs, leaving me feeling completely inadequate. It *was* the right person, I thought with relief, but now what did I do? For all my glib talk about the section, I didn't even know where it was located. And what in the world would I do when I got there?

On my way home I stopped off to see Lee, who was amused but sympathetic. The Harlem section, she said, was located on the second floor of a building on Lenox Avenue, near 131st Street. It was plainly labeled and I couldn't possibly miss it. Once there, I should just sit down somewhere and wait for Comrade H.; when she came I should show her my credentials and everything would straighten itself out.

I didn't like the idea of having to wander around Harlem alone at night, but in the face of Lee's serene courage I found I was ashamed to mention the fact. Moreover, all these strange conspiratorial arrangements worried me. I couldn't understand why in the world things had to be managed this way. I started to ask her why, then I abruptly stopped. After all, I was only a new recruit. I knew very little about the movement. Impressed as I was by the intelligence and sincerity of the Communists I had met, I was quite willing to concede that the Party knew better than I did. After all, they had had much more experience.

Although I was unaware of it at the time, by this decision on my part to trust the Party rather than my own judgment I had taken the first step toward becoming a Communist in deed as well as in name. One of the first phases in transforming a young idealist into a hardened revolutionary is to imbue him with a terrific sense of his own inadequacy, to make him so humble that he refuses to use his own powers of reason and relies confidently on the decisions of the Party. Why I, being the individualist that I was, confidently placed my future in the hands of others, I shall never know. I can only attribute it to that thing called "faith" that leads one to trust blindly in something that is bigger than oneself.

The following night I climbed the rickety stairs to the second floor of 415 Lenox Avenue and stared about me. It was, I discovered, much like the city office of the American League—bare, badly lighted, grimy. People were running about madly, operating the aged mimeograph machine, tying up stacks of literature, having hurried conferences. No one paid the least attention to me. I sat down on a wooden bench in a corner, forlornly, and waited. Fifteen minutes later, Comrade H. bustled in, followed by three other people. When she spied me, her face lighted up and she rushed over.

"I'm so glad you came," she said happily. "I didn't mean to be curt yesterday, but I have to be very careful in the office. The Bureau doesn't even approve of unions, let alone Communists. You never know who's listening in on conversations and reporting back to the authorities." Hurriedly, she introduced the three people with her. "There's only four of us and we can certainly use one more. Now, let's see if we can find a room where we can talk the situation over."

From then on, things moved so fast that I found my head spinning. In a daze, I tried to assimilate all the information that poured in. The main job of the Communist unit in our precinct, I discovered, was to build up the Home Relief Bureau workers' union, which later on was absorbed into the very left-wing United Public Workers Union. The going was rough, I learned, not only because the city authorities were definitely antiunion but because the social workers in this particular office knew nothing about unions, didn't understand their purpose, and hence were totally uninterested in the problem. It was our task to educate our fellow investigators, make them understand the principles of unionism, and get them to sign up. This would be difficult, in view of the fact that we had to work undercover, which seemed a bit odd to me. Then I remembered that, although legally every American had the right to join a union of his own choosing, in actual practice it worked out quite differently. Employers, I had discovered, often fought bitterly against unionization because it meant they had to pay more wages.

While I was still trying to straighten out the union situation, I found that the conversation had shifted to the problems of the unit proper. Before I knew what was happening,

I found that I had been elected agit-prop—or educational director.

"But, Comrade H.," I protested, "I've only been a Party member for a little over a month; I don't know the least thing about Communist theory!"

She laughed. "These other three comrades are even newer in the Party than you are. I'm the only one that's had any experience. But we have to have an agit-prop and you're elected to do the job. And don't look so upset. I'm sure you'll be able to handle the situation."

I stared at her helplessly. Not only did I feel inadequate to handle the job but I frankly didn't see where I was going to find time and energy to do all these things. From now on, I realized, I would have four meetings a week—unit, unit bureau, union, union "fraction"—and besides I would have the added responsibility of being the educational director! I started to protest again and then I fell silent. I had joined the Party knowing full well that it would involve hard work, and I wasn't going to back out now.

I threw myself enthusiastically into the work of building up our rather small local, because I felt that a good strong one was definitely needed in our precinct. Working conditions there were really frightful. Most of the investigators kept their jobs only because they had to eat. We were based in a fire-trap building, so overcrowded that there was often no place to sit down and write reports. The lighting was poor and the sanitary facilities worse. Case loads were unbearably heavy. This fact, plus the unnecessarily large amount of paper work involved, left most of us continually struggling to keep our heads above water. Theoretically, we were supposed to work from nine in the morning to five at night, with an hour off for lunch; but in practice a conscientious investigator had to skip lunch (or grab a bite in five minutes), work madly all day, and even take his case book home that evening.

After a month or two in the Home Relief Bureau, a new case worker would begin to look haggard and hollow eyed. The accelerated pace, the physical strain of climbing many flights of stairs during the day (most relief clients lived on the top floors of walk-up apartment houses where the rent was cheap), the long evenings spent writing up case histories—all these had taken their toll. The result was that, generally, if an investigator didn't become cynical, bothering little about clients, he either left his job or cracked up.

To me, conditions were intolerable. The interest, I found, was in saving money rather than in really helping the needy. An investigator's standing was judged more on his ability to "close up" cases (whether justly or unjustly didn't seem to matter) than on his handling of clients. Anything above a bare minimum of relief was given grudgingly. Even though little extras (such as cod-liver oil for the children and blankets) were available, I used to have to fight furiously to get them for my clients.

Perhaps the thing that horrified me the most was the immense amount of "red tape" surrounding the initial giving of relief. An applicant had to fill out innumerable papers and then wait three or four weeks before his first check came through. In the waiting period, he was given nothing, and if he had reached starvation level he simply had to go hungry.

Sometimes kind-hearted Home Relief Bureau investigators took money out of their pockets and gave it to these applicants. We had to be very careful, however, because if we were found out, we would lose our jobs. And yet it was very difficult to sit by and see such unnecessary suffering without being able to help. I remember the day I went to see an old colored Pullman porter who had applied for relief. I found him sitting quietly in a shabby furnished room, obviously unhappy that he had to beg for food. I needed to verify the fact that he had lived in New York City long enough to be eligible, so I asked him if he had any gas or telephone bills to prove his residence. When he shook his head, I told him he would have to go to a notary and sign a statement affirming that he had lived in New York the proper length of time. That, I said, would cost him a quarter. Sadly he looked at me.

After admitting he had been living on doughnuts and coffee, provided by his next-door neighbor, for the last week, "Miss," he said quietly, "if I'd have had a quarter, I'd have eaten it."

I walked out, seething with rage. It would take three weeks to get that man on relief and meanwhile God knows how he would eat. Brought up as I was in a small town where neighborliness prevailed, I considered it a disgrace to let a man go hungry. Most people did not try to chisel off the Home Relief Bureau. They were decent people, eager to work but unable to find jobs. It's not their fault that they're forced to beg, I thought; they have a right to be treated like human beings.

What especially upset me was that when I reported this to the supervisor at the Relief office she shrugged her shoulders. There wasn't any use bothering about it, she said cynically. After all he's only a Negro. (It was an area that dealt mainly with Negro relief.) That, sadly enough, seemed to be the general attitude at the Relief Bureau. I wondered how people could feel that way and still call themselves Christians.

In contrast, I was continually impressed with the humane and practical way in which a Communist dealt with social problems. If a family was dispossessed, he would waste no time in asking foolish questions but would act swiftly.

First, he would store the family's furniture temporarily in, say, the garage of a friend of his. Next, he would take the hungry group to his house and feed them. After that, he would find them a bed for the night and set about getting them a permanent home. When that had been accomplished, he would persuade the unhappy family to join a Harlem committee to petition the mayor to do something about better housing for the area. To me, that seemed the ideal plan for improving poor conditions; first, extend help to the individual as a person and then, when that was done, work out a long-range plan to solve the problem in general.

But the impact of what I had seen in Harlem was not the only factor in my increasing belief in Communism. There were many other experiences, some of which stand out vividly in my mind. There was the meeting that I had with an advanced student—whom I shall call Edwin—at Union Theological Seminary back in the spring of 1935. Harold Patch had introduced me to him because he wanted me to co-sign Edwin's application for membership in the Party. I asked him why he wanted to join, and with eyes aglow he tried to explain his beliefs.

"The old Christianity is dead, Elizabeth," he said thoughtfully. "Christ came to this earth to preach the brotherhood of man, but most people seem to have forgotten. They are too immersed in making money and getting

[41]

ahead in the world. I've always wanted to be a minister of Christ, but somehow, until I discovered the doctrine of Communism, I was nauseated with the rotten hypocrisy of the average churchgoer, not to mention the attitude of the clergy." Then he smiled, and I felt that at long last he had found what he was looking for. "I'm convinced that Communism is the Christianity of the future, that I, as a potential Christian minister, must *per se* be a Communist, even though it will be a very hard life. Does that startle you?"

No, it didn't. In fact, it only confirmed what I had been thinking for several months. Yet I was worried about his future. Would this new-found allegiance of his stand in the way of his being ordained the following year? I asked him whether or not he had broached his ideas to anyone at Union Theological Seminary and, if so, what they thought.

"Yes," Edwin said cheerfully. "I've talked to Dr. Harry Ward about the question of my joining the Communist Party. He's not a member, as you know, but he told me that I should follow the dictates of my own conscience. In fact, he indicated that my membership would make absolutely no difference in my being ordained." He paused for a moment and looked at me. "You know, it's funny, but I would swear he approved the step I am taking."

Yes, that was quite possibly true; Harry Ward was one of the big-shots in the American League and I had met him there. He was a lean, determined little man in his sixties, obviously one who would always fight for what he believed in, regardless of the cost. I had known he was sympathetic to Communism, so Edwin's statement didn't in the least surprise me. I felt, as I had before, that Communism was the religion of the future. Christianity had arisen as the advocate of the poor and oppressed, and in the course of natural events it had degenerated into the toy of the wealthy; now Communism would take its place as the exponent of the brotherhood of man.

Edwin joined the Party, and very soon thereafter two other students at Union Theological Seminary applied for membership. One was a prospective preacher who, like Edwin, had not yet been ordained; the other was a minister who had been doing missionary work in Japan for several years and had returned to the United States to take a few refresher courses. About the latter, I worried considerably, since I knew the Communist Party was illegal over there. Perhaps, if I certified him for membership, he would be going back to his death. He smiled tranquilly when I put the question to him.

"Don't worry, Elizabeth, I'm not afraid. Years ago I put my life into the hands of God and promised Him that I would live only for His purposes. I've lived austerely and worked extremely hard, but I've always been happy in the thought that I was living up to my ideals. I've thought about Communism for a long time now and I'm convinced that it is the Christianity of the future. I want to join the Communist Party and work for the brotherhood of man. It may cost me my life but that's immaterial. Will you deny me the right to fight for what I believe in?"

I shook my head and found, to my distress, that tears were flowing down my face. Hastily, I pulled myself together and signed his Party card.

"Goodbye and good luck for all the years in the future," I said, feeling that he was a far better person than I would ever be. "You now have three Communist Party members in Union Theological Seminary and that is sufficient to make a unit. Tell Edwin to check with the Harlem section and they will give him directives. You won't have to see me again."

He smiled gently. I knew with finality that I would never see him again. "Goodbye and thank you, Comrade Elizabeth. I shall try to make a very good Communist."

There was the time when I joined a citywide demonstration to induce the New York City authorities to put out more money for relief. It was a cold, dreary day and the dirty snow lay piled in heaps on the pavement; Mayor LaGuardia—who didn't quite know how to cope with the demands of the unemployed—had forbidden us to march, under the odd pretext that the streets were too slippery and we might fall and injure ourselves. But we marched anyway, led by Vito Marcantonio—at that time a small-time lawyer who had been a law partner of LaGuardia's and later Congressman from New York. It was perhaps my first experience with violence: I saw Marc bundled into a New York police "paddy-wagon"—after having been thoroughly kicked in the shins—for consignment to "protective custody" (LaGuardia claimed that Marcantonio's life was threatened by the mob!). I saw the New York police ride their horses into the crowd and knock the demonstrators sprawling into the gutters. For the first time in my life I found myself in the grip of an uncontrollable rage; people shouldn't be kicked around like that.

In the excitement, my hands were clasped in those of two marchers, one on either side of me. "Come on, comrades, we won't stand for this sort of nonsense. If they want violence, we'll give it to them."

Why I wasn't arrested that day is still a major mystery; carried beyond myself, I stumbled over fallen marchers and battled with the police, caring nothing about what happened to me. When we finally picked ourselves up and straggled on down to the Port Authority Building, via side streets, I found myself singing hoarsely the first words of the *Communist Internationale*—"arise, ye prisoners of starvation; arise, ye wretched of the earth!"

In the spring of 1935 I was approached by Pauline Rogers, executive secretary of the American League. Up till then, I had had very little to do with her, although I do remember that she had come out of her office to congratulate me when I announced that I had joined the Party. But then, so had almost everyone else; for, with few exceptions, the whole staff turned out to be Communists.

That day, however, she wandered out to where I was working and sat down beside me. She was, she said, sorry that I would have to leave, but was I still interested in the problem of combating Italian Fascist propaganda in this country? I replied that of course I was, but that I probably wouldn't have too much spare time, not with my heavy schedule in the Relief Bureau. She looked at me thoughtfully.

"I have a friend who's working in that field," she said, "and she badly needs help right now. Unfortunately, she doesn't know the language and besides she hasn't been over to Italy recently. You could be of great assistance to her if you could spare a little time."

"I don't know," I started dubiously, thinking of the many tasks I had lined up. Then my interest in Italian Fascism got the better of me: "Why, yes, I guess so."

"Good," she replied briskly, "but remember, you must never mention this to anyone—even in the Party. She's in direct contact with underground anti-Fascists in Italy and we can't afford to risk their lives."

[45]

None of this seemed in the least odd to me, because I knew from personal experience how dangerous it was to be against Mussolini in Italy.

The next day at tea time I met Pauline at Childs with a rather heavy-set woman in a shapeless brown hat and nondescript brown tweed coat. Pauline hurriedly introduced her as Mrs. Juliet Glazer and then said that she had to rush back to the office, leaving me somewhat at a loss. Mrs. Glazer seemed to sense my awkwardness. She smiled suddenly and I realized that, even with her straggly brown hair and rather plain face, she had beautiful brown eyes.

"Let's have some tea, shall we?"

The voice was cultured, the accent probably New England. We chatted inconsequentially for a little while. From her remarks I got the impression she came from an old American family, that she was a widow living on a small but adequate income and doing research work in the Columbia University library to keep herself occupied. No mention was made of Italian anti-Fascist work, although she did tell me she had been a Communist for some years. At the end she glanced at her watch and said she had an appointment. Would I, she asked, come over to her house the following week for a late tea?

The address she gave me was on west 74th Street, just off Riverside Drive. When I arrived there I found it was a brick building that had quite evidently once been a one-family residence. I pushed her bell and at the answering buzz went up the old-fashioned carpeted stairs to the second floor where Mrs. Glazer, waiting in the doorway, beckoned me into the living room. As I glanced around, I noticed that, while not richly furnished, it certainly wasn't shabby; the living room was fairly spacious and there seemed to be a bedroom to the right, behind curtained glass doors. Mrs. Glazer began to putter around in the small kitchenette that, together with the bathroom, led off the other end of the living room.

"I'll be right in," she said cheerfully. "I'm just getting the tea ready."

We chatted for a good two hours, at the end of which I felt that I knew no more about Mrs. Glazer—her personal life, her work in the Italian anti-Fascist movement—than I had before. She had, I realized, spent most of her time asking me about my family, educational background, political beliefs, present job. Well, I thought to myself, I really can't blame her for wanting to know all about me. After all, she has to be sure I am trustworthy.

Yet, when the third meeting over tea produced no further results, I began to wonder. After all, she seemed like a nice person and I enjoyed talking to her, but that wasn't the purpose for which I had come.

On my fourth visit she served me highballs instead of tea. I took one and then politely refused the second. "The little puritan!" she said mockingly. "Are you always this way?"

In those days I still felt annoyed when someone taunted me with being unsophisticated, but I bit my lip and explained again, patiently, that I wasn't being "holier than thou"—that I just didn't like alcohol.

To this she made no answer but shrugged her shoulders as if to suggest that she didn't believe a word I said. Then she began to talk vaguely about the underground movement in Europe, dwelling especially on the work of women there. They often had to perform unpleasant tasks and had to do a lot of drinking and sleep with many men. Although I prided myself on not being a "prude," I was nauseated not only by her choice of subjects but by her obvious relish in discussing them. Her talk didn't make sense to me (it sounded actually like something out of a lurid book) and I couldn't see why she took such morbid delight in dwelling on ugly details. When I tried to steer the conversation to another topic, however, she would laugh and say I was a "hot-house flower," that I didn't have the stamina to face the facts of life. Communists, she would say, should be made of sterner stuff and I had a lot to learn before I would make a good revolutionary.

Probably I was more disturbed by all this than I was willing to admit to myself, not because I believed anything she told me but because I began to wonder whether she was all there mentally. Finally I telephoned Pauline Rogers, intending to tell her that I felt I could not continue with Mrs. Glazer. After all, there was no reason why I had to sit around and listen to her talk like that when she seemed to have no intention of giving me any anti-Fascist work to do. Pauline, unfortunately, could not be reached. Well, I would see Mrs. Glazer just once more, ask her just what she wanted me to do, if anything, and then decide whether or not to continue seeing her.

A few days before our next meeting, however, the telephone rang at midnight; when I climbed sleepily out of bed and picked up the receiver, I found that it was Mrs. Glazer on the other end.

"Come on over," she said. "I want to talk to you."

"At this hour?" I said, shaking myself awake. "Why, Mrs. Glazer, it's twelve o'clock and I have to be at work at nine tomorrow. I can't come now!"

"You must!" her voice was urgent. "There's something important that's come up and I *must* see you."

At last! This must be the important work Pauline Rogers had mentioned. But why did it have to come in the middle of the night like this? Well, I was half awake anyway and Mrs. Glazer's house was only ten blocks away.

"All right," I said sleepily, "I'll be there just as soon as I can get dressed."

Hurriedly I threw on some clothes and stumbled down the service stairs. Outside, the wind was blowing furiously and I fought to keep my hat on my head. As I battled my way doggedly down Riverside Drive, the black shadows of the trees swayed ominously on the pavement and my footsteps echoed hollowly in the deserted street. By now, I was wide awake and beginning to feel frightened. What was I walking into anyway? All my previous doubts about Mrs. Glazer came back to haunt me. Was this a genuine thing—or was she drunk or crazy or what? I was half inclined to turn around and go back home but I fought down my panic. You're being childish, I said to myself firmly and, setting my jaw, continued on.

Mrs. Glazer, self-possessed as ever, greeted me cordially at the door, waved me to a seat on the sofa, offered me a drink and then sat down opposite me. Impatiently I waited for her to tell me why she had summoned me out at this late hour, but she continued to talk leisurely about the underground movement in Italy. I glanced at my watch. An hour had passed and nothing had been accomplished. The thought of my comfortable bed waiting for me at home became intolerable; my annoyance exploded into words.

"Mrs. Glazer," I said, and my voice was icy, "you have

dragged me out of bed at an ungodly hour to come down here on some supposedly urgent business and yet you have said nothing about it. Just what do you want?" As I talked, I found my anger mounting. "After all, I do have to earn a living and it's important that I get enough sleep to keep on going."

She smiled at me. "My dear, you don't have to keep that miserable job in the Home Relief Bureau. You don't like it and there's no reason why you should beat out your brains there. What did you tell me you really wanted to do? Oh, yes, you said that if you had the money you would get a Ph.D. in sociology and then find a teaching position. Well, that dream can easily be realized. I have inherited a great deal of money—more than I can ever use myself—and I will be glad to finance you until you get your degree."

She paused for a moment to note my reaction, then she went on.

"You see, my dear, I like you very much and I feel that you would be very valuable in the Italian anti-Fascist movement. But you really can't do much as long as you are tied down with a job that keeps you worn out all the time. Why don't you just give it up and let me take care of things from here on in?"

I stared at her, wondering whether all this was really happening to me. This sounded too good to be true. Here was the chance to get back into the teaching field and in a subject that my social-work experience had convinced me was a very important one. Above all, I could get away from Harlem and its misery and back into the old academic atmosphere, at the same time being able to contribute to the fight against Fascism. I wavered. The comfortable sofa, the drink, and Mrs. Glazer's seeming kindness were having a softening effect on me. She really is a nice person, I said to myself, even though she does have her peculiar moments. Who else that I have ever known has shown such thoughtfulness? All the doubts I had ever had about her vanished. She was a thoroughly good person and my heart warmed to her.

I found myself just about to open my mouth and accept her kind offer, when suddenly all my stiff-necked old Yankee pride rose up in defiance. I couldn't take money from someone else, no matter how well meaning they were. I had to earn my own way in the world. Disagreeable as it was to work in the Home Relief Bureau, I would have to stick it out. After all, many other people had far worse jobs than I had. Reluctantly, I said farewell to a beautiful dream. It had been nice while it lasted.

"I'm sorry, Mrs. Glazer," I said gently, "but I really couldn't accept money from you. It was very kind of you to suggest it. But, well, I just couldn't. Perhaps someday, when and if I do have a decent job, I can come back and help you."

Her face hardened and her mouth set in a taut, hard line. "Well, the little puritan again! The little girl who doesn't like to drink, who is shocked at my stories about underground life in Europe, who nobly turns down my offer of money. Why don't you grow up?" She looked at me a moment and then went on, mockingly, "You're living on illusions, my friend. You, with your bourgeois ideas of getting married and raising a brood of children! You, with your decadent New England pride that won't let you accept help! What kind of people are we getting in the Party these days?"

I felt as though I had had a blow in the pit of my stomach, but I got to my feet shakily while an icy rage seized me.

"I don't know what you're talking about, Mrs. Glazer, but one thing is quite clear. There's no use in our having any further relations. I'm going to call Pauline Rogers in the morning and tell her so. After all, I've only continued to contact you because I gave my word to a representative of the Party. But now I've had enough. I'm not going to take any more!"

She stood up then and came over to me, her eyes pleading.

"Please, Elizabeth, don't feel that way. I know it's very late and you're tired. But, believe me, I'm tired too, perhaps even more than you are. After all, I'm an old woman now and I've gotten too cynical. I really didn't mean to insult you." She looked at me sadly and continued: "Even if you don't want to accept my offer, would you help me? Although I have traveled extensively in Italy and am now engaged in helping the underground over there, I don't know the language. Would you give me lessons? I would be glad to pay you a fair price and that certainly would help you financially."

I felt a pang of remorse. Perhaps, after all, she did mean well. Besides, I could do with a little more money, and in giving her Italian lessons I was earning it decently. I told her I would be very glad to, and we arranged that I would come to see her the following Monday at six o'clock.

I dug my old Italian grammar out of my trunk and went over to keep my appointment the next week. To my surprise, I found that she had a visitor—a tall, dark, military-looking man with an accent that I took to be German. Suddenly I realized that, having been detained at the Relief office, I was almost an hour late. Undoubtedly I had barged in on a dinner date that she had arranged. With an apology I turned to leave, but Mrs. Glazer grasped me by the sleeve.

"Come on in and have a cocktail with us," she urged. "This is Mr. Smith and he is going to take us to dinner."

It was kind of her to be so polite, I thought. The least I could do was to have a drink with them and withdraw tactfully. Mr. Smith settled himself on the sofa beside me and for the next fifteen minutes he chatted charmingly and casually about art in Europe, while Mrs. Glazer sat across the room and watched with an odd smile. At the end of that time I got to my feet and said firmly that I must go. I had—I fell back on the time-worn social "white lie"—an engagement for dinner. I had the strangest impression, as they urged me to stay, that they both looked dismayed. But after making an appointment for an Italian lesson for the following week, I went on home.

The next week I made it a point to arrive exactly on time. To my great surprise, there was Mr. Smith again. As I hesitated in the doorway, wondering what to do, Mrs. Glazer waved me in.

"Don't tell me that you have another engagement," she said gayly. "Mr. Smith has come especially to take us out to dinner. We'll have cocktails here and then go out and eat."

I was tired. After climbing stairs all day, my feet hurt and I wanted nothing better than to go home and take my shoes off. Besides, I was annoyed; Mrs. Glazer had known I was coming precisely at this hour to give her an Italian lesson. Why, then, did she have one of her beaux around? Then I thought of the lonely dinner ahead of me and wavered. It would be fun to go out to a really nice restaurant and eat with friends.

It was probably one of the most unpleasant evenings I have ever spent. It was not long before I was wishing I had followed my first impulse and gone home. Mr. Smith—I thought at the time that he had had several cocktails too many—was in an amorous mood and kept moving closer and closer to me on the sofa, eyeing me fondly. More and more embarrassed, I looked helplessly at Mrs. Glazer. She certainly should help me out of this uncomfortable situation. But she only sat looking amused, as if she were savoring some secret joke. As I was trying to decide whether or not I shouldn't risk being rude and get up and leave, she rose abruptly to her feet.

"It's getting late," she said, with a glance at her watch. "Let's go eat."

Our dinner at Barbetta's—a nice little Italian restaurant in the forties, just off Times Square—was scarcely happier. The food was excellent, but Mr. Smith, who I now decided was definitely sober, continued to ogle me over the table while Mrs. Glazer watched silently. I became more and more annoyed; after all, he was most certainly her beau— she hadn't said so, of course, but it was obvious—and it was most rude of him to behave that way. Well, I said to myself philosophically, he's just one more middle-aged man who likes to make passes at younger women and it's too bad she has to put up with him.

At the end of the meal, to my great relief, he announced that he had an urgent engagement. Calling a taxicab, he gave Mrs. Glazer's address and put us into it. As the door slammed shut, Mrs. Glazer leaned forward in her seat and looked intently at me.

"Well, how did you like him?" she asked eagerly.

I hesitated. After all, she seemed to like him so much, and it wouldn't be polite to criticize him.

"It was kind of him to take me to dinner," I said carefully, "but it really wasn't necessary. And I'm sorry I barged into your dinner party, but I understood that you'd be free for your lesson at that time."

"You didn't barge in," she said airily. "I brought him up especially to meet you. He's a very wealthy businessman and he is going to give you a very good job at a high salary. You and he ought to get along together very well. I could see that he took to you from the start. Now you can leave your Home Relief job and not feel that you are accepting charity."

I shook my head. The idea of working with Mr. Smith definitely didn't appeal to me. Aside from my disgust at his behavior there was a hard, steely quality about the man that repelled me. The less I saw of Mr. Smith the happier I would be. I turned decisively to Mrs. Glazer.

"I'm sorry, but I'm going to stay where I am. It's not such a bad job after all. Besides, we are all going to be put on the Civil Service rolls. That will give us some permanency and perhaps a raise in pay."

She looked amused. "But that won't come for some time yet. I know. I read about it in the papers."

"Oh yes, it will," I said firmly. "Very shortly we're all going down to meet the examiner and have our finger-prints taken. That means that it won't be long now."

"You can't do that!" she said, her face turning white. "If you have your fingerprints taken you will be no further use to the revolutionary movement. You must leave immediately."

None of this made any sense to me. What did fingerprints have to do with the Communist movement? Then, looking at the expression on her face, I was frightened. I was sure by now that she wasn't crazy—in fact, she was alarmingly sane. And if that was so, then something strange was going on. Her ugly talk about the underground movement in Europe; her attempt to give me money and, when I refused that, to find me a job with an unpleasant man; her odd talk about fingerprints—what did it all mean? I didn't know, but I was quite sure something was wrong. She didn't behave the way a Communist should. Well, I wasn't going to stick around any longer. I would say goodbye once and for all and let Pauline Rogers know about the situation.

"Mrs. Glazer," I said firmly, "I haven't the least idea what you are up to, but as far as I'm concerned, I don't want to. I am going back to the Home Relief where I belong and you will have to find someone else to give you Italian lessons."

By now the cab had reached her home. As she paid the driver, I got out, said goodbye, and started off for home, ignoring her protests. The next day I telephoned Pauline but I couldn't reach her. All right, I said to myself, I'll have to handle this my own way, since there is no one else I can ask for advice. I'll never see Mrs. Glazer again, I decided. If she calls, I won't answer the phone.

For over a month Mrs. Glazer continued to ring me up and I persistently refused to go to the phone. Finally, one night, I answered a knock at the door to find her standing there, looking at me pleadingly. I had guests in my apartment, so I closed the door and went out into the corridor.

"What do you want?" I demanded.

"Why don't you reconsider?" she said. "You're really passing up a very good opportunity."

"There's nothing to reconsider," I said tersely. "I'm going to stay in the Home Relief Bureau." Then I thought of a clinching argument that ought to take her off my neck for good and all. "I'd be no use to you anyway, at least according to what you said. I've already had my fingerprints taken."

She stared at me and there was hate in her eyes.

"You fool! Why didn't you have sense enough to take my advice?"

"I have guests waiting," I said, opening the door to my apartment. "Goodnight, Mrs. Glazer, and goodbye!"

CHAPTER III

I FORGOT about this episode in the busy rush of my life at the Relief Bureau. With all the activities in which I was then involved, I felt that I was in the midst of a three-ring circus. As the weeks rolled on, I grew more and more tired and by the summer I was so weary that it was an effort to climb even a flight of stairs. One day, for the first time in my life, I fainted dead away, and I decided I would have to see a doctor. The examination showed I was completely tired out physically.

"How did you ever manage to get so run down?" the doctor asked, looking at me thoughtfully. "What do you do for a living?" When I told him, with deletions, he nodded comprehendingly. "No wonder. Well, you'll have to take a vacation and then find yourself a more peaceful occupation."

That was more easily said than done, I thought. I wouldn't be in the Home Relief Bureau if I had been able to find anything else. Perhaps, if I got a leave of absence, I could get back in shape and resume my job. I applied for the leave, but as usual it bogged down in red tape. While I was waiting for it to come through, I went to visit some friends one night and collapsed. It was quite clear now that I was in no shape to continue. Reluctantly I wrote to the Home Relief people and resigned.

When I got back on my feet again, I decided that now that I had background in the field the most sensible thing to do was to return to Columbia University and spent a year getting my master's degree in sociology. This decision stemmed not only from the practical interest I had in the subject but from the fact that, as the result of a job-hunting trip to Washington, D.C., the previous winter, I had discovered there were numerous government jobs available if only one had studied sociology. I had a little money left. By hoarding it carefully and taking odd typing and translating jobs, I could support myself for a semester. After that, perhaps something else would turn up.

In the meantime, I had been transferred back to the Communist Party unit in Columbia University. I found it much the same as when I had left, except that it was in the throes of trouble with Comrade Land, one of the old stand-bys in the Party, who was refusing to accept Party discipline and carry out the tasks given him.

I knew Comrade Land fairly well. All of us newcomers, who knew so little about Communism and were so eager to learn, had looked up to Land and respected him, thinking him the model of what a good Communist should be. It came as a great shock to discover that expulsion proceedings were being brought against him, and I was unable to understand it. His attitude left me even more puzzled, since he seemed to be making no serious attempt to disprove the charges against him—in fact, he appeared like a man who was sleepwalking.

Because it was my first experience with the application of Communist discipline, the memory remains vividly in my mind. The small top-story room where the trial was held overflowed with people. Not only all the members of the

Columbia unit were there but also representatives from the section, the district, the Central Committee, and a few unidentified people. Most of the outsiders, I didn't know. I did, however, recognize Louis Sass, the short, dark, energetic Hungarian who was the organizer for the Harlem section. And someone pointed out V. J. Jerome, a pale, cold-looking individual with a face like a sleepy fish. He was then the Party's authority on theoretical problems, although some years previously he had been a member of the Columbia unit.

It was eight o'clock, we settled ourselves, and the chairman rapped for order. As the hours ticked by, the charges against Comrade Land were stated. Not only had he refused to accept the directives of the unit and to carry them out but he had been guilty of insulting the leadership of the Party—he had called Comrade Sass an "idiot" and had remarked, over and over again, that Comrade Jerome was a "numbskull." The question of what should be done with Comrade Land was thrown open to the floor.

For the next few hours, comrade after comrade got up to give his views. Some defended Land loyally, some attacked him. My head began to ache with the noise and the smoke. Then Land got to his feet to answer the charges. He spoke slowly and haltingly, seeming to grope for words, and gave the impression that he cared very little about what happened to him. It was as if a shell of a man stood there. I found myself gripping the sides of my chair, and there was a hard knot in my throat.

It was almost four o'clock in the morning when the matter was finally put to a vote. As I had expected, the majority decision was that Land should be expelled. Then Comrade Jerome rose slowly to his feet.

"Comrades," he said slowly, and I found myself admiring the man, "I have known Comrade Land for a long time. He's basically a good person and a Communist with a long record of service. I don't think that he should be expelled summarily from the Party but should be given a chance to rehabilitate himself. I propose that he be put on a six-months' probationary period. If, during that period, he shows that he can carry out his duties, he should be allowed to return to membership."

As he sat down, a vote was taken. It was unanimously decided that Comrade Jerome's suggestion should be adopted —Land should be given a chance to show what he could do.

I walked wearily home through the deserted streets of Harlem. Tired as I was, I felt that the evening had not been wasted. I had now had a chance to see the Party's disciplinary apparatus in action. More than I realized at the time, I had been tremendously impressed by what I had seen. After all, Land had incontrovertibly made a very poor showing, yet the Party had been understanding in its treatment of him. How many people in the outside world would give a man another chance, especially when he had failed so often?

For the next two months, I lost track of Land. Then, one day, to my great surprise I saw him having lunch with Juliet Glazer in a Japanese restaurant on West 118th Street. I was with Lee Fuhr and two other fellow comrades from the Columbia unit, and I hoped fervently that I wouldn't be seen. Yet, somehow, I couldn't take my gaze from them. I was puzzled by the fact that Land and Juliet not only knew each other but were chatting in such friendly fashion. I came to with a start to realize that Lee was also looking in the same direction.

"What's he doing with *her?*" she muttered.

"What do you mean?" I asked sharply.

She looked at me, then at the two other comrades, and shrugged her shoulders.

"Perhaps I shouldn't tell you this, but—well, frankly, it worries me. I know that woman and she's no good." She paused for a moment and I saw an odd look come into the faces of the other two comrades. "A few months ago I was introduced to her by Land. He said she was a high-up comrade and needed my assistance. But she never told me what she wanted me to do. She merely said she would like to finance my nursing training—she had plenty of money—so that one day I would be useful to the Communist movement. I was all set to accept her offer—after all, I've had a pretty hard struggle to earn my living—when I suddenly had the uncanny feeling that I shouldn't do it. She was much too eager." She looked at us thoughtfully, then frowned and went on: "No, frankly, that's not the real reason. It's just that, as a nurse, I know all the queer quirks of human nature. She appeared much too fond of me, to the point where I felt embarrassed. You know, I'm convinced she's a 'homo.' And I don't want to be mixed up in anything like that."

The little red-headed comrade on the other side of me stared intently at the tablecloth.

"I know her too, Lee, only I've never mentioned the fact. The reason I didn't was that when Land introduced me to her, he stressed the fact that I should say nothing to anybody. But I've been worried too. She didn't seem to be a genuine person. She offered to pay my way through Teachers' College for the next two years and then find me a job.

[62]

I didn't accept because I felt there was something very odd about her."

I started to tell them about my experiences with Mrs. Glazer, but then I looked across the table and saw the expression on Margaret Hinckley's face. Good heavens, I thought, does Meg know Juliet, too? My mind suddenly went back to the spring of 1933 when I had first met her future husband, William C. Hinckley, who was then limping around the corridors of International House with a badly sprained ankle. He had told us he was going to marry Margaret Cummings, one of the members of Boston's Four Hundred, the following year. I had completely forgotten about Bill during the ensuing year when I had gone to Italy.

I did not run into Bill Hinckley again till the spring of 1935. By that time, they had been married and Meg was a member of the Columbia unit. Not long after she joined, she had brought me Bill's application card and I had signed as co-sponsor for him. Since he was then the executive secretary of the American Youth Congress (in actual fact, the ruling officer of the organization), it seemed wise for him to disconnect himself from the Columbia unit. After a couple of meetings he was transferred over to Gilbert Green, at that time an official in the Young Communist League and later one of the eleven Communists convicted after the marathon trial before Judge Harold R. Medina for membership in an organization advocating overthrow of the American government. Meg, however, had remained with the Columbia unit. Now she was talking, as if the words were being forced out of her.

"Lee," she said desperately, "I don't like this situation. I was introduced to that woman over there by Land just after

I joined the Party. I liked her at first. She came over to our house and met Bill and we all got along very nicely. She seemed to want us to help her in some project that she was engaged in. But she was never very definite about it. Then she started making passes at my husband and neither he nor I liked it. We decided that something very peculiar was going on. From then on, we never answered the telephone if we knew she was calling, and when she came to our home, our maid told her we were out. But now I'm upset. What is she doing lunching with Land?"

All three were staring at each other. I had, so far, said nothing. Then I told them about my experiences with Mrs. Glazer and we sat looking at each other thoughtfully. Meg was the first to speak.

"I think there's something very wrong about that woman," she said seriously. "Certainly she doesn't act like a Communist. She might be a counterrevolutionary sent into our ranks to corrupt the comrades. We ought to investigate her."

We all agreed, but somehow with the passing months, especially since Mrs. Glazer seemed to have disappeared from the Columbia campus, we forgot our resolution. Meanwhile I was having my own difficulties. My money had run out, there were no jobs of any kind available, and reluctantly I went on Home Relief, hoping to get on one of the W.P.A. projects. But by then the lists were closed. So, wearily I resigned myself to long days of walking around New York City, applying for any and every job I could think of.

Finally, in the spring of 1936 I found work typing manuscripts; when that ended, I had a succession of odd jobs— translating, tutoring, typing. None of them paid well, but

I managed to eke out an existence. In my spare time I was taking a course in education at Teachers' College—one that I had paid for the previous spring but which, due to my heavy schedule at the Home Relief Bureau, I had had to postpone; this, at least, kept me in touch with the academic world. I was still hoping that the several thousand dollars awarded me by an English court for injuries in a bus accident in 1930 would soon come through; with that in my pocket, I could afford to take a year off, get a degree in sociology, and return to the teaching field.

During the academic year of 1935–1936, I continued to function as a member of the Columbia University unit. My Communist duties kept me so busy that I had, luckily, no time to brood about my own misfortunes. I did, indeed, lead a hectic life. Looking back on it now, I wonder just where I found the time and energy to accomplish all I did. To begin with, my "inner-Party" duties were extremely heavy: I was financial secretary of the unit—which meant that I had to collect all the dues and spend long hours struggling with the Party's complicated bookkeeping system; moreover, such a position carried with it the responsibility of attending a weekly Bureau meeting, in addition to the unit meeting, plus the added duty of trotting up to Finnish Hall every Wednesday evening to hand in the money and attend a section finance meeting. Then, too, in the spring of 1936 I was made agit-prop for the unit—probably because no one else found they had the time; this meant that I had to read all the current Party literature and prepare reports for the unit, in addition to attending the weekly section agit-props' meeting.

By the summer of 1936 I found that I was more and more becoming a Communist in spirit as well as in name. In the

[65]

intervening period my convictions had been enormously strengthened. Perhaps it was because all the hectic activity incidental to the Party dulled my senses to the point where I was no longer able to look at the Communist Party objectively. To a certain extent, this was true. When a person lives on the ragged edge of existence, always overworked, always lacking proper sleep, he tends to lose perspective and keeps working automatically, like a squirrel in a cage, without questioning why he is going in circles. He has no time nor energy to sit down and view the problem dispassionately from a safe distance.

But more important was the influence of the Party's psychological devices, one of the most powerful of which was the educational program. It consisted in so saturating the new member with Party-slanted literature and in so insulating him from any outside sources of information, that he ended by accepting the Communist line as the only correct one. So subtly and naturally was this conditioning carried out that often the convert didn't realize he hadn't done his own thinking. Instead, he was convinced that he had arrived at his own conclusions unaided.

Like most of the new members, I had approached the Party humbly, realizing I knew very little about it and being vastly eager to learn. I was told that I had a long way to go and that I must study incessantly in order to get a firm foundation. After all, the older comrades pointed out to me, I couldn't very well be a Communist without knowing in detail just what I stood for. It was all very well to know the general program, but that wasn't enough. I must be well enough informed to be able to answer any questions put to me by outsiders, whether they pertained to the Communist position on China or the Party's stand on unemployment.

This made eminent sense to me and I followed their instructions faithfully, reading whenever I had a spare moment. Every day I went carefully through the *Daily Worker* from cover to cover. Every week I swallowed a number of current Communist pamphlets, and if I had any extra time I tackled some of the basic literature. This heavy schedule, standard for all Communists, left me with no time to do any outside reading. I could never seem to find a moment even to glance at the *New York Times*, let alone any of the current magazines, and I had to abandon any thought of getting around to non-Communist books.

In the winter of 1935–1936, too, I started going down to the Communist Workers' School, then located on the second floor of 50 East 13th Street—a rickety rabbit warren that housed the Party's national and district headquarters, the Communist newspapers, and the Workers' Bookshop. Here I took courses in Marxian political economy and struggled to learn the philosophical and economic bases of Communist theory. Actually, the whole concept of Marxism-Leninism (the technical name for Communism) is a highly complicated one and I found myself floundering hopelessly in "dialectical materialism," "economic determinism," and the "iron law of wages." I wished desperately that instead of concentrating on languages in college, I had enlarged my philosophic background and taken at least one course in economics. Certainly, I thought, I would understand more of what was going on.

The school itself impressed me very much, however, despite its unprepossessing appearance. The atmosphere in the classrooms was casual and informal and there was none of the rigidity that I had found in other educational institutions. The teachers, too, were friendly and helpful and

[67]

they seemed to regard their classes less as a group to be lectured at than as a group to discuss things with. The students themselves seemed alive and eager to learn. Although, undoubtedly, most of them had worked hard all day and were very tired, none of them slumbered in their seats. In fact, they sat alertly on the edge of their chairs, listening intently and firing questions at the lecturer.

At first I sat quietly in my seat, feeling incredibly ignorant in the midst of all this knowledge. But by the time the course was finished, I no longer had any questions. I had been so thoroughly convinced by the combined arguments of the class and the teacher that I no longer had any doubt that the Marxist-Leninist interpretation of the world's history was correct.

This combination of educational techniques on the part of the Party was slowly and inexorably having its effect on me. But there were other devices that supplemented it. In joining the Communists I had cut myself off from all but a very few outside friends. I was to find that more and more my social life centered in the Party. This partly resulted from the fact that my fellow comrades and I were thrown together so much in the work we were doing. We were continually having meetings and planning programs. Further, our erratic schedule made it all but impossible to keep outside engagements, since some emergency might arise and we would have to break them, inventing a plausible excuse that wouldn't betray our Communist affiliation. In addition, each Communist unit gave a party either weekly or biweekly in one of the members' homes for the dual purpose of raising money and talking to potential recruits. This more or less canceled out any other social dates. Yet, perhaps more than all this, was the feeling that we had a common bond, that because we felt the same way about life we were more at ease in our own company than anywhere else. Even when we had free time and a choice of places to go to, we tended to congregate at each other's homes.

The psychological effect of this close inner life on a new member was, of course, terrific; he came to feel that his only real friends were in the Party and that the outside world had very little relevance in his scheme of affairs. Yet this clever technique on the part of the Communist Party did not exhaust its store of devices. There was, even more effectively, the strong pressure of its rigid discipline, which slowly but surely tempered the new member into a steeled Communist.

Before I joined the Communist Party, I had been a strongly individualistic person: I didn't want anyone to do my thinking for me, nor did I want to lead a "regimented" life. Perhaps this attitude came down to me from my non-conformist forebears; perhaps it was a wholly natural reaction to an overly stern, old-fashioned New England upbringing. What had changed my point of view was the realization that, in order to improve the conditions of the world and build a new society, it would be necessary to have a strong organization with rules and regulations to which its members would have to adhere. It meant, I knew, that as an individual I would have to sacrifice certain rights and perhaps put up with many inconveniences but, in view of the importance of the goal to be attained, I was sure that it was worthwhile. After all, I decided, this is a step that I am taking voluntarily. No one is forcing me into it.

The Communist Party's discipline, in fact, was largely successful because it appealed to the responsibility of the individual himself and to his desire for the approval of his fellow comrades. I was told that each Communist should indulge in "Bolshevik self-criticism"—that is, he should be able to view his own actions impersonally and decide whether he had behaved rightly or wrongly, and he should be able to admit his mistakes without rationalizing. Moreover, his fellow comrades also sat in judgment on him. If, in their opinion, he had erred, he was publicly criticized at his unit meeting—an experience that was, to say the least, humiliating. Usually, once was enough to cure a comrade who had been slipshod in his duties or failed to pay his dues on time. After hearing himself denounced as a bad Communist and a disgrace to the movement, he generally reformed in a hurry.

I was told, too, that as a Communist I was responsible not only for my own actions but for those of my fellow comrades, since it was important to the movement that the wrong sort of people didn't get into our ranks. That meant if I knew Comrade W didn't pay his dues or attend meetings, if he got drunk frequently in public and set a poor example of what a Communist should be like, I should report that fact to the Bureau so that they could call him in and give him a talking-to. At first I disliked this idea—after all, talebearing is not a pleasant thing. Then I began to accept it as a necessary part of the work of the organization. Undoubtedly, it was important that we Communists give a good account of ourselves to the outside world. If one of us slipped up, he was bringing discredit on the whole Party and it was the duty of the organization to do something about it. Thus I learnt some should suffer for the good of all.

Although I was unaware of it at the time, we were also

being imperceptibly schooled in the practice of conspiratorial methods, although in those early days they were probably no more complicated than those used by the average secret society. In fact, that is probably why most of us failed to see the deadly implications of the tactics we were learning. They seemed little more than the shenanigans of a fraternity or sorority group. We did, of course, take a phoney name when we joined the Party, but none of us, I think, took this very seriously. It was a custom and we conformed to it. Moreover, it offered us a chance to escape from the name that had been foisted upon us at birth and to select one that possibly had more appeal. A good many people took names they had always wanted to have; others took the names of heroes they admired, as I did; others went under the pseudonyms of their pet enemies: at that time Nicholas Murray Butler was president of Columbia University and cordially disliked by the left-wingers—consequently we had a number of Comrade Nicholas Butlers. One Chinese student, just to confuse matters thoroughly, became "Comrade Levine."

If we joined other Communist organizations, we could, if we chose, take other pseudonyms, and a good many of us did. Why, I can't at the moment recall, except probably because it seemed to be the thing to do. The only difficulty with acquiring many names was that it was not easy to remember which one to use where, and this led to embarrassing moments—sometimes hilarious ones.

I remember I took an alias for my class at the Workers' School, filled out my application blank, and thought nothing more of the matter. The first night I was late for school; the teacher had already begun to talk and, embarrassed, I tiptoed up to the one vacant seat in the front row. The roll had evidently been called, for the professor stopped, consulted his list, and looked down at me.

"What's your name, Comrade?" he asked.

In the excitement, I completely forgot what name I had selected.

"I don't know, Comrade professor," I stammered.

The teacher suppressed a smile and a roar of laughter shook the classroom. It was sympathetic laughter, I realized with relief.

We were, I am afraid, very poor in undercover tactics in those days. Although we tried to keep our identities and meetings secret, I'm sure that anyone who really wanted to find out could have done so. Certainly, the Hearst reporters who were then investigating Communism on the Columbia campus had us pretty well spotted—even to knowing what drugstores we hung out in. But that, of course, was in the semiopen days of the Party and most of us were very new, inexperienced members.

In the late spring of 1936, while riding down Broadway on a trolley car, I saw Juliet Glazer again. She was two seats ahead of me, seemingly immersed in thought. I remembered our resolution to investigate her and I moved over beside her.

"Hello, Mrs. Glazer," I said cheerfully. "It's been so long since I've seen you. You know, I've been wanting to run into you for a long time to tell you that you were perfectly correct. I should have left the Relief Bureau and taken you up on your offer. But now, of course, it's too late."

Her eyes grew wary, then she smiled cordially and said in her friendliest manner:

"I *am* glad to see you again. Why don't you visit me

[72]

sometime? In fact, come for tea Wednesday next week; I live at the same address, you know."

She had taken the bait! Now I had to notify Meg so that we could go up and tell the section authorities about the situation. She wasn't home, however, so I went on up by myself and talked to Comrade Sass. His offhand opinion was that she didn't sound like a genuine Communist. However, he said he would check with the district and let me know. When I returned a couple of days later, he shook his head.

"No one down there knows anything about her. She's obviously a phoney sent in by the counterrevolutionaries to corrupt our people. She must be exposed. Keep that date with her and take a comrade from the section along. Comrade C will do. He looks like a college boy and won't arouse suspicion. Let him do all the talking and just stay in the background."

The following Wednesday, promptly at tea time, Comrade C—a long, lean, scholarly-looking man with glasses—and I arrived at Mrs. Glazer's place. I rang the bell and we slowly climbed the carpeted stairs. As usual, she was standing in the doorway, her face showing surprise at the addition of Comrade C. But then she relaxed. Undoubtedly, looking back on it now, she thought I had brought her a potential contact from the Columbia unit. As we stood in the middle of the living room, I started to introduce my companion, but Comrade C gestured me aside.

"Mrs. Glazer," he said firmly, "I am a representative of the Harlem section of the Communist Party. You have been posing as a comrade doing undercover work and trying to involve several of our people. Just who are you and what is your game?"

[73]

Her face went chalk white and the rouge stood out in blobs. I don't think I have ever seen such naked terror in anyone's eyes in my life. She moistened her lips, tried to speak, then caught on to the back of the chair behind her for support. What is she so frightened of, I wondered. She acts as if we were going to kill her. As she struggled to speak, I looked past her and saw that the glass doors to the small inner room were closed, but outlined clearly against the thin curtains was the figure of a man—standing motionless. For no reason that I can put my finger on, I felt an icy chill sweep over me and I wanted to get out of that room fast and run as far away as possible. I caught myself abruptly and moved closer to Comrade C. Mrs. Glazer had by now found her voice.

"You're crazy," she croaked. "I have nothing to do with the Communist Party. I never have. I don't know what you're talking about. I'm just a research worker at Columbia University."

"Come off that," Comrade C said, staring at her steadily. "I know what you've been doing. Well, in the future, stay away from our people."

He put on his hat and turned to leave; Mrs. Glazer, realizing that I was edging toward the door, turned on me savagely.

"You stay right here. I have a few things to say to you!"

I looked at Comrade C and saw that he was badly frightened, too. With one motion he pushed me out the door, stepped out after me, and slammed it shut.

"Let's get out of here fast," he muttered. "I don't like the smell of that place."

Down the stairs we fled, so fast that we tripped over each other and fell in a heap at the bottom. Picking ourselves up, we literally ran for a block until we reached Broadway. There we found a telephone and called Comrade Sass, who had been waiting for our call.

"She's definitely a counterrevolutionary and a dangerous one," said Sass, when he heard our story. "I'll report it to headquarters."

I thought, then, that I had seen the last of Mrs. Glazer but to my horror I found that I hadn't. Two nights later, when I was at dinner, I answered a knock at the door to find her standing in the hallway, accompanied by Pauline Rogers. I was about to slam the door in her face. Then I realized that with three other people in the apartment I didn't need to be afraid.

"I want to talk to you," she said curtly.

Silently, I led them through the living room and into my bedroom. Closing the door, I turned to a Mrs. Glazer whose face was distorted by hate and rage.

"I've brought Pauline Rogers here to guarantee my *bona fides*," she said. Then a cold menace came into her voice: "And now, my petty meddler, I'm going to tell you a few things."

She launched into a vituperative diatribe, which I was too stunned to take in properly, while Pauline sat silently by. I remember only that, interspersed with everything else, she called me a "Trotskyite," a "counterrevolutionary," an "enemy of the working class"—words that I had heard in the Party before and knew to be deadly insults, without ever quite knowing their meaning. At the end, she looked at me with a concentrated fury that left me weak and shaking.

"Just remember one thing," she said, and I have never forgotten her words, "if ever you meddle in my affairs again, I'll see that you're taken care of. You'll be put six feet under and you won't come back to do any more talking!"

Why I didn't keel over in a faint at this point I don't know. Perhaps because all my life I'd been accustomed to going calmly through emergencies and then collapsing later, when all the excitement was over. I got to my feet and found, to my great surprise, that I could still stand. Although my voice quavered, I could still control it.

"Look here, Mrs. Glazer, I don't know who you are or what you are up to, but I do know you aren't any Communist. No one knows you in the section or the district. I've checked on that. Whether you're dangerous or just plain crazy, I don't know. But I do know that I'm not going to take any more of this nonsense from you." I threw the door wide open. "Get out, Mrs. Glazer, and don't you ever come back again!"

She looked at me as if a mouse had suddenly risen up and defied her. Without a word, she stalked out the door, followed by Pauline Rogers. I walked slowly back into the living room. Then my knees buckled and I sat down on the nearest chair.

"What's the matter?" one of my fellow comrades asked anxiously. "You're white as a ghost and you're trembling."

"I don't know," I said, and my hands were shaking so that I couldn't light my cigarette, "but that's the woman I've been telling you about—the counterrevolutionary that we investigated. She talked wildly—said she was the power behind the Communist Party—that she could make or break me or all the rest of us. Then she ended up by threatening my life!"

[76]

We looked at each other thoughtfully; then Cy snubbed out his cigarette and spoke.

"She's probably not all there in the head," he said soothingly. "No normal person talks that way. Anyway, if she's really dangerous, we'll all be around to protect you."

I knew very well that he didn't believe what he was saying nor did the rest, yet there really was no sense in worrying about the matter. There was nothing we could do. Whoever she is, I thought hopefully, she wouldn't dare do anything to me. After all, I have friends around me.

I probably would have slept less soundly that night if I had had any inkling of who Mrs. Glazer really was. Indeed, if I had known that she was a member of the dreaded Russian Secret Police and if, in addition, I had known enough about that organization to know that they ruthlessly disposed of anyone who threatened their safety, I would probably have sat up all night, listening tensely for every squeak in the floor boards. As it was, this was something that I only learned much later on. And so I went peacefully to bed that night and slept.

CHAPTER IV

I N ABOUT mid-November 1936 I bumped into the girl who
had taken Pauline Rogers's place as organizational secretary of the American League Against War and Fascism. I
had seen her several times before, but only once since the
city office had been moved from Fourth Avenue to a new
location on the north side of Union Square. She greeted me
gayly and asked what I was doing. When I told her I hadn't
as yet found a permanent and lucrative position, her eyes
narrowed thoughtfully.

"Perhaps I can find you something," she said. "I have a
friend—a very wealthy businessman from Lithuania—who
badly needs a secretary. He wants a person who can take
shorthand and type properly and who can correct his English, which is still not perfect. You would be the ideal person." She paused for a moment and then went on. "He's an
old Communist and I have known him for a long time. But
remember, you must never mention this matter to anyone.
He doesn't want his political sympathies known in this
country."

I hesitated a moment—this was reminiscent of my ill-
fated introduction to Mrs. Glazer. Then I thought to myself that this was quite different—a bona-fide offer of a
job. I said that I would be glad to meet her friend. His name,

she said, was Joseph Eckhart, and she arranged that I come the following afternoon to a restaurant on Fourth Avenue.

Mr. Eckhart turned out to be a tall, broad-shouldered man with receding hair and a pair of bright-green eyes under heavy eyebrows. He was, I judged, a man somewhere in his fifties, and his accent, which was not too noticeable, seemed to be a cross between Russian and German. We chatted for a little while and he told me he was in the export business but that things weren't as yet set up completely.

About ten days later I met him again. This time he informed me that he had been called "home" and didn't know whether or not he would return to the United States. Would I give him a permanent address where he could reach me if he did come back? Something about the whole performance vaguely puzzled me. Although he strenuously insisted that he was only a "businessman"—and indeed a good many things about him confirmed that impression— some cryptic remarks made me wonder whether or not he didn't have some connection with the Communist International. I had, so I thought, never met one of its representatives before, although I had been told there were such people. Nor did I have more than the slightest notion of what their activities were, although I was under the impression that they acted as liaison men between the different Communist parties of the world. At any rate, I had by now been sufficiently trained as a Communist to ask no questions. I politely wished him *bon voyage*.

I continued on with my odd jobs and my Communist work in Harlem until the early spring of 1937, when I got a two-months' temporary position with Consumers' Union. This outfit had been set up not too long before by the striking left-wing employees of the old Consumers' Research to give consumers information on standard products.

While I was with Consumers' Union, I was startled one night to receive a telephone call from Joseph Eckhart; he was back in the country and wanted to see me. Over dinner at Longchamps he finally told me that he was a representative of the international Communist movement, that he had been to Moscow, and that now he had returned on official business.

"Then you're not just a businessman," I said.

"Oh, yes, I am," he smiled, sardonically. "I'm a purchasing agent in the airplane field. And that ties in with my Communist work. I've been sent over especially to buy American planes and ship them to the Spanish Loyalists via Mexico."

The Spanish Civil War had been going on for some time. Fellow comrades of mine had gone over there to fight for the Madrid government—in fact my old friend Lee Fuhr had sailed with the first medical contingent. I myself hadn't been too involved, although I had done some work for left-wing committees that had been set up to aid Republican Spain. Yet, like all Communists, I was intensely interested in the Loyalist cause. But I didn't see where I fitted into the picture and I said so.

"I don't know yet," he said slowly. "Things are in a state of flux right now, but I may need you as a secretary at any time. I'll keep in touch with you."

Then I remembered that, having just returned from Moscow, he must have some inside news about the Trotskyite trials which were then going on. They were discussed continually in the Party during that period. By now, I had learned that Trotskyites were dangerous, unscrupulous terrorists who hated the Communists bitterly and were out to smash them in every land. They were an organization of men who had rallied around Leon Trotsky, the Russian ex-Revolutionary who had been exiled from the Soviet Union. I had, at that time, never met any Trotskyites personally. I just knew, from what I had been told in the Party, that they were no-good people and my enemies.

The so-called "Trotskyite" trials, of course, concerned a group of old Bolsheviks—a great number of them Army men—who were accused of having become Trotskyites and of working with the Nazis to commit acts of sabotage and espionage against the Soviet Union. Outside Party ranks there was serious doubt that these men were guilty. In fact, a good many people thought, with justification, that this was just a frame-up. Yet, as far as I remember, none of us Communists ever questioned the charge that these men were traitors and criminals. Perhaps the only question that ever occurred to us on the subject was *why* these steeled old Bolsheviks had done such a terrible thing. I turned to Eckhart and asked him. For a moment there was a look of pain on his face and then it became inscrutable.

"I don't want to talk about it."

"But why?" I demanded.

"Because I'm an old Red soldier myself. I was an officer in the Civil War and I knew many of these people. You've been reading things in books and you don't know what it was really like."

I thought then that I understood his emotion. It must be dreadful to feel that old friends of yours had behaved in such an abominable way. Apologetically, I changed the subject.

For the rest of the spring I continued to have dinner with Eckhart occasionally, but when, by June, he was still not sure about my employment, I told him I was going to take a position as athletic counselor in the R. H. Macy camp. That, he said, would be all right; he would keep in touch with me.

In the fall, when I returned to New York, I saw Eckhart again. He told me that because of the passage of the Neutrality Act he would be unable, he thought, to do anything further about the purchase of airplanes for Spain. He thought that meant he would be ordered back to Moscow shortly. However, he would keep in touch with me just in case he did need my services. He seemed thinner and harassed looking and, although he was as charming and courteous as ever, his mind seemed to be on something else. Knowing that he suffered from frequent and very bad attacks of migraine, I asked him if he was feeling well.

"Oh, I'm all right physically," he said savagely, "but I'm worried about the people over there. What are they going to do with me? Why don't I get any word? Oh, never mind! You wouldn't know what I'm talking about."

One night at table he suddenly put down his water glass and stared across at me.

"If I go back 'home,'" he said slowly, "I'll never come back here. I'll be dead in a year."

I knew that in addition to his constant migraine he had a bad gall bladder and sundry other bad internal troubles.

"Don't be silly, Joe," I said soothingly. "You aren't going to die in a year. Your insides will hold out longer than that. And, besides, don't worry about going back to Moscow. They undoubtedly have as good doctors there as here."

He gave me a strange look, then he nodded absently. "Yes, I guess you're right. I'm just in a bad mood."

When dinner was over, he asked if I would like to come for a drive. As we crossed the George Washington Bridge and started up the highway toward New York State, I noticed that his usually quiet hands were clenched on the wheel and he sat rigidly in the seat. I wished then that I hadn't agreed to come, but it was too late to change my mind. As we branched off onto a road with little white guardian posts along the edges, he suddenly seemed to go to pieces.

"Look at those posts," he cried, and there was a wild look in his eyes. "All I'd have to do would be to give one little twist to this wheel and we'd crash into them. Then it would be all over with. There wouldn't be any more worrying, any more thinking! I've often thought about it, as I drove along. Why shouldn't I?"

He's mad! I thought to myself, feeling terror sweep through me. I must stop him thinking that way! Fighting to keep my voice steady, I talked on and on for fifteen minutes. To this day I don't know what I said, but at the end I saw him relax and wipe the perspiration off his forehead.

"I'm sorry," he said dully. "I guess I went a little crazy."

When I got home that night, I found that my knees were still shaking. The man must be out of his mind, I thought, to behave that way. Could it be that the tension he had gone under all these years had finally made his brain snap? I was greatly alarmed, but as I knew he was soon leaving the country, I decided I would somehow cope with the situation.

Late in 1937, I picked up an evening paper and saw on

the front page a picture of my old friend Mrs. Glazer. I hurried into a drugstore, ordered a cup of coffee, and with trembling hands began to read the attached story. On and on I read, unaware that a woman was waiting patiently behind me to take my seat.

I folded the newspaper and, almost in a fog, went home. As I swayed on the subway strap, I tried to sort out the facts in my mind. Mrs. Glazer was really Juliet Stuart Poyntz (somewhere along the line she had married a German named Glazer), a prominent person in the Communist Party who for years had held extremely important posts in the movement. Yet, not long before I first met her, she had somehow drifted out of sight and was no longer mentioned in Party circles. Some six months previous, she had disappeared from her room in the American Women's Hotel on West 57th Street. She had just walked out one evening and never returned, leaving her belongings intact. During all these months a search had been conducted for her but all efforts had failed.

None of this made any sense to me but I was seriously disturbed. There were so many frighteningly unanswered questions in my mind. Why, if she was a good Communist, had she behaved the way she had? Why, if she was a Party member, had Comrade Sass been unable to get any information about her at headquarters? What was going on? What had happened to her?

As I closed the front door, the telephone rang. It was Joe Eckhart, and he wanted me to have dinner with him. That's good, I thought to myself, as I accepted. He can give me the answers on this. As I hurriedly changed my clothes, I remembered that I had first spoken to him about Juliet a few months back, when he had taken me to dinner at Barbetta's. I asked jokingly if he and she were friends, since they both seemed to patronize the same restaurants. His eyes narrowed slightly and he considered his answer carefully.

"Yes, I knew her a few years back," he said.

When I told him about my experience with her and asked what he thought, he suddenly became very evasive. It had been so long ago, he said, that he couldn't really remember her very well—in fact, couldn't even recall where he had met her. His tone discouraged any further comment and I fell silent.

Now his strange behavior of that night returned to plague me. When I arrived at Longchamps, Eckhart had a cocktail waiting on the table for me. It was as if he knew I had read the article and was trying to soothe me down before I exploded. I sat down and ordered mechanically, then put the menu down and faced him across the table.

"What's happened to Juliet?" I demanded. "And why didn't you tell me who she was?" Then, suspiciously, "Come to think of it, how did you know that the Juliet *Glazer* I told you about because I didn't have any other name for her was Juliet *Poyntz?*"

"Very simple," he replied, staring at the tablecloth. "She was such a famous person in the movement that everyone knew her by her first name, regardless of what last one she hitched on. Besides, your description coincided. As for knowing her, everyone in the Communist Party—at least those who were in before your days—knew her at one time or another. I have met her several times." He stopped and took a sip of water. "There was no particular reason for telling you her history. You wouldn't know much more than you know now."

[85]

"But what's happened to her?" I persisted.

"Who knows?" He shrugged his shoulders. "I wouldn't bother about it, if I were you. Why should you get so upset, anyway? You didn't like the woman. In fact, you were always worried for fear that she'd turn up on your doorstep again. Well, just relax. You'll never see her again."

Something about the words or the intonation of his voice frightened me. "What do you mean?"

"Just what I said; she'll never bother you again." There was an icy look on his face that discouraged any further questions. "Now, let's have a good dinner, shall we?"

I lay awake for some time that night puzzling over what I had learned about Mrs. Glazer. I wished that Lee Fuhr weren't in Spain, so that I could talk it over with her. What did Eckhart know about the case that he wasn't telling me? Or was I, perhaps, silly to feel this queer sense of apprehension? And yet . . . When I finally fell asleep, I dreamed that Mrs. Glazer, with a hideous look of rage on her face, was chasing me over the edge of a precipice.

It must have been the end of December or early January of 1938 that Eckhart called up to say that he was leaving the country. Would I, he asked, have dinner with him once more? He wanted to introduce me to a friend of his with whom I could keep in contact after he left. When I sounded puzzled, he explained that perhaps I could be of some help to his friend, and anyway I could at least meet the man.

This turning me over to a perfectly strange person, for what seemed to be no good reason, was just as purposeless —or so I thought—as my continuing contacts with Joseph Eckhart. But I was a disciplined Communist, and as this was evidently a Party task I made no objection.

Eckhart's friend Marcel turned out to be a tall, well-fed

man about my age, with unruly dark hair and black eyes. I remember little about that first meeting with him except that he somehow managed the astounding task of eating almost everything on the table within reach and at the same time monopolizing the conversation. In rapid succession I learned that his parents were Polish, he had been born and brought up in Germany, had lived in Paris for at least ten years, was now in the United States as Joe's "assistant," and didn't know how much longer he would stay on. To this fund of information, he added that he was in the sauerkraut business. He excused himself for engaging in what he evidently considered a lowly occupation by explaining that he wrote poetry on the side.

When he left us, I was still bewildered by this strange new character. Eckhart chuckled.

"He is a bit queer," he said tolerantly, "and he does talk too much. But you'll get along with him."

Marcel, it seemed, had inherited Eckhart's dark-green Packard. One night, not long afterward, he drove by and took me to dinner. Over a good meal, he talked volubly, discussing everything from art to politics. Finally he referred casually to the current Robinson-Rubens case that had been occupying prominent space in the newspapers for some little time. I had not paid very much attention to the news stories, but I did remember that they concerned a Mr. Donald Robinson who had gone with his wife to Moscow, for some unexplained reason, and had quite suddenly disappeared. His wife, frantic, had contacted the American authorities. The State Department, investigating, had found that the name was phoney, that Mr. Robinson was really a Mr. Rubens, and that there were very odd angles to the case. Mrs. Robinson at that point was arrested by the Soviet authorities and placed in Lubianka prison. When the American Ambassador, Loy Henderson, went to see her, however, she suddenly clammed up and refused to say anything. None of this had particularly interested me. I had taken it for granted that Robinson must be some anti-Soviet agent who had sneaked into the U.S.S.R. for sabotage work. Now I came to and realized that Marcel was chattering on.

". . . and that case is still plenty hot. After all, he was one of ours, and his wife's talking out of turn like that spilled the beans. The whole organization's been shaken up. That was why Joe was recalled. I'm glad I wasn't too closely mixed up in it."

I stared at him. "One of ours"—that phrase meant that Rubens was a Communist. But if he was, what was he doing in Moscow under an assumed name, and why had he disappeared? I knew by long experience that asking questions not only was not done in the Communist movement but never brought answers anyway, so I kept discreetly silent, hoping Marcel would continue. But, seeming to feel that he had already said too much, he steered the conversation into other channels.

Marcel stands out in my memory as the oddest member of the Communist underground I have ever met, and I wonder to this day how he was ever selected for that task. When he came round to pick up telephone messages which he had asked me to take for him, he would sit down, leisurely drink a cup of coffee and talk about Paris. Then, taking a dramatic stance in the middle of the room, he would either recite from his favorite poet Heine or would read me poems in German that he himself had written. Since my knowledge of the language was confined to what I had learned in a summer-school course, I'm afraid that much of this was wasted on me. However, I would always pretend I understood, not so much from politeness as from the realization that if I admitted that it made no sense, he would sit down and explain every line and stay even later.

One foggy night he offered to take me for a drive. As we went out Riverside Drive he, as usual, talked volubly, but this time there seemed to be an undercurrent of something indefinably frightening. He began by telling me he had been a member of the "service" (as he termed it) in Paris for ten years. He had joined there, he said. Then he went on to describe how he had terrified a Communist there—a man who he said had run off with some of the Party's money—by sitting in a telephone booth all night and calling him up every five minutes; then, when the man picked up the receiver, he hung up. I had never heard of this Communist technique before, although I have certainly run into it since. At the time, it seemed silly and I said so. He laughed and I didn't like the sound of it.

"He knew what it meant, all right. He knew we were after him."

While I struggled to think of something to say, he shifted to another subject. On our way back he turned to me apologetically.

"I don't like this kind of work," he said grimly. "Maybe I'm not tough enough."

Not knowing what kind of work he was in, I could find nothing to say. After a pause, while he was strangely silent, I said tentatively, "Why don't you get into something else?"

He took his eyes off the road and stared at me savagely. "You don't know what you're saying! No one ever leaves the organization; it's not like the Catholic Church, where you only lose your soul."

[89]

It seemed to me that he was being unnecessarily emotional, but then everything about him was dramatic. He always behaved like a character on a stage. Good heavens, I thought wearily, just who are all these strange people? Juliet, Joe, Marcel? And why do they behave in such completely mad ways? It's as if I were wandering around in an Alice-in-Wonderland world, where the most absurd things seemed to be taken for granted as being the only normal ones. I found suddenly that I was fed up with queer characters, cryptic statements, and odd patterns of behavior. I wished that, for a change, someone would make sense.

Marcel finally departed in the late spring, leaving me an address where I could reach him in Paris. Thank goodness, I said to myself, he didn't introduce me to any more strange people. After that I lost track of him, except for two postcards from Hendaye, France, on the Spanish frontier. Undoubtedly, I thought, he was doing something to help the Loyalist cause in Spain.

All these strange experiences would, of course, have made a logical pattern if I had known that, from Juliet on, I had been dealing with the Russian Secret Police. As I was later to learn, Juliet Glazer had been detached from the open American Communist Party apparatus and assigned to the N.K.V.D. not long before I met her. She had been trying to recruit Lee, Meg, myself, and God knows how many other innocents for undercover work. She must have revolted against what she was doing and tried to get out of the apparatus, and the N.K.V.D., aware of this, "liquidated" her.

Joseph Eckhart, as I discovered later on, was part of the Soviet Military Intelligence. Undoubtedly upset by the framed-up Trotskyite trials, which not only involved many of his friends but threatened to engulf him, too, he was—at the time I knew him—living in terror of his life. I have no doubt that he will never return. He, like Juliet, was probably killed a long time ago. As for Marcel, he somehow survived; at the present time he is in New York City working in the Department of Public Information of the United Nations.

CHAPTER V

One day, the Columbia University Placement Bureau called to ask if I would like a job with the Italian Library of Information—a new organization. The prospect of getting back into my field appealed to me and I went down to see Ugo V. d'Annunzio, son of the famous Gabriele d'Annunzio of Fiume fame, at Rockefeller Center. I wasn't then sure whether it was Fascist, anti-Fascist, or just plain in the middle. However, the new director offered me a job as secretary and research worker and I accepted it.

I hadn't been there long before I discovered that the Italian Library of Information was indeed Fascist, a subdivision of the Italian government Propaganda Ministry. In fact, it registered later on as a "foreign agent." I could have left then but I didn't want to. This, I thought, was a golden opportunity to find out what propaganda the Fascists were foisting on the American people. When I get enough data, I thought jubilantly, I'll blow the whole works up and expose their machinations.

I went down to Communist headquarters and talked to a Party functionary on the ninth floor—a tall, dark Italian whose pseudonym was "F. Brown." I later learned that he had been a famous revolutionary in Italy, was extremely important in the American Party, and ultimately became editor of the Communist *Unità del Popolo*. He was finally unmasked and soon departed for his native Italy. Comrade Brown was very much interested. He told me to keep an eye on all that was going on there and collect publications and copies of letters. Then, when we had enough, we could do something.

By fall, however, I was beginning to be discouraged about the whole matter. Brown, seemingly very busy, had turned me over to a Comrade Nunzio, who was working in the Italian Labor movement and not only was little interested but never showed up for appointments. Finally, in despair, I went to Comrade Brown.

"Look," I said. "I think it is important to expose what the Italian Fascists are doing in this country. They're not only handing out their own slanted literature but they're also peddling anti-Semitic pamphlets and working for the Spanish Nationalists. But Nunzio never does anything!"

"I know," he said wearily. "He's only interested in the labor movement and I'm overworked. But you're right. It is important, especially to the international movement. I'll put you in touch with a comrade from the Comintern. Meet me here next Wednesday at seven o'clock."

By this time I was well on my way to becoming what the Party called a "steeled Bolshevik."

Although the discipline was rigid, I accepted it uncomplainingly because I realized that only through the unfaltering obedience of its members could our movement attain its objective. I asked no questions, followed orders unhesitatingly, and had no doubts about the good faith of the Party leaders. That I was unable to come out in my true colors and fight for my beliefs openly did go against the

[93]

grain. I disliked having to use phoney names, meet people surreptitiously, and masquerade as a "liberal." But I saw clearly that we were living in an evil and corrupt society, and I knew it would be unrealistic to ignore that fact.

Perhaps the only small doubt in my mind arose from my experiences with Juliet, Eckhart, and Marcel. They had been introduced to me as bona-fide Communists and, being well-disciplined, I had continued to work with them, even when their subsequent behavior had disturbed me. I had said to myself quite firmly that the Party knew what it was doing and that it was not up to me to question its workings; yet a vague sense of uneasiness remained, even though I hesitated to admit it to myself.

Now, as I walked down University Place with Comrade Brown on the way to meet my new contact, I found myself wondering just what he would be like. I had been told he was a leading agent of the Communist International, that I could trust him implicitly, and that I should obey his orders without question. Would he, then, be like the other three I had met? For a moment I felt a touch of panic and had to fight down an impulse to take to my heels.

At the corner of Eighth Street a small, stocky man in his mid-forties appeared seemingly out of nowhere. Brown introduced him briefly as "Timmy" and remarked that he had to leave because he was late for an appointment.

"We can drop you off at the subway," Timmy said. "I have my car here."

As we clambered into his antique Dodge sedan parked around the corner, I thought to myself that certainly my new contact was not impressive looking. On the contrary, he seemed rather colorless and shabby—a little man in a battered brown hat, nondescript suit and well-worn brown shoes. We drove in silence to Fourteenth Street, where Comrade Brown climbed out. "Goodbye and good luck," he said, as he shook hands with me. Timmy swung the car around and headed downtown.

"I know a restaurant on lower Second Avenue where the food is good and we can sit and talk."

Two hours later we were still sitting over dinner. I had told him all I knew about the workings of the Italian Library and a good many personal details about myself. Somehow I found myself pouring out to him all my disturbing experiences with Juliet, Eckhart, and Marcel. For the most part he had sat in thoughtful silence, his eyes guarded, now and then breaking in with swift, intelligent questions. I began to realize that I had underestimated the man: his mind was quick, keen, incisive. Also I revised my first impression of his appearance, which was decidedly not colorless. Although short in stature, he was powerfully built with a large head, very broad shoulders and strong square hands. His eyes were startlingly blue, his hair bright red, and I was intrigued by the fact that his mouth was very much like my mother's. His clothes were well worn, it is true, but they showed that indifference to dress which is characteristic of so many Communist Party workers.

We were still talking when he got to his feet.

"Let's take a drive," he said. "Then we can discuss things further."

As we drove up through Central Park, he began to digress from my problem and to talk about the Communist movement. He told me of the misery and suffering he had seen in Europe, and of the greed and selfishness of a few that had made these conditions possible. Someday, he said, there would be a new society in which men would live like human beings and not like animals. All over the world, Communists were helping to make this dream come true, although they knew that few of them would live to see it realized. Then he went on to tell me about what our comrades were facing in Europe—jail, death, and things that were far worse.

Sensing intense emotion behind his words, I said to him, "You sound as if you had gone through some of these experiences yourself."

"Yes," he said very quietly. "I have. But that is not important." The life of a Communist, he said, is not easy—only the strongest, mentally and physically, can survive. That is why, he added sadly, we lose so many people. They cannot take the hardships involved.

By now we had reached my house. He shut off the ignition and leaned back in his seat.

"You know," he said, "our movement is somewhat like a buggy overcrowded with people going up a steep and rocky road. At every curve someone loses his hold and falls off. That, of course, is what happened to the three people you met before. They started off as good Communists, but they weren't quite strong enough to hold on."

I felt as if someone had hit me in the pit of my stomach. Through the waves of dizziness that swirled around me, I heard his voice as though from a long way off. After a brief time, I steadied myself. What was he saying?

". . . and so you must see that the job you hold is vitally important to the Party. You must stay there at all costs, watch what goes on, and report it to me. We will also be interested in any documents you can safely bring out. You will contact me through a third party whose telephone number I am going to give you. She can reach me at any time. Do you understand?"

I nodded, unable to trust my voice. Inexorably he went on.

"You are now no longer an ordinary Communist but a member of the underground. You must cut yourself off completely from all your old Communist friends. If you happen to meet them and they get curious, you will have to tell them that you have dropped out of the Party. You cannot even be known as a 'liberal' and move in progressive circles. Instead, you must pose as an ultraconservative, with a slight leaning toward Fascism."

I leaned wearily back against the seat and tried to collect my thoughts. All this had happened too fast for me. As if he sensed what was going on in my mind, Timmy suddenly spoke in an oddly gentle voice.

"I know that all this is going to be very hard for you. You will be completely alone except for me. Your fellow comrades may even think you a traitor. But the Party would not ask this sacrifice of you if it were not vitally important."

Then he smiled, and the hard, watchful look seemed to drop from his face. I saw with amazement that he was a very human person, and I found myself liking him.

"Good night and sleep well," he said.

But sleep did not come easily that night. I lay awake trying to sort out my thoughts. I was glad to know that my "unholy trio" had turned out to be traitors—I had never really trusted them anyway. Now the last small fragment of doubt was gone. Even though I didn't fully understand him, there was something reassuring about my new contact.

I liked his simple direct manner, his quick intelligent mind, his obvious air of sincerity. And then, as I thought about my future, a wave of terror swept over me. Without quite knowing why, I felt that I was entering a land from which there was no return.

In the weeks that followed I saw Timmy quite frequently. We usually met in small, out-of-the-way restaurants where we would not be seen, and after eating drove around in his car. He would look over the material I had brought, listen to what I had to report and then, going over the situation with me, point out what was important and what trivial and tell me what to look for in the future. Undoubtedly my "greenness" at undercover work exasperated him, but he was always very patient. He would carefully explain why I had done the wrong thing and then proceed to set forth the correct methods. My amateurish attempts to listen at closed doors and search wastebaskets especially annoyed him.

"That's not the way to operate," he declared flatly. "No one does it except in mystery novels. It's too risky. Concentrate on impressing the Library with the fact that you are trustworthy, so that more and more they will take you into their confidence. Then we shall be able to get all the information we need."

During these weeks my liking and admiration for Timmy became greater. He was a stern taskmaster, it is true, but I felt that no matter how much pressure he was putting on me, he was driving himself still harder. I would look at his tired eyes and haggard face and wonder how he managed to keep going. Strangely enough, even though he had told me that his birthplace was in Russia, he reminded me of my New England parents. There was the same simple, plain way of life, the same capacity for hard work, the same un-swerving loyalty to an ideal, the same shy kindness and generosity, the same feeling for human pain and suffering. I began to look on him as the ideal Communist—a man who, despite his small stature, was head and shoulders above anyone else I had ever known.

It was on a cold, snowy night in December that I discov-ered I was in love with him. He had parked the car while we went to eat, and when we came out sometime later on we found it wedged firmly in a snowdrift. After a great deal of pushing and tugging we finally managed to free the wheels and climbed panting into the car. I surveyed my ruined hat sadly.

"Let me shake it off for you," he said, and reached over for it.

His hand touched mine, I looked at him, and then quite suddenly I found myself in his arms, his lips on mine. We both drew away simultaneously and stared at each other. Time and space seemed to stand still, and in my heart there was a strange sense of peace, as though at last I had come home. Then he smiled shakily and put his hand over mine.

"I've been afraid this would happen. Don't you know I've been in love with you since we first met?"

I could only shake my head, still trying to comprehend what had happened to me. He switched on the ignition and started the car.

"Let's drive for a while."

It was then well after midnight and the snow was coming down heavily, but I don't think either of us was aware of it. He drove furiously up Riverside Drive and out along the Hudson River, through sleeping town after town. With my coat pulled tightly around me, I settled back and let myself float away into an ecstasy that seemed to have no beginning and no end. Nothing mattered any more—I had found the man I loved. His silence was not a barrier between us, even if I momentarily wondered what his thoughts were. There was an inexplicable comfort and warmth in our nearness. As the first streaks of dawn began to touch the sky, he slowed his speed and turned to me.

"Perhaps we'd better go back now."

In a little while the first edges of the sun began to show above the hills. We stopped the car and sat hand in hand, watching it. It was the most beautiful sunrise I had ever seen. Finally he started the motor and we drove on again, still in silence. As we neared the outskirts of New York, he seemed to come out of his reverie.

"I love you very much," he said, almost as though he were talking to himself, "and I should be very happy at this moment. Yet there is the shadow of pain in my heart because I know what lies before us."

I didn't understand what he meant. In my exaltation I had not thought of our love as something that would be a pain or a problem to him. It bewildered me and I sat quite still, listening.

"It would be so very simple if only we were two ordinary Communists, moving in Party circles. Then we could live together as good comrades do. Perhaps, if you wished, we could even be married legally at City Hall in order to conform to bourgeois conventions. That is what we would do under normal circumstances. That is what you would want, isn't it?" he asked, turning to me.

I was surprised at the question. Actually I had not thought about it; indeed I had not thought beyond being so

ompletely happy. After almost four years in the Party I
ad taken the Communist pattern of marital life quite for
ranted. Marriage, we had been told, was an institution in-
ented by the ruling class to perpetuate its power. Commu-
ists who adhered strictly to Party doctrine lived together
; man and wife without bourgeois legal sanctions; others
ade a compromise with the world around them and took
ut a marriage license. Why, then, was he asking me this
id looking at me so sadly?

"I can see that you are puzzled," he said. "But then you
on't understand the situation we are in. The underground
perates very differently from the open Party that you are
;ed to. As you have discovered, each of us is cut off com-
letely from all normal Communist life. We can have no
ontacts that are not strictly necessary for the work of the
arty. Even these few relationships must be kept on an en-
rely impersonal level, otherwise the whole organization
ight be endangered. We are forbidden to form close
iendships and, especially, to fall in love. You and I have
） right, under Communist discipline, to feel the way we
） about each other."

The whole fabric of my world seemed to be collapsing
ound me.

"But that's absurd," I cried. "They have no right to de-
and that!"

"Yes," he said gently, "they do. If personal relationships
e allowed to get in the way of the movement, we shall
ver achieve our goal. That goes without saying. And,
t, at a time like this, it is very difficult to obey instruc-
ns."

"What are you going to do?" I asked dully, experiencing

[101]

directly what I had long known—the fact that, with Com
munists, Party discipline intrudes even into their intimat
personal affairs.

"I don't know," he replied, gripping the wheel very hard
"I should give you a new contact and walk out of your lif
forever. But I don't seem to be able to do it."

We again fell into silence and had reached upper Man
hattan before he spoke again.

"There is only one way out," he explained reluctantly
"and that is to stick together and keep our relationship un
known to everyone. It will be a hard life for both of u:
We will not be able to live together; we will only be abl
to see each other occasionally. You will have to take m
completely on faith, without knowing who I am, where
live, or what I do for a living. Do you think you would b
able to do that?"

I sat staring at the road ahead, only half aware that w
were nearing my neighborhood. What should I say? An
then I knew that I had already made my decision. Here w:
the man whom I admired, loved, and trusted. I belonge
with him, no matter how hard the road ahead might be.

"I'll stick with you." And on these words we parted.

By early spring, 1939, my days with the Italian Library
Information were running out. The director had someho
stumbled over an anti-Fascist article that I had written fo
the *Columbia Spectator* back in 1935. He flung it angrily o
my desk and asked me what I was doing in the Library
I had such violent objections to Fascism. So I was not su:
prised when I was told my services were no longer neede

Meanwhile Timmy and I were shaping up what life te
gether we could. Obviously we had to live apart. Most
our meetings were on business, but whenever he could fin

time from his work, he would snatch a few hours with me. Occasionally we could take a brief week end, get in the car, and drive to some out-of-the-way place—an inn or motel. After I left the Library, I expected to be sent back to the open Party, but Timmy emphasized I would be more useful if I continued to work with him. This pleased me very much, for it meant that I would be able to see him more often. On his instructions, I left the Columbia University area, where he felt that I was too well known to the Communists, and took an apartment in Greenwich Village.

During the rest of the spring and summer I did "odd" jobs for Timmy, meanwhile earning my living as a translator and secretary. I acted as a "mail drop," receiving letters postmarked "Canada," addressed to me but meant for Timmy, and turning them over to him unopened. Much later I discovered his correspondent up there was Fred Rose, a leading Canadian Communist and later Member of Parliament, who was sent to prison for espionage in 1946. I made copies of letters and documents Timmy brought to my apartment. Mostly, however, I did research work for him, digging up facts on people and situations in which he was interested.

Underground methods were now beginning to seem quite natural to me. I no longer thought it odd that I had to communicate with Timmy via a third party, that I must always use a pay telephone when calling him, that if he could not come to my apartment we could only meet on out-of-the-way street corners. Whenever I had an appointment to see him, I was almost automatically on the alert to determine whether or not anyone was following me. Then, too, I had learned all sorts of elaborate precautions to protect the documents and material I had in my possession. If

I had to leave the apartment, I was careful to put them in my black trunk and tie a thin black thread around it so that I would know if they had been tampered with in my absence. And to make doubly sure, I arranged two books in a certain way behind my front door so that anyone who came would inevitably knock them out of position. I never questioned why this pattern of behavior was necessary; I took it for granted as being part of the normal underground procedure.

In the summer of 1939 a number of leading Canadian Communists came down to New York and Timmy, who by now had a great deal of confidence in me, asked if I would help him in his dealings with them.

"I want my meeting with them to look as natural as possible," he said. "So we will take them out to lunch or dinner, and you keep their wives occupied while I transact my business with the men."

What this "business" was, he never told me, and I never asked. I think I had some vague idea that he was a liaison man between the American Party and the Canadian one. So, on numerous occasions we entertained the visiting Canadian functionaries. Two of them I remember quite clearly: Sam Carr, the Communist official who, on his arrest in 1949 by the F.B.I., was deported and is now serving a long prison sentence for espionage in Canada; and Tim Buck, the head of the Canadian Party. The latter I got to know quite well, because he stayed in New York longer than the others. He was a long, lean, rather likable man with a yen for Russian food and "Vat 69" Scotch whiskey. One night I recall that we took him out to the Soviet Pavilion at the New York World's Fair, where he was received with a great flourish and given not only a superspecial dinner but all he could drink of his prized "Vat 69."

It was during this same summer of 1939 that two members of the Mexican Communist Party began shuttling between Mexico and New York. One of them was a tall, dark, fierce-eyed young man by the name of Leopolo Arenal; the other was a short, excessively fat man. I had no idea who Arenal might be, but the fat man I later learned was a Mexican painter. They, too, had business with Timmy, and because Leopolo always brought his wife Helena along, I was taken to lunches and dinners to perform the same role that I had for the Canadians. With wifely pride, I began to realize that Timmy was a much more important man than I had suspected. Obviously, he was a liaison man not only with the Canadian Party but also with the Mexican one.

What I did not know until later on was that the two of them were not just Mexican Communists but part of the Russian Secret Police's hatchet squad. Even then they were laying plans to "liquidate" Leon Trotsky, the Russian ex-revolutionary and Stalin's bitterest enemy, who had taken refuge in Mexico. Timmy needed a "mail drop" where he could receive letters from the Mexicans, and he was unwilling to use my address since it might arouse suspicion were I to have correspondents in both Canada and Mexico. After some thought, he decided to have the letters sent to Leopolo's sister-in-law, Rose Arenal, a school teacher then separated from her husband and living in the Prospect Park section of Brooklyn. I was introduced to Rose, who was told only that I was "Elizabeth," a good and trusted comrade, and it was arranged that I go out to her house every so often to pick up whatever mail she had.

[105]

One night at the end of August 1939 Timmy and I were talking in my apartment when the news of the Nazi-Soviet Nonaggression Pact came over the radio. It hit me like a bombshell. Like all Communists, I regarded the Soviet Union as the land of hope, the one country that had achieved Communism, the leading force in the struggle for a better world. Nazism and Fascism represented all the evils we were fighting against. How, then, could the Soviet Union make an alliance with Nazi Germany? It couldn't be true—the report must be wrong. Timmy, however, didn't seem perturbed.

"No, the news is probably correct."

"But it can't be," I protested. "Here we are working to promote a united front of all progressive forces to fight the evils of Fascism and Nazism. How could the Soviet Union make an alliance with the enemy?"

"You don't understand the dialectics of the situation," he explained, looking at me thoughtfully. "Our ultimate objective of building a new world always remains constant, but we must be realistic and adjust ourselves to the facts as we find them. In the words of a very famous revolutionary, 'we will reach Communism even if we have to crawl there on our bellies.' This means that we may have to twist and turn and do seemingly contradictory things, but we never lose sight of our final goal. Now, take this present move. The Soviet Union is the only Communist country in the world, and as such she is a strong force in our world movement. She must be preserved at all costs if our hope for a Communist world is to come true. Yet you and I know that she is surrounded by a vicious group of capitalist nations waiting to pounce on her and crush her. The situation at the present time is such that if she hadn't signed that pact,

Hitler would most certainly have attacked her. Not only is she totally unprepared to fight but neither the United States nor Great Britain would have come to her aid, for all their noble speeches. In fact, they would have been secretly glad to see her destroyed."

He sat forward on his chair, his blue eyes intent. "Don't think this alliance," he continued, "means the Soviet Union either likes or trusts Germany. It's merely a stalling move to give her time to build up her resources to face a future war of aggression. Don't worry," he concluded grimly, "we shall continue to fight Nazism and Fascism just as vigorously as we did in the past, and the Russian Party will be secretly aiding us."

I thought it over. As a matter of fact I knew relatively little about Marxism-Leninism, compared to a man like Timmy, who had spent his entire life as a revolutionary. And what he said made sense from a practical viewpoint— and that was obviously the most important thing. Certainly the Soviet leaders, with their vast experience, should know precisely what they were doing. Who was I to criticize?

This conviction was confirmed about a week later when Timmy came to me, obviously in a very serious mood.

"We've got to step up the fight against Nazism because the world situation is growing very critical. And so I need your help."

The problem as he explained it to me was this: the Party suspected that Richard Waldo, then president of the McClure Newspaper Syndicate on lower West Street, was a German agent. Every effort had been made to find out what he was doing. They had ransacked his office at night after entering with a skeleton key; they had sent in Communist undercover people in the guise of employees. Since none had been particularly successful, it would be necessary for someone to get a job as his secretary.

"That's where you come in," he said. "Waldo is notoriously hard to get along with. He continually fires his secretaries, and right now he's in the market for a new one. You're a secretary, and with your background with the Fascist Italian Library I think you can get in there. What do you think?"

At first I balked at the idea. I was certainly anxious to fight Nazism, but my short experience with undercover work in the Italian Library had shown me just how nerve-racking such a job could be. Moreover, I still disliked having continually to act out a role. Timmy eyed me sternly.

"A good Bolshevik has courage and discipline," he said, "and he is strong enough to overcome his weaknesses and accept the will of the Party. I wanted so much to be proud of you and instead you are letting me down."

I was ashamed of my momentary rebellion. I did love him very much and I wanted to be a good Communist. He did not force me to make an immediate decision; instead I was left to thrash out the matter for myself.

On Labor Day week end we drove up to Connecticut and found a quiet place near New Haven. We were both utterly exhausted and wanted a complete rest. But we were rudely interrupted. Monday morning the radio blared out the news that the Germans had invaded Poland. Timmy's face grew very set.

"This is it," he announced. "From now on we will be on a wartime basis, with little time for rest or pleasure. Pack your things and we'll get back to the city."

The next day I mustered my courage and went down to the McClure Newspaper Syndicate, pretending that I had been sent there by an employment agency. To my great surprise, Mr. Waldo liked me and the job of being his personal secretary was mine. Shortly after, on September 17, Russia invaded Poland.

"I don't understand," I said to Timmy. "Making a non-aggression pact for self-protection is one thing and invading an innocent country is another."

"You don't know the facts," he replied. "The Polish government now in control is quite as beastly and vicious as was the old Czarist one in Russia. The vast mass of people in Poland have been ground under the heel of a ruthless, greedy clique of men. Germany's invasion has given our Soviet comrades the opportunity to go in and liberate the Polish workers and peasants."

On the heels of the Russian invasion came a swift shift in the policy of the American Communist Party. Ever since I had been a member, our entire program had revolved around building a united front of all peoples and nations to fight against the Fascist aggressors. Internationally, we stood for collective security; domestically, we upheld the New Deal and its "progressive" policies. Now, suddenly, the Party denounced this second world war as an "imperialist" one and demanded that the United States stay out of it. It continued, however, to support the "liberal" domestic ideas of the Roosevelt administration. This abrupt about-face in tactics puzzled me. I took my problem to Timmy.

"Will you please explain to me what's going on?" I asked.

"It's very simple," he said. "We worked to build up a united-front program because we hoped that through a coalition of peace-loving nations we could avoid war. Now it's happened. And as you can see from what I told you about Poland, it's not a people's war. It's just the same old conflict between greedy 'imperialist' powers that's been going on for centuries. Each side is fighting for its own self-ish interests and doesn't care anything about the welfare of humanity. Why should we let our country get into this struggle? Thousands of good Americans would be killed and nothing would be gained by it."

By now I had arrived at the point where I relied almost completely on Timmy's judgment in matters of Communist doctrine, and I accepted his explanation of the change in "line" without any question. It was perfectly clear from the work I was doing that the Party was continuing to fight Fascism, even though publicly it was pursuing a seemingly contradictory policy. It never occurred to me to question the good faith of the Party leaders. I was quite sure they were following the best course possible in view of the circumstances.

Isolated as I was in the underground, I was completely unaware of what was going on in the open Party. Only much later on did I learn that the double news of the Soviet Union's invasion of Poland and the change in our program had spread consternation throughout the Party ranks. Many members, among them old friends of mine, became disillusioned and turned in their cards; others still in the grip of Communist ideology managed to rationalize their misgivings and remained.

During the early fall of 1939 public opinion in this country began to turn against the Soviet Union, which was denounced as an aggressor nation and excoriated for her brutal attack on Poland. This same violent feeling was directed against the American Communist Party, always vigorously defending the Russian point of view. It was called "Russian-inspired"; it was accused of having deserted the anti-Fascist movement in its hour of greatest need and of being itself Fascist dominated. With growing amazement and alarm, I watched the hysteria build up. Was this the beginning of a Communist witch-hunt?

In the midst of all this furor I was at work in the McClure Newspaper Syndicate—a hard, grueling job. Mr. Waldo was difficult to please, and I lived in constant terror of his acid, biting criticisms. Indeed there was no peace anywhere in the office, for all his employees were so afraid of displeasing him that they were jumpy and on edge. But I carried out my Party task as well as I could, hating each moment of it but happy in the thought that I was helping to fight Fascism. I kept track of all the strange people with whom Mr. Waldo was in contact, watched what was going on in the office, and smuggled out copies of interesting documents and correspondence. At night I would come home frazzled and exhausted and tumble into bed; in the morning I would set my teeth and go back to work. And always there was Timmy—sympathetic, encouraging, instructing.

I tried to make friends with the other employees but I found them rather aloof and uncommunicative. Just why, I thought to myself, do they behave that way, and why in the world do they continue working in an office where the salaries are not good and the atmosphere so uncongenial? Five years later I learned with amusement that I wasn't the only "plant" in Mr. Waldo's office. His activities were evidently known to a number of anti-Fascist organizations— not to mention actual intelligence agencies—and most of the other employees were also there to spy on him.

Sometime that fall I suddenly discovered, quite by accident, who Timmy was and where he worked. Up to then I had vaguely assumed he was some sort of journalist, because he seemed to know so much about the newspaper world. I met him on this occasion in Madison Square Park. While we sat for a while on a bench watching the pigeons and talking, he pulled a bunch of tickets out of his pocket.

"I've been able to get some passes to a good play and I'm going to give them to my friends. Would you like a couple?"

He handed me two and I idly noted what I thought was the name "Golos" written on one of them.

"These must be earmarked for another friend of yours," I said, pointing to the penciled notation. "My name isn't Golos."

I was quite unprepared for his reaction. His face went very white and his eyes became wary. With an abrupt motion, he got to his feet and started to walk away.

"I've got to get back to work," he stated coldly.

Completely puzzled, I followed him out of the park. A week later, as we sat over dinner in a restaurant on the lower East Side, I started to ask him a question, "Timmy, I would . . ."

"Why do you keep pretending you don't know my real name," he broke in angrily. "You've known it ever since I gave you those tickets."

I stared at him in bewilderment and then light dawned.

"Then your name is Golos?" I asked.

"Don't put on an act," he said crossly. "You know perfectly well I am Jacob Golos."

His tone implied that any Party person ought to know who he was, but the name itself meant nothing to me. In the Communist circles in which I had previously moved, knowledge of Party personages and activities in this country was scanty. Yet, to anyone who had had a long experience with the Communist movement in the United States, Jacob Golos was a famous person. He had been extremely active in the early days of the Party, among other things helping to set up the Technical Aid Society for Soviet Russia—an organization for the training of men and women to be sent from the United States to the U.S.S.R. Later on he became increasingly well known, especially as one of the editors of the Russian Communist newspaper *Novy Mir*, published in New York. By the early thirties he was head of World Tourists, a travel agency set up by the American Communist Party in 1927 for the dual purpose of making money and encouraging tourists to go to Russia. Moreover, he was high up in Party circles, being one of the three-man Central Control Commission, that ruthless disciplinary committee which keeps the American comrades in line. He was one of the "behind-the-scenes" manipulators who actually gave the orders in the Communist Party—I remember his telling me much later that he attended all the top Communist meetings, where he sat behind a black curtain so that he wouldn't be seen.

Not wanting to hurt his feelings, I refrained from telling Timmy that I hadn't the slightest idea who Golos was. Perhaps, too, I was somewhat bewildered and upset at his attitude.

"Well," he admitted resignedly, "now that you know, I suppose it does make things simpler. From now on you can phone me at World Tourists when you want me and forget that other telephone number. But remember to be very careful what you say. I am never sure whether or not my wires are being tapped." Then he smiled. "I didn't mean to jump on you but you know the rules of the underground. Perhaps in a way I'm glad because I don't have to pretend to you any more. And you'd better call me Yasha and not Timmy."

A deep sense of relief filled me. Of his love I was always sure, and now I knew that what bothered him was not that he personally didn't trust me—it was Party discipline again. For the next month or so Yasha (occasionally I forgot and called him Timmy) told me nothing further about himself personally, although he did let me know more about World Tourists. It was, he said, a travel agency. Although World Tourists handled travel reservations to every country, its main business was sending individual tourists and groups to the Soviet Union, on which it got preferential treatment. The result was that during the thirties it did a land-office business in Russian travel and the profits rolled in.

"Don't think I'm a millionaire," he said laughingly. "Although the books don't show it, World Tourists is really owned by the Party. I just run it for them and receive a salary for my services. All the money that we make goes to them."

I puzzled over this revelation briefly. I hadn't realized that the Party engaged in "bourgeois" industry. Somehow I had thought, as a good many Communists did, that its income derived solely from the dues of its members and from the contributions of sympathizers. It seemed there were a good many things that I didn't know.

What I knew about Yasha personally was very little. I learned that he lived somewhere in a cheap rented room and spent the minimum on himself. A life of poverty—at one time he and his roommate at college could never attend classes at the same time because they had only one pair of pants between them—had taught him to be frugal. At first I tried to get him to buy a new hat—his battered brown felt was a particular bone of contention between us—but he so consistently refused that finally I gave up.

While Yasha and I were getting to know each other better in the little things of life, the general feeling of antagonism toward the Communist Party was growing in the United States. Even the Roosevelt administration, with which the Party had been friendly and whose "progressive" policies it had supported, was growing hostile. Yasha began to be alarmed at these developments.

"It looks as if the American government is going to crack down on us," he said. "Perhaps the Party will be outlawed and driven underground."

Not long after, the blow fell. One night Yasha came to see me looking white and strained.

"I'm afraid it's happened. Our offices were raided this morning by the Department of Justice and they've planted agents at the front door to question anyone who comes in. It's very lucky that I told you under no circumstances to come up there. Otherwise you might have been involved."

"But what excuse do they have for doing that?" I demanded indignantly.

"They say that since we have a contract with Intourist, we should have registered as foreign agents. That's absurd, of course. The American Express has a similar contract and they haven't been bothered."

He got to his feet and began to pace up and down the room.

"I've been served with a *duces tecum* subpoena," he said wearily, "and that means I've got to appear in court with all my files and documents. There's no time to destroy anything, and some of that material is going to involve our comrades badly. Why didn't I get rid of it before?"

He sat down on the couch and put his head between his hands. Quietly I moved over and put my arm around him. This was going to be a bad strain for him, and already he was so tired and overworked.

The indictment of World Tourists went before the Federal Court in New York and the trial began. It seemed to drag on endlessly, first in New York and later in Washington. Yasha was on the stand hour after hour. The American authorities were trying to get him to admit that he had been mixed up in illegal activities, but solidly and unwaveringly he stood his ground. After his death one of his lawyers, Joe Brodsky, told me what a magnificent fight he had put up.

"I remember one of the last days in court," he said. "Golos had been battered for days but, tired as he was, he refused to give in. During the recess one of the prosecuting attorneys, his nerves frayed by the long battle, rushed up to Golos, grabbed him by the coat lapels and shook him. 'You ——,' he cried. 'Why the hell won't you talk?' Golos just looked at him quietly, disengaged himself, and walked away."

But the frightful strain was telling on Yasha. His red hair was becoming grayer and sparser, his blue eyes seemed to have no more fire in them, his face became habitually white and taut. When he came to see me, he would fall on the couch, trying to catch his breath after the three flights of stairs he had climbed, and he would complain of a queer pain on the left side of his chest.

Increasing worry about him was beginning to make me edgy, and occasionally I would blow up and ask why he didn't take things easier. He would smile crookedly.

"I can't rest," he would say. "I still have a job to do.

What happens to me personally doesn't matter, but the fate of our movement is important."

What was aging Yasha was not alone the grueling trial but the sense that he had let down his old comrades. The files which the Department of Justice had seized in their World Tourists raid proved conclusively that Earl Browder had gone abroad under a pseudonym and with the aid of faked papers. He was arrested on the charge of passport fraud. This seemed to upset Yasha more than anything else.

"Earl is my friend," he kept saying, over and over. "I have known him for many years and I like him. It is *my* carelessness that is going to send him to jail."

Night after night, I would hold him in my arms, trying to make him relax. Then, after he had finally fallen into a restless sleep, I would lie awake for hours trying to straighten things out in my mind. I was so terribly tired myself: the combination of the nerve-racking job at Wallo's office and the strain of worrying about Yasha was beginning to tell on me. Over and over I wished we could get away from this driving life and go off by ourselves and lead a normal existence. I knew this was impossible, that Yasha had always been and would always be a Communist revolutionary, and that in accepting him I had automatically accepted this sort of life.

Mingled with my fatigue and apprehension for him, too, was a smoldering indignation against the United States government. What right did they have to persecute his friend, Earl Browder, for going abroad on a false passport? Obviously he had done so to avoid difficulties with the authorities of the Fascist countries through which he had to pass in order to get to Moscow. A good many top United States officials traveled under assumed names—as did famous personages wanting to be incognito—and no one seemed to think it illegal. The Justice Department was just using this episode to "get" our people, and in the process they were killing the man I loved. I began to hate them bitterly.

Meanwhile, it looked as though more and more Communist organizations were being caught in the Justice Department's net. First there was the *Daily Worker*, the American Communist Party's official organ; then International Publishers, headed by Alexander Trachtenberg, a famous Communist; and many others. In each case the charge was the same: the organization was tied up with the Soviet government and had broken the law by failing to register as a "foreign agent." The strategy of the Justice Department was rapidly becoming clear. It intended to force all our organizations to register as "agents of the Soviet government," thus labeling the whole American Communist movement as Russian inspired. In the current atmosphere of hysteria against the Russian invasion of Poland, it would be extremely simple to pass laws in this country outlawing the Party as an un-American group, thus forcing us underground.

In spite of the fact that the Justice Department seemed to be getting nowhere, American Communist officials were worried. Long experience with Justice Department operatives had taught them that these people were tenacious and did not give up easily. Because of this, Yasha told me, a meeting of the Central Committee was being called. When I saw him the evening after, I was frightened at his appearance. With a gesture of utter weariness he sank into a chair and in a few brief words told me what had happened.

It had been a long session. As the hours had dragged on the room had become choked with smoke and the members had begun to doze in their seats. Finally a decision was reached. The Party would give the Justice Department a "victim" in the hope, as a *quid pro quo*, that the witch-hunt would be called off. One by one the various organizations involved in the raids had been considered, then the members of the committee had settled on World Tourists as the sacrificial goat.

"I protested against the decision"—Yasha spoke like a beaten man—"but I was overruled. And as a good Communist, I'm obliged to carry it out." Then he got to his feet and paced up and down the room. "I never thought," he stated in a tone of complete despair, "that I would live to see the day when I would have to plead guilty in a bourgeois court."

He threw himself down on the bed and turned his face to the wall. Very gently I covered him with a blanket and in a few minutes he was sleeping the sleep of utter exhaustion.

For some time I sat staring at the wall. Why did the Party have to demand this added sacrifice of him when he had already given so much? Why did they have to crucify him like this?

According to the Party's instructions, he went before a Federal judge and pleaded guilty to the charge of not registering as an agent of the Soviet government. He was given a suspended sentence of one year and an order to fill out the foreign agents' registration forms immediately. However, the cases against the other Communist organizations were not pressed and so International Publishers, the *Daily Worker*, and the rest did not have to declare themselves as agents of the Soviet government. Temporarily, at least, the American Communist Party had escaped from a bad situation.

CHAPTER VI

AFTER THE TRIAL was over and done with, Yasha became more like his normal self. He looked more rested, the color came back to his face, his step was buoyant again.

But the next few months were very difficult ones for him. The office of World Tourists, formerly an important organization in left-wing circles, became overnight a place to be avoided. Promptly after the trial's conclusion, Communist officers in the business, among them Alexander Trachtenberg, hurriedly tendered their resignations and took to their heels. Old customers, afraid of being involved with an organization now labeled a Soviet agency, drifted away. Yasha sat in his empty office, feeling himself an outcast.

"The rats are deserting the sinking ship," he said grimly to me.

Meanwhile, back in February 1940 I had been fired by Mr. Waldo in one of his habitual fits of rage. Walking home that night, I felt a sense of relief at being out of that weird place, but I did hate to tell Yasha that I had let him down. He took the news quite calmly, however, lost no time in instructing another comrade to take my place while I found a job in an advertising agency, and continued to carry on with the usual odd jobs he gave me.

On my way home one May afternoon I stopped at a

drugstore and telephoned Rose Arenal to see if she had any letters. She sounded tense and as if she were on the verge of hysteria.

"No," she said. "There's nothing. But please come see me this evening. Something terrible has happened."

Wondering just what was going on, I sat down at the counter and ordered a Coca-Cola, meanwhile glancing over the evening paper. Then I froze in my seat. What I found was only a small item, datelined Mexico City, but I had to reread it five times before I was able to take it all in. Leon Trotsky's personal guard—an American named Robert Sheldon Harte—had been kidnaped and later found shot in the back, "Mexican style." The murderers were named as Leopolo and Luis Arenal. I folded the paper and walked into the nearest telephone booth. Yasha would still be at the office.

"I must see you immediately," I said, putting what urgency I could in the words.

An hour later we sat on a park bench in Sheridan Square in the Village. Wordlessly, I handed him the paper and pointed out the item to him.

He read the article thoughtfully and then put the paper down on the bench. His face was noncommittal.

"It shouldn't have been done," he commented at last. "That's the trouble with dealing with those hot-headed Mexicans. They go off and act on impulse."

I was weak with relief. More than I realized, I had been worried and fearful that Yasha had been mixed up in this murder. Obviously, judging from what he said, he not only had had nothing to do with it, but he did not condone it.

Later on I realized ironically that I had completely misunderstood his words. He was condemning not the murder but the bungling job the killers had done. For, as time showed me, Jacob Golos was one of the Russian Secret Police men who were assigned to engineer the assassination of Leon Trotsky. The murder of Robert Sheldon Harte, Trotsky's personal guard, had occurred in an abortive attempt to get the Russian ex-revolutionary himself. Another attempt was more successful. Several months after this a G.P.U. killer who was thought for some time to be a member of a rival Trotskyite faction, was apprehended a few minutes after he had plunged an alpenstock into Trotsky's brain. What Yasha thought about this latter murder I never learned from him. But Harte's death, because of our contacts with the assassins, came close to home and he was instant with his directions.

"Break off all connections with Rose immediately," he snapped, "and stay away from that neighborhood. This thing's too hot."

"But she's expecting me tonight," I protested, "and she's in trouble."

"We can't take a chance," he said. "She's probably under suspicion already, being Luis's wife. Maybe he's even hiding out there. I just hope she doesn't go to pieces and talk too much."

The words sounded callous but I realized he was right. What happened to an individual Communist was unimportant compared to the welfare of the Party. Certainly I had seen Yasha go through hell for his convictions.

All that spring before Harte's death, World Tourists had continued steadily downhill and Yasha finally accepted the fact.

Yet he still had his dreams and he meant to make them

come true. One night in the summer of 1940 he came to my apartment with some typewritten sheets.

"Here is a plan I drew up in 1932," he said. "Read it and see what you think of it."

The project called for an agency to handle all the passenger and freight traffic between this country and the Soviet Union. Yet, unlike the Amtorg Trading Corporation, a Russian commercial agency that handled all the Soviet business interests in the United States, it was to be an American outfit, run not by Russians but by Americans. It sounded interesting and I said so.

"This should have been done a long time ago," he declared. "The Amtorg's been too long in sole control of all business relations between this country and the Soviet Union. And they've certainly messed things up. They're inefficient. They don't know the least thing about modern American business methods and they've done nothing but antagonize the decent businessmen over here."

I looked surprised and said, "But I thought that Communists, no matter from what country they come, would make it a point to do a good job."

"Most of them aren't Communists," he pointed out acridly. "They are riffraff and remnants of the old Czarist regime. When you're building up a new society, you have to work with what you have. We picked them because they had been in private enterprise over there before the Revolution and we thought they knew more about business than we did."

He got up from his chair and paced the floor.

"I had hoped to use World Tourists as the base for this new organization," he continued. "But we're too well smeared now. Therefore, we'll have to set up a completely new outfit. I've talked to Earl Browder and he says that the Party's Finance Committee will put up the money to get it started. Now, we need an ultrarespectable businessman, with good connections, to head the thing. I'm going to work on that now."

Sometime in the fall of 1940 he came in a jubilant mood to see me.

"Earl's found just the right man," he said happily. "His name is John Hazard Reynolds and he lives in a swank apartment up on Fifth Avenue, in the sixties. Good old American family, Social Registerite, moves in the top circles, both social and business. He himself has a fair income but his wife has a million. Reynolds was a Wall Street broker but got out before the 1929 crash and doesn't seem to have done much of anything else since. He's getting a little tired of the life of leisure and would like to get into some business."

"Do you mean to say he would run a business for the Communist Party?" I asked in amazement.

"Certainly," Yasha replied. "He's a radical from way back. Spoke on a platform with Scott Nearing, the old Communist propagandist, around 1919. He's a contributor to the Party and one of the three angels of our publication *Soviet Russia Today*. In fact, that's how we happened to find him. Ted Bayer, the managing editor of that magazine, recommended him."

"When do you start?"

"Just as soon as we can find one of our own men to handle the practical operation of the business. Reynolds isn't much of a businessman and, anyway, we wouldn't trust him that far. We just want him for a front guy to give the proper tone to the enterprise."

"Does he know that?" I queried.

"No, and he won't. He's been told that he will be in complete charge of the whole agency. I don't think he'll object to our sending someone in to do the real work. He's the sort of person who likes to sit behind a desk and look important."

Two weeks later, Yasha dropped in for dinner and sat down dejectedly in a chair.

"I'm getting discouraged about this idea," he said. "In addition to being temperamental, Reynolds is a complete snob and he won't accept any of the men we've suggested because they don't have the proper background. Would you like the job?"

"Me?" I said in amazement. "But why?"

"Because," he explained, "you have the sort of background he would go for—New England family, Vassar education, and so forth. You had a lot of experience with your father in department stores and you've been working in various New York businesses. I'll teach you everything I know about the field, and then with my coaching and some good, hard work I think you can swing the job. What do you say?"

"I'd love it," I said enthusiastically. "That is, if you think I can do it."

"Good," he said and smiled. "But remember that you will have to sell yourself to Reynolds on your own merits. I can't force you on him."

In November, Yasha called me over to his office during my lunch hour and introduced me to John H. Reynolds, a tall, lean man in his early fifties, with fading reddish hair and a prominent nose. From his carefully matching tie and breast-pocket handkerchief to his expensive-looking shoes, he was impeccably dressed. His slightly arrogant manner and his accent said loudly Park Avenue, the Racket Club, and the Plaza.

We talked for about an hour. Three weeks later he telephoned me and asked if I would meet him at the Vanderbilt Hotel. We lunched and finally he got to the point and asked me if I would accept the position of vice president in the new firm. With secret amusement and feeling very much like the cat that had swallowed the canary, I was properly overcome but accepted.

During the next two months, negotiations with Intourist, the Soviet agency in Moscow which handled all such package shipments, went on at a slow pace. Although Yasha apparently had contacts in the Soviet Consulate in New York who had great influence in Moscow, the Intourist people obviously were determined to force upon us a one-sided deal and refused to give an inch. Reynolds, accustomed to having his own way, was getting more and more annoyed. This fact, combined with the Russians' mulishness, had by now gotten Yasha thoroughly angry.

"I'll put the screws on them," he told me, "and see if we can't break the deadlock. They're just a bunch of traders."

Meanwhile, at least the routine arrangements for setting up the business were progressing. Earl Browder gave Reynolds $15,000 in bills as initial capital for the enterprise. Reynolds split this sum five ways and very cautiously made deposits in five different banks so that he might cover up the fact that he had been receiving money from the Communist Party.

During this period I continued at my advertising job and spent my nights and week ends at World Tourists, where Yasha explained to me how the package business operated. Although the ultimate goal of the new business was to handle all freight and passenger traffic to the U.S.S.R., the current war situation in Europe made it necessary for us to start on a small scale, handling only the shipment of parcels containing food, clothing, and medicine to individuals in the Soviet Union.

I read innumerable files and documents and learned the practical aspects of the business so fully that I could make up a package and wrap it myself and type a Soviet import license on a Russian typewriter. Late at night I would wearily drag myself home and fall into bed. But somehow I didn't mind the fatigue. I was enthusiastic about the new business and I wanted to be qualified to do a real job.

The only thing that worried me then was Yasha's health. The strange pains on the left side of his chest had disappeared after the trial was over but seemingly were bothering him again. He never mentioned them, but every so often he would suddenly put his hand over his heart. One night he arrived very late, his face ashen, walked slowly over to the couch, and leaned back against the cushions. I was immediately frightened and rushed over to him.

"I'm afraid there's something wrong with my heart," he said shakily. "While with Earl Browder tonight on the street, I suddenly couldn't get my breath. I leaned up against a building and fought for a half hour before I could even talk."

I sat beside him and held on to his cold hands in a sudden wave of panic.

"You must go see a doctor right away."

"There's no use," he shook his head sadly. "I spent four years in medical school myself and I know."

Long after he had fallen asleep, I sat up worrying about him. Somehow I had to get him to a doctor. Obviously, insisting that he go wouldn't work.

I was pondering this problem one night when Yasha came up, his arms laden with packages of documents. "Not long ago the Dies Committee raided our offices," he announced. "Needless to say, I've had my lesson and they didn't find anything. However, I've decided that it's foolish to keep all this material around, even though it's in a fairly safe hiding place. We'll burn it up in your fireplace. I'm living in a cheap hotel now and there's no place to destroy it there."

He opened the packages and spilled the contents onto the floor. As he did so, I threw them piece by piece on the fire. There were sheaves of what seemed to be reports in English and Russian, and then I discovered to my great surprise a heap of red passports stamped with the official seal of the United States of America.

"Why are you throwing away perfectly good passports?"

"They're not genuine," he answered absently, as he rifled through a batch of documents. "World Tourists sent a lot of Americans to Spain to fight during the Civil War and they all traveled on fake passports."

I nodded and methodically tore the covers off the passports, ripped the pages out, and tossed them into the fireplace. Then as I gathered up another bunch of papers, a small folder fell out and dropped at my feet. I picked it up and casually looked at it. On the inside cover was a picture of Yasha evidently taken many years earlier; on the right was some printing in Russian. With my meager knowledge of the language I could only make out his name in Russian characters and "G.P.U." Beneath was the date 1925.

I thought to myself that the initials were vaguely familiar. Hadn't I heard many years before that the G.P.U. was some sort of Russian terrorist organization? Unfortunately, in my pre-Party days I had had absolutely no interest in history or current affairs; I hadn't even cared about reading the newspapers. And after I had become a member of the Communist Party, quite naturally I would never have learned anything about the G.P.U.—the one organization, I found out later, that was never mentioned in Party circles under any circumstances. Otherwise I would have known, as many non-Communist Americans did by that time, that the G.P.U. was the dreaded Russian Secret Police, a far more ruthless group than Hitler's famous Gestapo ever was. So, puzzled, I forgot I should not ask questions and held the card out to Yasha.

"What's this?"

He looked at it for a moment in silence, tossed it on the burning heap in the fireplace, then picked up the poker to stir the half-burned papers so they would catch fire more easily.

"It's just an identity card," he said, without looking at me. "I was in Russia after the Revolution, and as part of my work I was a member of the police force. We were issued those cards so that we could identify ourselves and get free rides on trains and buses."

Fully accepting this explanation, I resumed my work at the fireplace. I did think to myself that my memory must be very unreliable—certainly Yasha, who was born and brought up there, ought to know all about Russia.

By the last days of January 1941 Yasha's pressure on his Russian contacts was beginning to produce results and Intourist was ready to deal with us on a fair business basis. The starting capital was larger than we had expected, for at the last minute Reynolds had decided to add $5,000 of his own to the Party's $15,000.

Reynolds and I finally found a good office on the nineteenth floor of 212 Fifth Avenue, where we had a fine view of the Hudson River over to the New Jersey shore. We signed the lease and, anxious to get started, moved into a bare office next door while the alterations were being made. Before we did, however, Yasha told me he had some Party work for me to do.

"Up till now you've had only the Penguin to take care of," he said. "Now you'll have to take on some additional undercover contacts." The Penguin was one of the "odd jobs" that I had at the time. His real name was Abe Brothman and he was a chemical engineer who, because of his usefulness to the underground, had been removed from his Communist Party unit and put in direct contact with Yasha. The previous spring I had been introduced to him, and from then on it had been my job to meet Abe periodically and collect the blueprints which he had painstakingly gotten together. Since Abe seemed constitutionally unable to be on time for his appointments and often kept me waiting on street corners in the cold or rain, I heaved a sigh of relief when, in September 1941, I was told to turn him over to someone else. Who the new contact was I didn't know at the time; it was only in the summer of 1950 that I discovered that he had been taken over by Harry Gold, who was convicted of espionage in December 1950 and sentenced to thirty years. Brothman is now serving a seven-year sentence in the federal penitentiary for obstruction of justice.

Yasha now explained that he would soon introduce me to Mary Price, a Communist of many years' standing. She was a charter member, under the name of Mary Watkins, of the United Office and Professional Workers of America and then was Washington secretary of the well-known writer and columnist Walter Lippmann. Yasha said Mary had told him that Lippmann had very interesting material in his files on inside politics in the American government which Yasha felt the Party should have. She belonged to an old American family, was born in Greensboro, North Carolina, and Southerners were the last people to be suspected of being Communists. Yasha added that this background made her perfect for undercover work.

That evening, at Schrafft's on Fifth Avenue and 13th Street, Yasha and I had dinner with Mary, a brunette of average height, slender, attractive but not pretty, with steady, cool eyes. After we had gone over all the ins and outs of the situation, it was decided I would go to Washington once a month to pick up any material she had. She on her part would come up to New York once a month. Our traveling expenses would be paid by the Party. This meant that the information would be coming through every two weeks.

On my first visit to Washington I spent Saturday and Sunday with Mary in the charming old Georgetown house she shared with two other girls, both of them fellow comrades who worked in the American government. Mr. Lippmann was away just then, presumably on business, and it was decided that Mary would go through his back files and bring home all the "interesting" stuff so we could make copies of it. For two days we typed madly until our backs ached, and we somehow managed to finish everything. Then Mary returned the files to the office, and I tucked the copies into my briefcase and returned with them to New York. Yasha was delighted with the haul.

"That's excellent material," he said happily.

Soon after, the U.S. Service & Shipping Corporation, our new firm, was installed in permanent offices, and they were elegant ones, befitting the exalted position Reynolds considered he occupied. He had ordered the most expensive furniture available, beautiful linen paper had been put on the walls of the private offices, and he had even brought down some of his mother's antique furniture, including a love seat for his office and some shaky-legged tables—definitely not utilitarian and of questionable beauty. Yasha eyed all this grandeur with contempt.

"All it needs is lace curtains," he said scornfully, when Reynolds was out of hearing.

He was even more appalled the morning Reynolds came down with a tremendous oil painting of one of his ancestors who, as he pompously pointed out, had been the first elected mayor of New York. In silence, we watched while Reynolds proudly put it on the wall.

"That's my great-grandfather hanging there," he declared with an air of superiority.

Yasha could stand it no longer. "My great-grandfather was hanged, too," he said thoughtfully, "but under slightly different circumstances."

Yet Yasha tolerated Reynolds acting the aristocrat, because obviously he was a perfect front for the business. He was well known and respected in the Chase National Bank where we did business; he hired a socially top-notch firm of accountants; his lawyers were apparently impeccable. So impressed was the State Department by his eminent respectability that they told us we didn't have to register as "foreign agents" even though we did have a contract with a subdivision of the Soviet government. Moreover, as a subagent of the U.S. Service, World Tourists was being rehabilitated. Since it no longer had any direct connection with the Soviet government, it was permitted to withdraw its registration as a "foreign agent." The former "red" taint seemed to be disappearing in the minds of the general public. Old customers returned in droves to send packages and the future looked good.

With all these preoccupations, I had little time to worry about Yasha's health, but I was brought up short late in March. Yasha had another attack; he couldn't get his breath and I decided that something drastic had to be done about getting him to a doctor. At last I realized he was procrastinating because he really didn't want to know the truth about his condition. I hit on a ruse.

"I'm going up to see my sinus specialist," I told him. "Why don't you come along and see him, too? I think all that's the matter with you is a bad bronchial condition."

Somewhat reassured, he drove up to 64th Street with me and was ushered into the doctor's office. I sat down on a chair in the comfortable waiting room. Outside, a cold March rain was lashing against the windows and the wind was howling like a lost soul. I shivered a little, in spite of the warmth of the room, and lit a cigarette. Twelve years before, almost to the day, while a storm raged outside, I had sat in a similar waiting room and stared unseeingly at a picture on the wall. Inside the hospital somewhere my mother lay on an operating table. Then the doctor, grave faced but kindly, had appeared and told me gently there was no hope.

A sudden sense of panic now gripped me. I sprang to my feet and began to pace the floor. Was that same pattern of death going to be repeated? Was I again going to lose the only person I loved? The door opened and Yasha walked out, followed by the doctor.

He looked very grave. "I'm afraid Mr. Golos has an extremely bad heart condition, technically called arteriosclerosis," he said. "However, I think we've caught it in time, and if he takes very good care of himself he may live for some time yet."

Numbly, we walked out of the office and got into the car.

"I'm not very hungry," Yasha said after a while, "but I suppose we ought to eat."

We stopped off at a cafeteria and ate halfheartedly in silence. Then we drove on home. I closed the door of the apartment behind me and threw the keys on the table. Yasha had sat down on the couch with his coat and hat still on. I moved over beside him, trying to pull myself together, trying not to give way to my emotions. Suddenly, with a gesture of desperation, he threw his arms around me and held on as though I were the only stable thing in a world that was crashing around him.

"This is the end," he said.

"No, of course it isn't," I said reassuringly, holding him very tight. "It only means that you've got to take better care of yourself. There will be many years ahead for us."

But even as I said it, I knew with the awful feeling of finality that this really was the end. Yasha was a revolutionary and he would keep on driving himself, no matter what his physical condition was. Someday soon I would lose him.

[134]

Things went along quite as usual until May, when Yasha suddenly walked into my office one day and closed the door. He put a folded copy of the *New York Times* in front of me and pointed to an article.

The story, with picture, stated that a Russian engineer by the name of Ovakimian had just been taken into custody by the F.B.I. on charges of espionage. I looked at Yasha inquiringly.

"That's the man I've been in contact with," he said somberly, "although I didn't know his name until I saw it in the paper. Now I'm afraid we're in the soup."

I still couldn't quite get my bearings.

"But you aren't mixed up in Russian espionage," I said dazedly, and then, seeing the look on his face, "You mean, you are?"

"I thought you knew," he said in some surprise. "I am a member of the G.P.U., that is the Russian Secret Police. We are responsible for doing intelligence work for the Soviet Union all over the world. That man whose picture you see in the paper is my superior officer."

I stared at him in silence, wondering why I hadn't guessed all this long before. I had had all the pieces of the puzzle in my hands: Yasha's contacts with members of the Canadian and Mexican Communist Parties, his G.P.U. card, his friends at the Soviet Consulate, his influence in obtaining our contract with Intourist so easily. I had just taken all these things for granted as they came, one by one, and had not stopped to put them together. And now I found that I wasn't too shocked by this revelation. After all, Yasha had been born in Russia, had lived there for many years and, despite his American citizenship, still felt that he owed his primary allegiance to that country.

"Then all this information we are gathering is going to the Russians?" I asked.

"Why not?" he demanded. "They certainly need it, and we need to help the one Communist country that exists in the world if we are to achieve a new social order in this country. Moreover, it's not just going to the Soviet Union. The information is filtered out in Moscow and what is useful to other Communist parties is sent on to them. Remember the Soviet Union is our spiritual Fatherland, our one hope for a new world society, and we should assist her in any way possible." Yes, I thought, that is true. But I was worried about Yasha.

"Are you going to be involved in all this?" I asked anxiously.

"I'm afraid I am," he said thoughtfully. "I wouldn't be surprised if the F.B.I. agents turned up on my doorstep. That's why from now on we'll have to be very careful. I don't want to lead them to you. And for heaven's sake, don't let Reynolds know that anything is wrong. He'd fall apart at the seams."

A few days later the taxi driver who had a regular stand in front of the World Tourists building and who had driven Yasha on numerous occasions came up to see him.

"A couple of agents from the F.B.I. questioned me the other day," he said. "They wanted to know where I had let you out the other day, the time you went up to Seventh Avenue and 34th Street. I thought you'd like to know."

Yasha thanked the man for his kindness and rushed over to see me.

"They're after me, as I feared," he said grimly. "And they may very well have found you, too. Be very careful in the future. Watch to see if you're being tailed and be sure you've thrown off any surveillance before you go to see Mary or Bob or the Penguin."

"But what do I do?" I said in a panic.

"Just keep your head, appear casual, and don't let them know you've noticed them," he said soothingly. "Then after an appropriate interval dash onto a subway when the doors are closing, or else find a building with more than one exit. Go in one way and out the other."

I shook my head dubiously. It was one thing to read about dodging pursuit, as all the heroes in the murder mysteries did, and another to find that you had to do it yourself.

He patted my shoulder gently. "Don't worry," he reassured me. "You'll do all right." Unconvinced, I watched him go out of the office and close the door.

A few nights later on, Reynolds invited Yasha and me up to his house for dinner. We left my office late and as we reached the lobby of the building we saw two men, one standing at each exit. There was no doubt as to who they were, for the building at that hour was always completely deserted. My stomach seemed to turn upside down and I realized we were trapped. There was no other way out.

"They've followed me here," Yasha said to me out of the corner of his mouth. "I don't want to take them up to Reynolds, so go on ahead without me and I'll get rid of them and come later."

For the next hour I sat over cocktails with the Reynoldses, my nerves in tight knots, trying very hard to appear nonchalant and not show my anxiety. The hands of the clock seemed to crawl as I kept saying, "He'll be here any moment," and hoped that it was true. Suppose he had a heart attack from all this excitement? Just as the Reynoldses were becoming unbearably impatient at holding up dinner, Yasha walked in. He gave me a brief nod as if to say, "All is well," and sat down.

My turn was to come next. On the heels of this occurrence I had my first experience at being tailed. I had an appointment that night with Bob Miller, editor of the pro-Communist Latin-American newsletter *The Hemisphere*, in New York City. Yasha was to join us later. As I left World Tourists, where I had been conferring with him, I noticed it was getting late, so when I walked out of the lobby into Broadway I quickened my steps. Then I stopped very suddenly. The street as usual at that hour was deserted except for two young men, one on either side of the next corner, where they could effectively block my progress up Broadway. My heart felt as if it had stopped. This was it!

With terror, I realized that I was carrying, carefully wrapped in a newspaper, a package of documents to be returned to Bob. What should I do? I pulled myself together and casually walked past the men and into a candy store, intending to phone Yasha and warn him what had happened. As I dropped my nickel into the slot I saw one of my pursuers slip into the adjoining booth. The walls were too thin, I realized at once, and so I dropped the receiver back on the hook and walked out into the street.

My knees were shaking and a cold sweat was breaking out on me. I tried desperately to think what to do. If I returned to World Tourists I would let my pursuers know that I suspected I was being tailed—something I had been told not to do. Blindly, I headed up Broadway and then thought of a plan. The Pennsylvania Station was not far away. One could enter the Ladies' Room there from the upper waiting room, go down the stairs, and then leave on the lower level.

With seeming nonchalance, I walked through the door marked "Ladies," automatically noticing that my "tails" were still behind me, then made a frantic dash down the stairs and out the lower exit. No one seemed to be behind me. Still not satisfied, I walked over to the Public Library on 42nd Street and Fifth Avenue, went in one door and out another. I appeared to have lost my pursuers but I didn't dare take any chances on meeting Bob. Wearily I took a bus home, figuring that Yasha would call me there when I didn't show up at the restaurant.

As I sat on the couch waiting for the telephone to ring, I gradually stopped trembling and I could feel the blood returning to my face. Then quite suddenly an intense wave of anger swept over me. What right had these people to persecute us like that? Yasha was right. They were no better than the brutal old Russian Cossacks. Now the chips were down and it was they or I. I said to myself quite savagely that if the F.B.I. thought it was going to find out anything from me it had another think coming.

I drew a deep breath and with a pang of nostalgia I realized that the good old days were over. Now I was one of the hunted, and no matter where I went, the footsteps of the hunters would be hot behind me. Although I was not aware of it, this was the last thing needed to make me a completely "steeled Bolshevik."

CHAPTER VII

During the next two or three months I became quite
accustomed to the F.B.I.'s almost constant surveillance,
and I began to accept it as a game played for high stakes. I
must learn its rules and think and act as unemotionally as
possible. Coolly, I studied the techniques used by the F.B.I.
agents. With Yasha's help I mastered all the old underground methods and even devised newer and better ways
of outwitting them. I soon discovered that the Bureau
agents were all long-legged, athletic young men whom I
could not outrun; I had to rely on strategy. In a very short
space of time I had developed an incredible number of
ruses: running in and out of buildings with more than one
exit; walking up to the "tail" and asking his help in finding
a street address, which always seemed to disconcert him;
going to a movie and sneaking out the fire exit; sometimes
even changing direction abruptly and following the erstwhile pursuer. Eventually I acquired that strange sixth sense
of danger common to all the hunted, for I could, as we used
to say, "smell trouble in the air," but I never left anything
to chance. Whenever I was to meet a Communist contact,
I spent at least a half hour methodically checking and re-
checking to be sure I was not under surveillance. Often
Yasha and I would use the "double tail" method: I would

leave the office first, he would follow a few minutes later and stay a block behind me. If he determined to his satisfaction that the coast was clear, he would speed up and pass me, blowing his nose loudly on his handkerchief; if he found that I was being followed, he would continue to trail along. I used to think wryly that we must make a very odd procession going down the street—first me, then the F.B.I., then Yasha.

Strangely enough, I could never manage to work up any particular animus against the agents who were tailing me. They were just a group of hard-working young men assigned to this detail—too bad they were on the wrong side of the fence. Perhaps the strongest emotion I ever felt was sheer annoyance; they always managed to turn up in hot, muggy weather when I was tired and my feet hurt or else on stormy days when I had forgotten to bring my umbrella to the office. After one long trek in the rain in order to shake them off, I complained bitterly to Yasha that the feathers on my brand-new hat had been completely ruined.

"Why don't you send a bill to J. Edgar Hoover?" he suggested cheerfully. "He ought to be willing to buy you a new hat."

Yet, in spite of our jesting, neither of us underestimated the force that was pitted against us, and we took what might seem ridiculous precautions to protect ourselves and our organization. We were convinced that our telephones were being tapped, hence our conversations over the wire were purely business ones. Every so often a Communist electrician would check the walls of Yasha's office, inch by inch, to make sure that no dictaphones had been planted. To be doubly secure we never talked there unless the radio was turned on or one of us sat and continually jiggled the telephone receiver to break any sound waves that might be picked up by a hidden microphone. In general, we made it a policy not to keep too many incriminating documents in our possession. Those which it was absolutely necessary to preserve were carefully placed in the World Tourists safe (only Yasha and I had the combination), and a complicated set of booby traps was rigged up to insure against tampering. Any other dangerous papers were immediately destroyed after reading—we tore them into small pieces and burned them little by little in a large metal ashtray on Yasha's desk. I am sure his secretary was considerably puzzled by what was going on. More than once, alarmed by the smell of smoke, she dashed into his private office to find both of us calmly stirring a flaming mass in the ash tray.

In the latter part of June 1941 the worst blow of all fell —Germany attacked the Soviet Union. White-faced, Yasha and I were listening to the news bulletins pour in over the radio: the Soviet forces were retreating before the German onslaught. Suddenly Yasha switched off the radio and nervously paced the floor in the form of a square, six feet one way, six feet the other. With an awful feeling of terror, I remembered he had learned that habit in prison, where the cell space was limited, and only reverted to it when he was extremely agitated. Yasha sat down on the couch opposite me, his face cold and set.

"This is the final showdown," he said in a tone that frightened me. "Our Fatherland has been attacked and the future of all Communism lies in the balance. Over there our comrades are being ruthlessly slaughtered; over here we must work night and day, without any thought of rest, until the Fascist beasts have been wiped out."

I sat watching him silently, realizing with a sick pain in

[142]

my heart that this was the end of any personal future we might have planned.

Almost immediately, with the precision of a well-thought-out plan, Yasha received his instructions from the Russian police. Late one night, as I was curled up on the couch reading a book, I heard his key in the lock. He came in and sat beside me wordlessly.

"What's the matter?" I asked, wondering what had happened to make him so preoccupied that he had even forgotten to kiss me. He smiled then and put his arms around me.

"I'm sorry to be so absent-minded," he said, holding me very close. "It's just that I had a long conference this evening with my contact Charlie, and I was still thinking over the orders he transmitted to me."

"What does he think about the war?" I asked interestedly.

Yasha frowned. "He's worried. Right now the Soviet forces are taking the full brunt of a terrific land offensive. They're short of materiel and no one knows how much help, if any, the United States government is going to give. Perhaps Great Britain and the United States will sell the Soviet Union down the river to save their own skins. And even if the United States adopts the official policy of aiding the Soviets in their war effort, there is a powerful Fascist clique in the government that can—and will—effectively sabotage any help that is being given."

"Then it's completely hopeless," I said, wishing passionately that we could run away to some quiet spot and forget all about world problems.

"Not at all," he reassured me. "It only means that we have a difficult task before us. Moscow must be kept completely informed about what is going on behind the scenes in the American government so that she can be prepared to forestall any treachery. That's where we come in. I have received orders to get as many trusted comrades as possible into strategic positions in United States government agencies in Washington, where they will have access to secret and confidential information that can be relayed on to the Soviet Union."

He paused for a moment and then, looking at me tenderly, went on: "I hate to ask you to get mixed up in all this. It's going to be a very dangerous job. I do need your help because for many reasons it is going to be practically impossible for me to go to Washington, and you could see these people for me. Unfortunately I am torn between anxiety over you and my duty to the cause. Therefore, I am putting it up to you. Knowing all the risks involved, are you still willing to go on with me?"

Thoughtfully I looked at him, and for the first time the full impact of the situation hit me: we were now engaged in a total, all-out struggle that would determine the fate of the world. Yasha, with his usual single-mindedness of purpose, had unhesitatingly accepted his orders; why then should I waver? Through my mind flashed the words of the *Communist Internationale*—" 'Tis the final conflict; let each stand in his place"—and I realized all at once that never before had I completely understood their meaning. Heretofore, like most American Communists, I had been playing at being a revolutionary; now I was about to become one in dead earnest. I found, with a strange detachment, that I was not frightened. I had made my choice and I would stick to it.

"Of course," I answered quietly.

Looking as if a great load had fallen from his shoulders, Yasha kissed me very gently. "I thought that would be your answer, *golubishka*."

In my preoccupation with vital issues, I had forgotten what a terrific effect the war would have on our business. Very soon, however, I became aware that we were in for a bad time. Not only would no one ship any parcels to the U.S.S.R. in the midst of active warfare, especially when the Russians were retreating, but we might have difficulties with the shipments that had already gone out.

While we were going through this hectic business period, I took on an additional duty as an undercover agent. Worried about his health and the continued presence of the F.B.I., Yasha thought it wise to have an alternate channel of communication with the Russian Secret Police; hence, I was "introduced" to an intermediary through whom messages could be sent. Our first meeting was meticulously prearranged, since even Yasha was not to be allowed to know who my contact was. Carefully, I was given written instructions which I was to memorize and destroy: I was to be in front of a drugstore on Ninth Avenue in the Fifties at twelve noon; a man carrying a copy of *Life* magazine would walk up to me and say: "I am sorry to have kept you waiting," and I was to reply: "No, I haven't been waiting long." But if, after twenty minutes, no one appeared, I was to leave and return at the same time the following day. Under no circumstances was I to give him any personal information about myself. He was to know me only as Miss Wise (a translation of the Russian word *umnitsa*, which means, roughly, "smart gal"). For my part, I was to know nothing about him except his code name, which was John.

My new contact, who appeared promptly at five minutes

past twelve, turned out to be a thin, pale, blond young man of about my height, who was dressed in badly fitting clothes of obviously European make. Indubitably, he had not been in this country very long. He had that half-starved look so characteristic of new Soviet arrivals, his English was so meager I had difficulty in understanding him, and he displayed an astounding ignorance of American life. Indeed, I remember with some amusement his stubborn and unshakable belief that American workers were so terrorized by the police they had to carry revolvers to the polls on election day. Evidently, too, he had not been too well briefed on undercover work in the United States; not long after I met him he almost got us into serious difficulties.

One day the switchboard operator came into my office, complaining that there was a Russian on the phone who insisted on speaking to "Miss Wise." She had told him firmly that there was no such person in the company but he had refused to be convinced. With a cold feeling of terror, I realized it must be John. Having missed an appointment the day before, he was obviously trying to contact me, although how he knew where I worked was a mystery. What should I do? I couldn't speak to him because that would let the office force know that something very odd was going on; besides, with the F.B.I. still interested in me, the wires might easily be tapped. I thought fast.

"Don't be upset," I said as calmly as I could to the telephone girl. "Probably some girl who wanted to get rid of a wolf gave him the wrong phone number. Just hang up on him."

I marched across the street to Yasha's office, shaking with fear and anger.

[146]

"What's going on?" I demanded. "Doesn't he know better than to do a dangerous thing like that?"

He shook his head. "He's still green at the work. I'll have someone give him a talking-to."

Before long, however, it became increasingly clear that John was too unmistakably Russian for me to be seen with him openly. Moreover, he seemed quite unable to detect when he was under surveillance. We therefore decided to take the Newsreel theaters, of which there are quite a number in New York, as our base of operations. According to the plan, I was to enter the theater precisely on the hour, carrying a small brown attaché case containing any information to be passed on, and sit down on the extreme right near the back. Ten minutes later he was to take the seat next to me, without any sign of recognition, and place an identical case on the floor next to mine. After a sufficient interval of time had elapsed, I was to pick up his briefcase and leave the theater. With this elaborate ritual went an equally complicated schedule of times and places that went something like this: Tuesday, 8 P.M., theater opposite Grand Central Terminal, twenty minutes waiting time; if no contact, 9 P.M. same day theater on Times Square, half-hour waiting time; if no contact, next day, Wednesday, 8 P.M., theater at Fiftieth Street and Lexington Avenue, waiting time twenty minutes. Inasmuch as this timetable changed weekly and had to be committed to memory, it is not surprising that two or three times we slipped up and arrived at the appointed time in different places.

During the year and a half that I was to know John, he became steadily more Americanized. He bought new clothes and his English improved. But he never lost that tense, frightened air I later learned so characterized the Russian Secret Police agents. He seemed almost afraid of his own shadow. For no reason at all he would suddenly give a nervous start and his hands would begin to shake. At the time I attributed all this to a quite understandable fear of the F.B.I. I was not then aware that what really terrified him was the merciless and inhuman discipline of his own organization. One time, quite innocently, I gave him a fright which became one of the standing jokes of the Russian Secret Police. On this occasion, he was the first of us to leave the theater, and I noticed that in his agitation he had forgotten to pick up my briefcase.

"Wait a moment," I whispered, clutching him by the sleeve. "You've left your attaché case."

He turned completely white and the sweat stood out on his forehead. With a wild look at me he grabbed the valise and bolted out of the theater. "What in the world is the matter with him?" I said to myself, and after waiting five more minutes to give him time to get out, I went home to find Yasha. Puzzled, I told him what had happened and was completely nonplussed to see him throw back his head and roar with laughter.

"I'm sorry," he said after a moment, wiping his eyes. "Of course you wouldn't understand. Quite obviously your man is one of the military *attachés* at the Soviet Embassy. Your remark about *attaché cases* upset him because he thought you had discovered his identity. Most Russians don't know that briefcases are called *attaché cases* in English."

"Oh," I replied, finally comprehending, yet thinking to myself that the Russian Secret Police had a very brutal sense of humor. Yet, as I was later to discover, this was very typical of their jokes. They seemed to think it excruciatingly funny when someone was terrified.

Meanwhile, back in July, although hampered by Earl Browder's absence (he was then still serving his sentence for passport fraud in the Federal Penitentiary in Atlanta, Georgia), Yasha had finally made contact with a group of Communists who worked for the United States government in Washington, D.C. Jubilantly he came to my office one day to announce that he had just had a long and satisfactory conference with the leader of the group, who had come up to New York.

"Who is he?" I asked curiously, knowing that I shouldn't ask such a question. But Yasha was quite willing to tell me.

"His name is Nathan Gregory Silvermaster and I used to know him quite well in the Party way back in the early thirties. He's a trusted comrade whose record of revolutionary activity dates very far back—almost as far as mine." He smiled reminiscently. "You know, he's a Ukrainian like I am. Only, while I was working there for the underground he was over in China where his family had taken him after a particularly vicious pogrom. Yet he, too, was pulled into the movement. Even in his teens he used to help the Bolsheviks smuggle revolutionary literature across the Russian border.

"Not long after World War I he had come to America and spent some fifteen years on the West Coast, during which time he got his Ph.D. degree in economics, became an American citizen, and was a very active member of the Party. As a matter of fact, he worked very closely with Sam Darcy, who was organizer for California, and during the San Francisco general strike in 1933 he hid Earl Brow-

[149]

der in his apartment while the vigilantes were making a house-to-house search for him."

"But how was he able to get a position in Washington if he was such a well-known Communist?" I asked, puzzled.

"Oh, he was never an open Party member," Yasha explained. "In fact, he was generally known as a very respectable, bourgeois member of society. He always held good, solid positions, too. At the time he was protecting Earl, he was working for the California State Labor Department, and before that he taught for some time in St. Mary's College, which was a wonderful cover because no one would suspect that the Catholics would harbor a Communist." He chuckled at the thought and went on. "With that background he was able to get a job with the Farm Security Administration, a subdivision of the Agriculture Department, in the mid-thirties and he and Helen moved to Washington."

I sat amazed at this recital while Yasha enjoyed my bewilderment.

"Then the authorities have never discovered him in all these years?" I asked.

Yasha smiled. "You mean the American intelligence agencies? No, and that was Browder's doing. He realized that Greg would be very useful to us in the future, so he told him to lie low and not join any Communist unit in Washington. Hence he's in a very good position now. He's refrained from associating with known Communists and he's been very careful to act respectable and not express any radical ideas. Moreover, on Browder's instructions he's been gathering around him a group of people— some Party members, some sympathizers—employed in sensitive jobs in the government where they will be able to collect invaluable information for us."

"He sounds like a good person," I said thoughtfully.

"He is, and so is his wife Helen, whom you will soon meet. Surprisingly enough, she is the daughter of the Russian Baltic Baron Witte, who was known in Czarist days as the Red Baron because of his Communist sympathies. Hence she is very familiar with the workings of the underground, because in her childhood she helped her father hide prominent Bolshevik leaders in their home. Later on she married a White Russian nobleman by the name of Volkov and had one child, Anatole. However, she quite soon divorced her husband and some years after married Greg on the West Coast. She is, I might add, a very intelligent woman and completely trustworthy."

He added, "Greg is here in town right now and will stay on a few more days. Tomorrow it has been arranged that you will go to Washington and make contact with Helen at her home. On your return I will report to Greg what happened and we can make the final arrangements."

"But why do I have to go all the way to Washington to see Helen when Greg's in New York? And what in the world do I say to her?" I asked, somewhat confused by this odd arrangement.

He laughed, then became serious.

"The answer to both questions is very simple. Both Greg and Helen, being Russians with a long background in the revolutionary movement, are extremely distrustful of Americans and would rather not deal with them. I am trying to persuade them to accept you as an intermediary. Your job is to sell yourself to Helen—make friends with her

[151]

and give her the feeling that you are completely reliable. Incidentally, don't tell her anything *at all* about yourself. Although both the Silvermasters know who I am, because of our past acquaintance, it is better for you to remain incognito. She will know you only as Helen and will have your telephone number in case of emergency. Oh, and one more thing. Unlike the other American Communists you have been dealing with, both Greg and Helen know who they are working for and where the information will go. So don't act cagey and arouse her suspicions."

It sounded like a tall order. The next day, however, found me in Washington on my way to 5515 35th Street, N.W. Deliberately, I gave the cab driver a street number about a block from my destination, and as I watched him drive off I saw that I was in a prosperous, fairly new neighborhood not far from Chevy Chase Circle. The door of 5515 was opened by a slight, wiry woman of about forty, with dark brown hair done in a knot at the back of her neck and rather wary brown eyes set in a face that seemed more Polish than Russian.

"I'm Helen," I explained. "Greg said you'd be expecting me."

"Oh, yes." The voice had the slightest touch of an accent. "Come in."

The spacious living room, just off the hall, was cool and restful, and as I sat down on the comfortable sofa, with Helen opposite me, I found myself liking the casually charming way in which it was furnished. With a smile, I looked over at her.

"You have a beautiful home," I ventured.

"Do you like it? We made most of the furniture ourselves." Sitting there barelegged, in a cotton print dress and red play shoes, she didn't look like a baroness, yet there was an indefinable air of quality in her tone of voice and in the way she held her head. We sat and chatted for over an hour. She was friendly and gracious, yet somehow distant. Optimistically I hoped that I had made a good impression on her, but I had a strong feeling that she was still very suspicious.

A week or so later Yasha informed me that the Silvermasters had agreed to accept me as their contact, albeit somewhat reluctantly.

"You'll have to let them get used to you gradually," he said with a sigh. "Greg is satisfied with the arrangement but Helen suspects you of being an undercover agent for the F.B.I. We've tried to argue her out of that idiocy, but she's the kind of woman who relies heavily on feminine intuition and she insists her hunches are invariably right."

I laughed ruefully. It was bad enough to spend a good share of my time dodging the F.B.I. without being accused of working for them. Yet, looking back on the episode now, I wonder whether Helen didn't have a deeper insight into human nature than all the rest of us. She sensed instinctively that I didn't belong in the Communist movement.

It was arranged that I would go down to Washington every two weeks to pick up the Silvermaster material and relay instructions on what information was needed. I was also to collect the Party dues for the group and bring them not only the American Communist literature, as I was doing with Mary Price, but also Soviet publications, such as *Pravda*, the *Bolshevik*, and others.

Meanwhile, U.S. Service had announced that we would ship any useful articles to the Soviet fighting forces without import duty and with minimum freight charge. The response was terrific. The heretofore-deserted offices of World Tourists were jammed with people—some former customers, some left-wingers, and some just ordinary people. They brought presents that ranged all the way from vitamin pills to shotguns (the latter, of course, for obvious reasons had to be rejected). It seemed as though everyone, rich or poor, wanted to help the Soviet Union. Even political beliefs seemed to have been swept away in the tide of sympathy for the besieged Russians. People who bitterly hated the Bolshevik regime contributed along with the rest.

One day I was holding down Yasha's office in his absence. I looked up to see one of our customers who had been sending parcels regularly to his mother in Moscow. He clicked his heels and bowed from the waist.

"Madame," he said, looking pathetically threadbare in his shabby overcoat with moth-eaten fur collar, "I was a colonel in the White Army of the Czar in Russia. I fought the Bolsheviks during the Civil War and I shall continue to fight them as long as I live. But, Madame, I am a *Russian*. My country is being attacked by the barbarians and the Red Army needs help." He held out a leather case. "Here are my binoculars. Please send them to some Soviet Army officer who can use them. I am going now to contact all my White Army officer friends. They will have equipment that will be useful."

As I watched him march proudly out of the office, I felt a lump in my throat. How he must love his country to give his treasured binoculars to his bitterest enemies! He was not the only one. During the war about fifty per cent of the White Russians all over the world supported the Russian cause. In the fall of 1941 Sasha Pogorelsky, the Russian-born husband of one of our employees and an ex-White Army man with Communist sympathies, set up an organization of White Army officers for the purpose of aiding the Red Army. The project was quite successful. I remember attending one fund-raising affair held under their auspices at the Manhattan Opera House on West 34th Street where, to my amazement, Communists and left-wingers mingled with the White Russian colony, all united by a common purpose.

Meanwhile, by the end of the summer of 1941 *The Hemisphere* was deeply in debt and Yasha suggested to Bob Miller that he close down the enterprise and get a job somewhere in the United States government. With his experience in the Latin-American field, he was soon offered a position with the Coordinator of Inter-American Affairs, then headed by Nelson Rockefeller. Yasha urged him to take it, saying he could give us information that would be valuable to the Central Committee of the American Communist Party. Bob, unhappy over the prospect of undercover work, demurred, saying that the State Department regarded him as a Communist (he had quite evidently shown his sympathies in Moscow, and the American Embassy had become aware of the fact) and would probably send an unfavorable report on him to the C.I.A.A. After a long struggle we finally succeeded in overcoming his objections and he accepted a position as head of the political research division. Moreover, he was able to sell *The Hemisphere* files, carefully expurgated, to the Rockefeller Committee for a substantial sum of money.

Bob and his wife Jennie packed up their belongings, left their Knickerbocker Village apartment, and departed for Washington, thereby adding yet another person to my list of Communist contacts in the United States government. That was only the beginning. As time went on, the number grew so large that it was almost physically impossible to handle. Over a period of many years Yasha had built up a series of "look-outs"—people strategically situated in Communist-front organizations or in the Party itself—through whom he could contact Communists who would be useful for espionage work. Among these were Grace Granich, head of the Intercontinent News Service and sister-in-law of Mike Gold, columnist for the *Daily Worker*; Joseph North, editor of the now-defunct *New Masses* and at present on the *Daily Worker*; Michael Tkach, editor of the Communist-owned *Ukrainian Daily News*; Avram Landy, head of the Party's work among minorities, and V. J. Jerome, head of the theoretical organ of the Party. Both Landy and Jerome were behind-the-scenes powers in the American movement. With increasing amazement I asked Yasha how in the world he had been able to get together so many people. He laughed.

"Very simple. This organization has been built up solidly over a period of years and is always ready in case of emergency. Moreover, I'm only a small part of a vast machine. Other agents have the same facilities at their disposal. You haven't forgotten how you met Juliet, Joe, and Marcel, have you?"

"Then they were part of your organization?" I asked interestedly.

"Another branch," he replied. "Let me explain it to you. All Soviet intelligence work outside the U.S.S.R. is handled by the N.K.V.D., that is, the People's Commissariat for Internal Affairs. It was formerly known as the G.P.U. The N.K.V.D. has several branches, one of which is Military

[156]

Intelligence. We refer to these people in our reports by the code name of the 'neighbors.' It was to this branch that your trio belonged."

"Oh," I said, realizing for the first time what a powerful and far-flung network our International had at its command. I thought of all the new agents Yasha alone had taken on. Multiplied by the number of Soviet agents operating, it made a staggering total. Our new world is not too far away, I said to myself exultantly.

Yet, for all our quick expansion, we were not taking on new contacts haphazardly. Each new person was thoroughly checked before he was added to the apparatus. The Central Control Commission kept detailed dossiers on every American Party member—his background, record in the movement, weaknesses, and so on. These files were enlarged from time to time when the comrade himself or his friends added more material. To these records Yasha, as one of the three-man Commission, had ready access, and he could quite easily find out whether a person was reliable or whether he was a bad risk. This latter category included people who were ideologically unsound (they periodically had doubts about the Party's position or refused to carry out instructions) or those who had grave weaknesses (they drank too much, had too many affairs with women or, by kinship, friendship or marriage, had too-close ties with anti-Communist elements). Not satisfied with the Central Control Commission's information, Yasha would then send an inquiry through to Moscow, where the files were much more complete, just to be sure that in taking on a new agent we were not endangering the organization.

We were particularly leery about people who were "unstable elements," people who were weak and would not

[157]

stand up under pressure. For a brief period I contacted a young girl, whom I shall call Barbara Landers, a stenotypist in the War Production Board, where she had access to a certain amount of data. Unfortunately, although her record was good, she later became involved in a disappointing love affair, which left her weepy and nervous. We therefore decided to drop her as a contact and let her return to the open Party. This she did, later turning up in the "street" unit to which belonged Angela Calomiris, the plucky little Greek girl who for seven years worked undercover for the F.B.I. in the Communist movement.

Perhaps our greatest fear along this line was that an agent might crack up and land in a psychiatrist's office. If we detected any indication of such a possibility, he was dropped like a hot cake. One case I remember was that of a man whom I shall call Harold Sloan, a young Canadian whom I contacted for over a year and a half while he was working for the Canadian government in Washington.

He had been sent to us highly recommended for his trustworthiness by Tim Buck and Sam Carr, leaders of the Canadian Communist Party, and had a long and excellent record as a Party member in Canada, including a period of service in the Spanish Civil War. For a long time he functioned efficiently, giving us information which he obtained from his friends in the Canadian Legation. Then he began to have trouble with his wife and became moody and nervous to the point where he insisted he was going to consult a psychiatrist. When it became increasingly evident we could not keep him from going to pieces, I was ordered to stop contacting him.

Many of the contacts that we took on as agents were already in government service. If they were in positions that we considered productive, we left them where they were, otherwise we encouraged them to pull strings and move into more sensitive agencies. Typical of one of these latter cases was J. Julius Joseph from Allentown, Pennsylvania, a Communist of long standing, whom we had added to the organization in the summer of 1942. After a brilliant career in college and afterward as an economist, he went into social-security work in the United States government.

I still remember with amusement the way I was "introduced" to him. I was to go to his apartment in Washington, knock three times, and when he opened the door, recite the number of a dollar bill which he had in his possession.

After I had been working with him for about a year, by which time he was holding down an important post in the War Manpower Commission, he was due to be drafted. Since we would have no use for him in the United States Army's infantry, we suggested that he use his personal contacts to get a position in the Office of Strategic Services. Joe worked fast and furiously. Although he was inducted into the Army and put in basic training, he was fished out by the O.S.S. in three weeks' time and given a job in their "hush-hush" Japanese division. Here he was of invaluable use to us, not only because he knew in advance of the Americans' plans concerning Japan but because for a period he worked in the Library of Congress next door to the confidential Russian division, whose people trustingly gave him all the information that was of interest to us.

Joe, incidentally, for all his zeal, never seemed to learn the correct underground procedure. He was continually getting into difficulties that had us alternately worried and amused. One famous time, having been told either to burn documents or flush them down the toilet, he crammed a mass of flaming papers into the toilet, with the result that the seat was set on fire. His puzzled landlord, surveying the damage, finally walked out of the apartment, muttering to himself, "I don't see how that could possibly have happened."

Sometimes we had potential agents who, we thought, had the necessary qualifications to secure good positions in the United States government, so we sent them down to Washington to try their luck. This was not such a difficult procedure as it sounds. During the war the American government expanded quite suddenly to many times its former size. As a result, the Civil Service Commission and other similar agencies were swamped with work, and many times government employees remained in their jobs for as long as eighteen months before anyone got around to examining their records. Sometimes Yasha and I were actually horrified at the ease with which notorious, open Communists wandered into sensitive departments and obtained positions. We lived in terror lest someday one of the American intelligence agencies would trip over them and in the process uncover one of our carefully planted agents.

One case that comes to my mind was that of Leonard Mins, son of a charter member of the American Communist Party and a well-known revolutionary, who somehow turned up as a Russian interpreter in the O.S.S. J. Julius Joseph's wife, Bella, then working for the O.S.S.'s Movie Division, which made confidential films for the use of the United States General Staff, met him in the corridor of her building and fled in a panic. Years before, she had known him quite well; and remembering that he was an open Communist, she was terrified at being seen with him. Mins, incidentally, was finally uncovered by the United States government and fired. Nothing daunted, he fought the case for several months, then gave up and vanished from sight. At the time I complained bitterly to Yasha about the stupidity of the Communist movement in allowing Leonard to take such a position. He snorted indignantly.

"I don't know what is the matter with those people," he said in a rare burst of anger. "Mins is so well known that he might just as well go around Washington with the hammer and sickle painted on his chest and waving a red flag. He worked quite openly for the *Moscow Daily News* over there and he's been used by our organization in the past. Worse than that, I know for a fact that the F.B.I. has a collection of photographs showing him marching in May Day parades as a representative of the American Communist Party. I'll send word through to Moscow and tell Bella for goodness' sake to run like hell when she sees him."

As we passed from the fall of 1941 through 1942 and into the spring of 1943, we added more and more agents to our apparatus. Meanwhile, our two businesses were more or less drifting along. The shipments of gifts to the Red Army had been taken over by the Russian War Relief, who could send them in bulk more cheaply than we could, and although our old customers were returning to send personal packages, there were not sufficient of them even to pay our expenses. All this alarmed the American Communist Party which, having furnished $15,000 as initial capital for the U.S. Service & Shipping Corporation, wanted either dividends on their investment or their money back. Periodically, they would send messages to Jack Reynolds, asking for a complete financial statement covering the business or demanding that he return some of the cash he had received.

Yet, even in their anxiety, they were careful to choose a

suitable messenger—a man whom Jack, with all his snobbery, would accept and deal with. Lemuel Harris, a Communist of many years' standing, Moscow trained, was a perfect selection. He was the son of a wealthy Wall Street broker, came from a good old American family, and had known Jack intimately for a number of years. Looking back on the situation now, I feel very sorry for Lem. He was so pathetically idealistic and naïve, and in spite of his inside dealings with the Party he never seemed to become aware of what an ugly outfit he was mixed up with.

But Lem had another mission besides that of checking up on the financial status of the U.S. Service & Shipping Corporation. Being assistant to Welwel Wartzover (alias William Weiner), head of the Party's Finance Committee, he was responsible for collecting money from sympathizers and stowing it away in a safe place. For obvious reasons, the American Communist Party did not want to put all their assets in an account under their own name; they split their cash up and gave it to trusted people to keep in safe-deposit vaults. Jack Reynolds had one of these repositories. From the fall of 1941 on, the U.S. Service's safety-deposit box in the Chase National Bank was filled with money belonging to the American Communist Party, in amounts ranging through $10,000. Lem would bring the money to our office; then either Jack or I would take it down to the bank in a sealed envelope and cache it away in our box, after having carefully counted the bills to be sure there was no discrepancy.

By the summer of 1942 Jack Reynolds was becoming restless at the lack of activity in his business. He spent less and less time at the office and finally went back into the Finance Corps of the Army (he had served in Washington as a major in World War I). In fact, his commission was dated December 7, 1942, the anniversary of Pearl Harbor—a fact which he never let us forget. He made a great to-do about going to war, fussing loudly about how he was about to give his life to his country (even though we all knew that at his age and with his lack of front-line experience he would undoubtedly be given a nice, cushy job behind a desk), and it was with great relief that Yasha and I said goodbye to him. One of our lawyers eyed the whole proceedings cynically.

"You know," he said thoughtfully, "I think this time Jack has bitten off more than he can chew. He wants to get into a uniform so that he can swagger around and impress people, but he's going to find that even in the chairborne troops it's hard work. And that guy hasn't put in a good eight-hour day in a long, long time."

With Jack's departure I was made the operating head of the U.S. Service & Shipping Corporation, which left me free to go to Washington whenever necessary without being forced to make complicated excuses. Yet my burden of work in the business did not let up. In fact it increased to a point where I wondered daily just how long I could keep going.

Besides, I had to spend at least half my time across the street. The World Tourists packer left to get a better paying job, Yasha insisted on packing the eleven-pound cartons of food and clothing himself, and to ease the physical strain on him I pitched in and helped. Packing is not a clean job, and I often looked as if I had come out of the nearest ashcan.

While I was wrestling with the problems of the two businesses, I had the infinitely more nerve-racking job of relaying information from our Communist agents in Washington to Yasha and the Russian Secret Police. Of these people, by far the most valuable were in what we loosely called the Silvermaster group.

One of the most important members of the group was Harry Dexter White, Under Secretary of the United States Treasury and right-hand man of Secretary Morgenthau. He was in a position not only to give valuable information but also to influence United States policy in a pro-Soviet direction. According to Greg, he had been tied up with the revolutionary movement for many years, although no one seemed to know whether or not he had ever been a Communist Party member. He had been giving information to the Russians during the thirties but ceased abruptly when his contact, who was later identified as Whittaker Chambers, turned "sour" in 1938. Some two years before I came into the picture, Harry became very friendly with Greg, told him all about his past activities, and offered to give him what help he could. Before this episode, Greg had already suspected that Harry had some connection with the Russians. One evening he and Helen had visited the Whites and seen what they thought was a magnificent Russian rug on the living-room floor—the same rug that later was proved to have been a gift from Whittaker Chambers. They asked the Whites if it had come from the Amtorg Corporation, whereupon Harry and his wife turned quite pale and vociferously insisted that it was Persian. Immediately after, as they later admitted to Greg, they went up to their attic and hid the rug.

Harry had access to almost all the Treasury's top-secret material. In addition, because of Morgenthau's policy of exchanging information with other government agencies, we also received "hush-hush" data from many other strategic departments. Harry was also one of our friends at court: he pulled strings to help any of our agents who were in difficulties. Thus he used his influence when Greg Silvermaster was under fire in the Board of Economic Warfare in 1942. He gave recommendations to any of our people who needed to get into more sensitive positions (he swung his weight around when Ludwig Ullman was shifting to the Air Corps), and he placed new contacts in the Treasury Department (when he needed an additional office worker in 1943, he took on a Communist who had been recommended by the Silvermasters).

For all this, he was essentially a timid man and, as Greg put it, "he doesn't want his right hand to know what the left is doing." To keep him peaceful, Greg had to tell him that his material was going to one man of the American Communist Party's Central Committee and nowhere else. Although he indubitably knew that it was in reality going to Moscow, he didn't care to think about such things. After the unhappy outcome of his dealings with Whittaker Chambers, White had promised his wife, who was not a Communist and disliked his revolutionary activities, that he would stay out of espionage in the future, and he lived in terror that she would find out he had broken his word.

Very important, too, was George Silverman. At first a statistician with the Railroad Retirement Board and then a civilian employee of the Air Corps in the Pentagon, he had access during most of the war to many military secrets. He was a tall, broad-shouldered, heavy man with thick glasses and untidy hair who was regarded by most of his associates as being an expert in his field but slightly odd.

Even more than Harry, he was nervous and worried about his espionage activities; although he was a Communist of long standing, the realization that he was giving information to the Russian Secret Police gave him the jitters. He was offered a colonelcy in the Army but, possibly fearing a court-martial if he were found out, he refused to accept it, remaining a civilian employee. His caution drove him to insist that Greg go up to New York and deliver the material to the Russians there, in the strange belief that that would be a safer procedure.

One time we had a very narrow escape. As I sat in the kitchen talking to Helen Silvermaster, George arrived quite unexpectedly at the front door, his briefcase bulging with papers he had abstracted from the Pentagon. It was inevitable that we run into each other, and if he discovered that I was a Soviet agent, he would undoubtedly bolt out of the house in a panic and never return. With commendable presence of mind, Helen introduced me as Mrs. Something-or-Other, a personal friend of hers. George seemed slightly reassured, but I shall never forget the initial look of terror that came over his face. He was, indeed, frightened of his own shadow. He saw F.B.I. men behind every bush, and he would arrive at an appointment dripping with cold sweat, yet somehow—I could never figure out how—he kept on going. Periodically he would threaten to resign, and wearily the Silvermasters would invite him over for a meal of his favorite broiled lobster. Then, when he was well fed and at peace with the world, they would argue him into continuing.

In addition to these, there were the three central figures in the Silvermaster group, with whom I dealt personally: Greg and Helen Silvermaster and William Ludwig Ullman. Like Helen, Greg made an indelible impression on my mind, even though there was nothing outstanding about his physical appearance. I met him soon after I started shuttling down to Washington every two weeks in the summer of 1941. He was in his mid-forties, slight and of average height, with close-cropped steel-gray hair, lightish eyes, and a Hitler mustache. Generally he spoke slowly and with a pronounced British accent (he had, I learned, attended an English school in China in his youth). When he was excited, which was very rarely, he tended to stutter, and his sentence construction and pronunciation revealed him for a Russian. In a sense he reminded me of Yasha: he had that same passionate devotion to the movement—to which he gave every ounce of his energy—that same strong and inflexible will that drove him on relentlessly; that same impersonal and detached mind that refused to be bogged down in petty problems and personal emotions.

How he managed to carry on, I often wondered. He had an extremely bad case of bronchial asthma that often left him battling for breath, especially in the summertime when the foliage was out. He constantly carried an atomizer of medicine, and his air-conditioned room and automobile were stripped of anything that might harbor dust. He carefully avoided the country in summer. He once broke this rule, attending the Bretton Woods Monetary Conference in the White Mountains and coming down with a bad attack. I remember his saying to me, after one bad bout of asthma:

"You know," he said, "there aren't any medals being given for what we are doing. But I don't want any. My time is strictly limited, and when I die I want to feel that at least I have had some part in building a decent life for those who come after me."

The third member of the trio, Lud Ullman, whom I met quite soon after the Silvermasters, was a rather colorless-looking young man of average height, with receding brown hair and sharp features. Born in Missouri of a wealthy family, he had gone to college and then wandered from job to job until he finally ended up in the Treasury Department sometime in the thirties. He had met the Silvermasters at one of their parties. Helen, realizing that in spite of his shy, retiring manner he was a man with an extremely facile brain and a tremendous amount of vitality, carefully cultivated his acquaintance and finally persuaded him to join a Communist Party unit in Washington. Lud was a lonesome person with few friends, and before long he became very attached to Greg and Helen, at length moving in with them. Moreover, because of his future value to the cause, he was asked to drop out of his Communist unit and become a member of the Silvermaster group. Under Greg's training he became one of the best agents we ever had. His only weakness was that he was unable to operate under his own steam for any period of time, and so he continually needed encouragement and guidance.

It was not long before I got to know the Silvermaster ménage quite well. Once their initial suspicions were allayed, we came to be the best of friends. Every two weeks regularly I visited them, choosing a Tuesday or Wednesday or Thursday in order to avoid their week-end parties. If an emergency arose, they could telephone me at my home in New York and I would grab the next train down. Usually I would go out to their house late in the afternoon, using either a taxi or a combination of buses that landed me in front of the Washington home of Boston's ex-Mayor Curley, not far away. I would chat casually with Helen for a little while, then when Greg and Lud arrived, the three of us would adjourn to the living room to discuss politics while Helen was cooking. Dinner was served on a long, wooden table in the kitchen, or during the summer months on a screened-in porch in the back—a casual, friendly affair with Greg and Lud telling me interesting or humorous incidents in their work while we ate heartily of Helen's excellent food.

Then, when the dishes had been cleared away, we would get down to the business at hand. Greg would give me the Communist Party dues for the group, for it was his job to calculate and collect what each member owed. This procedure was usually accompanied by the explanation that the amount was not complete because so-and-so was behind in his payments. Next I would give them what literature I had brought—current American Communist Party pamphlets by such leaders as Browder and Gil Green, and the Soviet publications *Pravda*, the *Bolshevik*, and others. Almost invariably Greg would complain bitterly that the Russian material was out of date, and I would be forced to explain patiently that the wartime situation had held up shipments.

At this point I would relay to Greg any requests from the Russian Secret Police on people and subjects in which they were currently interested. Usually I had jotted these down in shorthand for safety's sake, but sometimes I handed him the original instruction sheet, typed in Russian, which had been given to Yasha by his Soviet superior. This latter invariably started out: "Please have the courtesy to ask Sam (Greg's code name) the following:" and proceeded to itemize the various questions.

What the Russians wanted to know was practically limitless. They asked for information on Communists they were considering taking on as agents, on anti-Soviet elements in Washington, on the attitudes of high-up government officials in a position to help or hinder the Soviet Union—such as William Batt of the War Production Board. They sought military data: production figures, performance tests on airplanes, troop strength and allocation, and new experimental developments such as R.D.X. and the B-29. They were avid for so-called political information: secret deals between the Americans and the various governments in exile, secret negotiations between the United States and Great Britain, contemplated loans to foreign countries, and other similar material. As Greg read down the list, he would run his fingers through his hair and groan audibly.

"How do they expect us to find out all this?" he would say hopelessly.

Aside from their disconcerting habit of asking for the impossible, the Russian Secret Police had the annoying trick of repeating the same question over and over again, even though it had been answered adequately several times. I particularly remember one case when they asked Greg for information on a Russian-born furrier, then working in the War Production Board, whom they evidently thought sufficiently sympathetic to the cause to be useful to them. Greg carefully dug it up and relayed it on. But that did not end the matter. Every so often the same request turned up until Greg began to mutter angrily:

"What's the matter with those people over there? Don't they keep their files in order?"

At the end of two years of this, his irritation turned to sardonic amusement and on my arrival he would greet me: "Well, are you going to ask me about Mr. X this time?"

Basically, however, Greg was completely devoted to the revolutionary cause, and he forgave the Russians' shortcomings because he understood the heavy difficulties under which they were operating. Even these minor outbursts, I realized sympathetically, were due mostly to badly frayed nerves and unbearable fatigue, so I would sit quietly while he poured out his resentment and then, when he had calmed down, we would proceed to look over the information he had been able to collect. During the next two hours we would discuss and put in order the Silvermaster group's material (microfilms of important papers, carbon copies of documents, and so on); meanwhile I made stenographic notes on information which Lud Ullman had sneaked out of his office on small scraps of paper.

By this time it would be quite late and we would be very tired. Helen would make *chai* (Russian tea) and we would sit around the kitchen table sipping it and laughing and joking. Then, our goodbyes said and the material safely stowed away in my knitting bag, one of them would lead me through the backyard to the garage, which fronted on an alley, and from there would drive me to Connecticut Avenue, where buses to the center of town ran at all hours of the night.

CHAPTER VIII

W<small>HILE OUR MEETINGS</small> continued in a fixed pattern, the life and activities of the Silvermaster group fluctuated considerably. Not long after I took over the group, Lud Ullman, being single and in his mid-thirties, was about to be drafted. Fearing to lose a valuable agent, we encouraged him to apply for Officers' Training in the hope that we could keep him in this country. Rejected because of flat feet and sinus trouble, he entered basic training in the Army. His facility for learning easily and his ability to take hard, grueling discipline without whimpering (he even won the respect of a particularly hard-boiled first sergeant) impressed his superiors. Immediately he was sent to Officer Candidate School, from which he emerged a lieutenant in the Air Corps. Then, with George Silverman and Harry White desperately pulling strings, he was finally assigned to the Pentagon in Washington, where he became even more valuable to us than he had been in the Treasury.

Quite early, the Russian Secret Police decided that Greg Silvermaster's valuable talents were being wasted in a nonproductive agency and he was encouraged to move into a more strategic part of the government. With the aid of Lauchlin Currie (administrative assistant to President Roosevelt) and Harry White, he became head of the Middle

East Division of the Board of Economic Warfare (on loan from the Farm Security Administration), where he had access to highly confidential economic data.

For about six months he functioned very efficiently, winning the rarely given praise of the N.K.V.D.; then one day I arrived at the Silvermaster home at six o'clock to find Greg sitting wearily on a chair. A glance at his face was enough to tell me that something very serious had happened.

"What's the matter?" I asked, my heart giving an extra beat.

"This," he said succinctly, holding out a page-and-a-half letter. It was addressed to his superior in the Board of Economic Warfare and signed by General Strong, head of G-2 (Army Intelligence).

I looked through the letter rapidly. After a long preamble stating that the F.B.I., O.N.I. (Naval Intelligence), and G-2 had sufficient evidence in their files to prove that N. Gregory Silvermaster was a Communist, it demanded his dismissal from his present post on the grounds that he was disloyal to the United States government.

"It's no use fighting this thing," he said despairingly. "They've probably got enough information to hang me. I'd better resign now before they kick me out."

"No," I said, coming to a rapid decision and hoping I was right. "That would only be admitting the charges are true, and we can't afford for that to happen. Stand your ground, put on an air of injured innocence: you are not a Communist, just a 'progressive' whose record proves you have always fought for the rights of labor. Rally all your 'liberal' friends around. There must be plenty of them. If necessary, hire a lawyer to fight the case through on the grounds that your reputation has been badly damaged. Meanwhile, pull

[173]

every string you can to get this business quashed. Use Currie, White, anybody else you know and trust. It's going to be rough, Greg, but just hold on."

Yasha and his superiors in the Russian Secret Police agreed with my analysis of the situation. Greg was told to stay on in his position and fight back, and I was told to continue my contacts with him while exercising the utmost caution to avoid surveillance.

After three months or so relief came to Greg Silvermaster: Under Secretary of War Robert E. Patterson, convinced by various pleas that an injustice had been done, forced the War Department to withdraw its demands. Greg was permitted to resign from the Board of Economic Warfare and return to the Department of Agriculture—and with a clean slate! After a sigh of relief that must have echoed throughout the entire Russian Secret Police apparatus, we went back to our normal routine.

As time went on, under the guidance of Yasha and myself the Silvermaster group steadily stepped up its intelligence operations. This, plus the shifting of personnel and the adding of new agents, meant that the information I handled varied considerably in type and volume. At the very beginning it was fairly meager and consisted largely of so-called political data obtained mostly through the Treasury Department. This varied all the way from downright gossipy items (such as the one about the White House attendant who, infuriated by Madame Chiang Kai-shek's arrogance, said he was going up to Chinatown and kick the first Chinese he met) to important secret information, such as United States plans for allocating Lend Lease. Moreover, it was handled in an extremely slipshod and unsystematic manner. What I took back to New York was only a few typewritten sheets on which Helen or Lud had briefly jotted down confidential information, plus a few carbon copies of important documents and letters.

Very soon, however, all this changed. The Russian Secret Police, their appetite whetted by the value of the material, demanded more extensive and detailed information. Almost simultaneously, due to the shifting of group members into more sensitive positions, we had access to extremely confidential data which, while it could not be abstracted from the United States government files permanently, could be "borrowed" for at least overnight. The old haphazard methods no longer sufficed. From then on, members of the group brought secret material to the Silvermaster home at night, where it was photographed on microfilm, and then returned the files the first thing in the morning before their absence could be discovered.

At first the output was on a relatively small scale and consisted of around three or four rolls of microfilm, averaging about thirty-five exposures to a roll. These, the Silvermasters developed themselves. I would then take the rolls back to New York where Yasha and I would look over the photographed documents. As time went on, however, the number of rolls increased until I was carrying back about forty of them every fortnight. It became impossible for the Silvermasters to handle both the filming and the developing and so, by the spring of 1943, the rolls were being transmitted undeveloped to the N.K.V.D., to be developed in the Soviet Embassy's laboratory. They were accompanied by an itemized list of what documents were contained on each spool in case the negative was blank or unreadable. In the latter case, we would try to get the material back and rephotograph it.

Difficulties soon arose—and such serious ones that they often drove the Silvermasters, worn out from lack of sleep, into a state of near hysteria. It was hard enough to take pictures of clearly typed documents on good paper, but when they ran into blurred carbon copies on poor stock, none of which ever came out legibly or, worse still, papers typed in three colors, a secret process used by one or two "hush-hush" United States government departments to prevent enemy spies from photographing them, they threw up their hands in despair.

The Russian Secret Police itself often contributed to the confusion—a fact which irritated the Silvermasters far more. The spools of microfilm were furnished by the N.K.V.D., because it was deemed unwise for the group to purchase them openly and further because, during part of the war years, it was impossible for a civilian to obtain them. Many times the Russians, obviously handicapped by a lack of supplies, could only send down a fraction of the quantity needed. Often they had to give me rolls of a less sensitive, slower speed film that made photographing documents extremely difficult, if not impossible. On such occasions Greg, with his nerves stretched to the breaking point, would explode in a burst of anger.

"How do they expect us to carry on when they can't furnish us with adequate films?" he would demand angrily. "They must have plenty of that material over there." Then, with a glint of sardonic amusement: "Or has something gone wrong with the United States government's Lend Lease program to the Soviet Union?"

In spite of these difficulties, the Silvermaster group managed to collect a fabulous amount of confidential material which they photographed and passed on to the Russian

Secret Police. As month succeeded month, I was more impressed by the amount and the value of the information which flowed through my hands. Our most fruitful source of material had by then become the Pentagon. Through Silverman and especially through Ullman came every conceivable piece of data on aircraft—production-figure charts showing allocation of planes to combat areas and foreign countries, performance data, new and secret developments in numberless fields. I remember when I returned to New York from one trip, loaded down with miscellaneous material.

"What have you got this time?" Yasha asked interestedly.

"I think I've brought you the entire Pentagon," I answered.

I was not far wrong and was rewarded by a glow of appreciation.

Besides this purely military information, we had a steady flow of political reports from the Treasury which included material from the Office of Strategic Services, the State Department, the Navy, the Army, and even a limited amount of data from the Department of Justice. We knew what was going on in the inner chambers of the United States government, up to and including the White House. In fact I doubt if there were very many people who were quite as well informed as we on what was happening in Washington.

Meanwhile our list of Communist agents in the government was steadily increasing. Yasha's look-out men were proving to be exceedingly efficient in producing people, and Earl Browder, released in the spring of 1942 before his prison term expired, was of great help to us in this matter. As each of these new Communists was detached from the open Communist Party and annexed to the N.K.V.D., thus being responsible only to Yasha and myself, he became an individual contact and not a member of a group. Unlike the Silvermasters, they were born Americans and hence were trusted even less.

Many of them were definitely "problem children," due to their youth and nervousness about undercover activities. One of these was William W. Remington, whom we always referred to as our "infant prodigy." A brilliant student in economics at Dartmouth College and later at Columbia University, he had by the early part of 1942 obtained a position in the United States government, at which time he came to our attention. Stranded in Washington without a Communist unit, he approached his friend Joe North, then editor of the *New Masses*, on one of his trips to New York and asked him for a contact. North, sensing his potential usefulness as an agent, promptly alerted Yasha, who looked up his record with the Central Control Commission and found that Bill had been a member of the Party in good standing for some time. He looked like a promising prospect, and Yasha arranged to confer with him over lunch, after which Yasha came to see me.

"I think we've got another good contact," he said hopefully. "Not only is he a reliable Communist but he's brilliant in his own field and should go far in the government. Moreover, he's got a good solid middle-class background —fine family, education in well-known schools—and he has a reputation for being respectable. I doubt if any of his friends or acquaintances have the slightest suspicion that he has any radical tendencies. I don't know how useful his present job will prove. But with proper training we can always move him into some more productive government agency. I'm going to introduce you to him and his wife and you can make arrangements to see him in Washington."

The four of us had dinner at Schrafft's restaurant on Fourth Avenue at the corner of 31st Street. Bill was a tall, lanky young man with sandy hair and blue eyes—the typical clean-cut American lad, I thought to myself. His wife Anne, whom he called "Bing," was much shorter, with brown hair and eyes and the look of a solid, steady person.

In accordance with a prearranged plan we chatted on general topics for a little while. Then, while Yasha discussed details of the undercover work with Bill, I kept Anne's attention with desultory conversation. We always made it a rule not to let any more people than were strictly necessary know about intelligence operations—this minimized the danger to the apparatus in case any agent turned "sour" and talked too much. At the end of the meal I made arrangements with the Remingtons to call them when I was in Washington.

From then on, until he went into the Navy in 1944, Bill was attached to our organization. I met him on my trips to Washington, brought him current Communist literature, and collected what data he had been able to smuggle out of his agency. I also, of course, collected both the Remingtons' Party dues—a task rendered difficult by the fact that Bill seemed to be perpetually broke. For a good share of the time I knew him, Bill held a position in the War Production Board, where secret data on aircraft production, allocation, and performance crossed his desk. These he would give me, plus any inside information on policies and attitudes of higher-ups in the agency or items of interest to the Russians, such as a formula for making synthetic rubber out of garbage.

Whether or not Bill ever suspected that his material was going to the Russian Secret Police, and not to the American Communist Party, as he had been told, I never knew, but certainly he was one of the most frightened people with whom I have ever had to deal. It was difficult to get him to bring out carbon copies of documents. Usually he would jot the information down on small scraps of paper, giving them to me furtively and with many admonitions about not letting them fall into the wrong hands. Moreover, lacking the courage to break with the Party and refuse to continue his undercover activities, he often resorted to elaborate and quite transparent subterfuges to avoid doing his Communist duties. He would deprecate the value of the information that he gave, saying that it wasn't worth bothering with. He would be tied up in nonexistent conferences on the days when I was in Washington, or he would be simply unreachable. All this reminded me very strongly of a small boy trying to avoid mowing the lawn or cleaning out the furnace when he would much rather go fishing. Sometimes I would suggest hopefully to Yasha that we ought to return Bill to the open Party.

"No," he would say firmly. "While the material he is producing is not outstanding, it does help to corroborate or supplement what we are getting through the Silvermasters. And, besides, there is still the possibility that we can push him into a really good position."

Despite my private conviction that Yasha was wrong, I continued the painful process of trying to extract information from Bill. This was further complicated by the fact that both he and his wife were seemingly trying to get into left-wing or Communist-front organizations, doubtless in the hope that by becoming well known as Reds they would

[180]

lose their value to our organization and be sent back to the open Party. Although I told them sternly to avoid any such activities, I could never be sure they carried out my orders. I began to feel that the Remingtons were more bother than they were worth, particularly in view of the many other contacts I had to handle.

In the meantime Mary Price was proving to be an extremely valuable person to us, and not only because she was relaying very interesting material which she found in Walter Lippmann's files. On our instructions she had left the house which she shared with her two Communist friends on Olive Avenue in the Georgetown area. We felt she was running too great a risk, since they were both well known as Reds, so she eventually took an apartment by herself on the top floor of an old house at 2038 Eye Street, N.W. She had an extra bed on the screened-in porch where I could stay overnight, thus eliminating the risk of registering at one of the Washington hotels—places we had been told to avoid because the F.B.I. kept a strict watch on all of them. The bed was narrow and hard, and in the wintertime the supply of blankets was so limited that I had to put newspapers under the mattress to keep out the cold. I would often awaken in the morning stiff in every joint, yet in those days I was so fagged out that I could have slept on anything.

Besides serving these useful functions, Mary brought into our apparatus one of our most important agents—Duncan C. Lee, a direct descendant of General Robert E. Lee. Born in China of missionary parents, educated first over there and then in the United States and England, he became a brilliant young lawyer and worked for "Wild Bill" Donovan's law firm in New York City. He had been a member

[181]

of the Party for some time, and when we first heard of him, he was attached to the Communist group that functioned within the Institute of Pacific Relations.

In the early summer Duncan took a position as a confidential assistant to General Donovan, then head of the O.S.S. He and his red-haired, Scottish-born wife Ishbel moved down to Washington. Yasha and I briefly considered my contacting him. Mary, however, vetoed the suggestion, saying that he was so high-strung and nervous that the sight of a stranger would send him into a state of panic.

"What does he look like?" I remember asking her.

"Nothing outstanding," she said thoughtfully. "Average height, medium-brown hair and light eyes, glasses, rather studious looking. He's a good person, only he's never before been mixed up in this sort of thing."

I looked at her sharply, wondering if she herself knew just whom she was working for. I had taken pains enough to keep her in complete ignorance, even though I did trust her sufficiently to give her my telephone number in New York. Whatever her surmises, however, they did not seem to affect her attitude, for she continued to carry on her duties imperturbably. During the summer and fall of 1942 she was my intermediary with Duncan, bringing him Communist literature and collecting his Party dues. Besides which, Mary brought him instructions from us and collected his information. His wife, being a British subject, was not at that time a member, due to the American Communist Party's policy in those years of not accepting aliens for membership.

His material at that point, while valuable, was meager. He would only give Mary small bits of information orally, making her promise she would not write it down but would carry it in her head. Since a Communist does not regard his promise as anything sacred—except, of course, when it is made to his superior in the Party—Mary would memorize the data and then rush home to write it down in shorthand. Nevertheless, this procedure was hazardous, because there was always the chance she might not remember the information correctly. We tried to get Mary to change Duncan's attitude, but unfortunately she was still "green" at the espionage business and had great difficulty in handling people. The Russian Secret Police were becoming more and more impatient and it was arranged that I contact Duncan instead. He was one of the most nervous people with whom I had to deal. His innate fear had been greatly heightened by the "cloak-and-dagger" attitude that was then rampant in the O.S.S. He was unwilling to have me telephone him, for he was convinced that his phone might be tapped. He sat quite close to me in the living room and almost whispered his information for fear that the walls might have ears. Moreover, although I succeeded in getting from him more and better information than had Mary, he almost always gave it to me orally and rarely would he give me a document, although under pressure he would hand over scraps of paper on which he had written down important data.

It was in the summer of 1942 that I finally met Earl Browder. He had taken a summer cottage on a lake near Monroe, New York, where he could rest and do some writing. As Yasha and I drove into the front yard, Earl was standing on the front steps, nonchalant in baggy trousers and a sport shirt, with his pipe in his mouth. He made no gesture of recognition until we were quite close to him, then he took his pipe out of his mouth and nodded in a friendly manner. Yasha smiled at him cheerfully.

"Comrade Browder," he said, "this is Comrade Bentley."

I stood speechless, trying to think of something suitable to say while Earl, after having looked me over briefly, shook hands with Yasha and asked how the trip had been. Then, as I was still standing embarrassed, Earl waved toward the front door.

"Come on in," he said. "I think lunch is almost ready."

As I followed him up the front steps, I found myself studying him covertly. Yes, he looked very much like his pictures, only much older and quite tired. Yet in spite of his general air of weariness and flabbiness, I sensed that there was a terrific amount of vitality and energy.

The large table was loaded with all sorts of food—salads, meat, cheese—and, as we sat down, Earl's wife Raïssa came bustling in from the kitchen with plates and napkins, shouting imperious orders in Russian to her servant, whom she called Nyanya. She acknowledged her introduction to me briefly, almost without interest, and then launched into a long conversation with Yasha. I thought to myself, as I gazed at her, that she must once have been a very beautiful woman but now, in her fifties, she was fading fast. The former seductive curves of her body were thickened by fat; the flesh on her arms was no longer firm, and the obviously gray hair had been dyed in a pathetic attempt to restore it to its original color. She's the sort of woman who refuses to admit she's growing old, I thought to myself, as I watched her gazing with seeming coyness at Yasha. Then, as I continued to watch her, I realized that beneath this pathetic exterior she was a dangerous woman. There was an air of arrogance and thinly veiled cruelty about her that repelled me. She would go to any lengths to get what she wanted, I decided, and I wondered to myself just why Earl, who seemed so nice, could ever have been attracted to her. What I did not then know was that Raïssa, even as far back as the Revolution, had been a powerful figure in the G.P.U. organization in Russia and that she still worked for it. One of her duties was to keep her husband in line and make reports on him. Browder had evidently had no choice in his marriage; the powers-that-be in Moscow had issued the orders and he had had to follow them.

Soon after Browder was back in circulation, he made an agreement with Yasha to give us all the help we needed in getting contacts for information gathering in Washington. In return, he wanted to see the data we were collecting down there so that he would be *au courant* with the situation. He was continually writing articles and books, and he needed this inside dope for background material. He did, however, insist he had no desire to see military information. At the time I was puzzled at this exception, but I later learned that he was fearful of being mixed up in any espionage of a military character. Activity of this nature, if discovered by the American authorities, subjected one to a heavy penalty and Earl had already spent two terms in prison. Although he had had an enjoyable time playing chess with the other inmates, he was not anxious to return for a third term.

Why Yasha needed to make special arrangements with Earl baffled me. I took it for granted that Communists all over the world helped each other without any trading. Much later on, however, I learned that a quite-savage struggle for personal power goes on in the ranks of the Communist Party and that every man who wishes to maintain his position or to advance must use every ounce of ingenuity and ruthlessness he possesses. Earl Browder, surrounded by power-hungry rivals, knew he must keep one jump ahead of them to stay in his precarious position. To do this, he must be able to convince his Moscow bosses that he was a valuable man who knew how to anticipate every twist and turn of the Party line. By having access to inside information on the policy of the United States government— information which he knew was also going to the Soviet Union—he could guess what Moscow's next move would be and swing in the right direction.

On the other hand, Yasha's superiors in the Russian Secret Police were continually demanding quick results of him. They accepted no excuse for failure and inflicted merciless discipline. Hence, to prove that he was a good agent, he had made this secret deal with Earl whereby he was able to get more information for the N.K.V.D. The Russians, incidentally, knew nothing about this agreement and did not approve when they later found out. They were against building up the personal power and prestige of any of their puppets like Earl, because this meant that sooner or later they might have difficulty controlling them.

One result of Yasha's agreement with Earl Browder was that the latter approved of his continuing use of Louis Budenz, then the editor of the *Daily Worker*. Although I did not know it, Louis and Yasha had been friends for some time, and I only became aware of the tie-up between them in the spring of 1943 when Yasha suggested I pick him up as a contact.

"I've got so much to do myself," he said apologetically. "And I don't think it will take much of your time."

My heart contracted with pity for Yasha. He was growing weaker and weaker physically, but his pride would not let him admit he no longer had his old strength. Tired as I was, I was glad to relieve him of an added burden. It was therefore arranged that I would go downtown with Yasha the next day and meet Budenz.

Our rendezvous was near the headquarters of the Communist Party, a building in which the *Daily Worker* was also located. After Yasha had gone up to the eighth floor and brought Budenz down, I was introduced under the name of Helen and we adjourned to a bar and grill on the corner of University Place and 12th Street. There we settled ourselves in a wooden booth where we could not be overheard, ordered coffee, and began to discuss our business.

The most important of Budenz's contacts we discussed that day was Louis Adamic, the Jugoslav-born novelist who, although not at that time a Communist Party member, was quite close to the movement. Budenz knew him and had occasional conferences with him, during which he learned quite interesting items. Moreover, Adamic became an unofficial adviser to the O.S.S. on the subject of his native Jugoslavia, and what he learned in this position filtered back to us.

It was arranged that Louis and I would meet in the future in the same bar and grill. There would be no prearranged meetings. Instead, when I wanted to see him I would call the *Daily Worker* (if he was not in, I would leave word that "Helen Johns" had called); when he had information to be passed on he would call me at World Tourists, leaving word in my absence that "Mr. Louis" had called.

Meanwhile, Yasha had taken on Communist agents whom he handled himself and about whose existence I knew nothing—or very little. In the fall of 1942 he announced that he had acquired a Communist cell of engineers, many of whose members could be placed in strategic places in the United States government. The leader of this group, he said, was named Julius. Since Julius worked around New York, he would be the contact man. It was arranged that whenever he had information available he would call me at my apartment and I in turn would notify Yasha so that they could get together. Julius has since been identified as Julius Rosenberg, sentenced to death in April 1951 for atom-bomb espionage activities.

In addition to all these activities, Yasha also had the job of counterintelligence covering the various Russian agencies. In almost every Soviet business he had a contact who apprised him of the operations of both the Soviet and American employees.

One of Yasha's oddest contacts was Vladimir Kazakevich, a tall, hungry-looking Russian with glasses and a perpetually absent-minded air. He had been born of White Russian parents, his father being an official in the Trans-Siberian railroad. Up until the late twenties or early thirties he had had no particular Communist sympathies. But later, when he came to this country via the West Coast, he had there fallen in with a group of Communists who had succeeded in converting him. While he never became a Party member, he moved from then on in left-wing and Communist circles, eking out a precarious existence writing ar-

[188]

ticles and making speeches. He was in the strange predicament of being neither a Soviet national nor an American citizen, and he traveled on a Nansen passport. His one conquering ambition was to return to the U.S.S.R. and become a Soviet citizen. The Russians, however, seemed to feel that he was more useful here as a propagandist for the Russian cause.

When I first met Kazakevich in 1941, he was haunting Yasha's office with monotonous regularity in the pathetic hope that by bringing odd bits of information to the G.P.U. he could earn permission to go back home. These visits were always carefully timed to coincide with our lunch hour, for he knew that Yasha would be kind-hearted enough to buy him a decent meal. Most of what he reported was trivial, yet Yasha always let him come, thinking that perhaps he would one day have something important to offer. Many times I would look out the door of his office and then whisper to Yasha:

"Don't look now, but here comes Kazy—right on time for lunch."

Yasha would sigh. "Poor devil! I don't suppose he's got anything important for me, but he always looks so hungry I can't refuse to feed him."

At one point, indeed, Kazakevich did get a position teaching for the Army at Cornell University; but just as we rejoiced at this and began to get good information from him, he was exposed as a Communist by Frederick Woltman of the New York *World Telegram*. Yasha took the news philosophically.

"I'm afraid he never will be much good to us," he said. "And besides, in spite of my orders he's taken to running in and out of the Soviet consulate, doing errands for the consul in the hope that he can get back to Moscow. That could endanger the apparatus."

Thereafter, except for infrequent visits, we never saw Kazakevich on business, although once in the spring of 1944 I ran into him in the Four Continents bookstore and took him to a nearby cafeteria for a cup of coffee. After my testimony naming him before a Congressional committee in 1949, I read in the paper that he had left for Russia. Evidently the Russians felt that he wasn't a safe person to have around the United States, even with his middling knowledge of espionage activities. I often wonder whether he is six feet under now, along with the rest of the Soviet agents who are no longer useful to Moscow.

I remember the case of one Russian Army major who got himself talked about because he insistently patronized Café Society downtown, night after night, and sat gazing amorously at Lena Horne, who was then a singer in the club. Soviet intelligence was distressed about this incident additionally, because the owner of the club was fairly well known as a Communist and we knew that the F.B.I. kept it under constant surveillance. Evidently the major was stepped on firmly, for after a while no more adverse reports came in about him.

Most of the reports from Yasha's undercover man in the Amtorg Corporation, however, dealt with shady business transactions that were sabotaging the Soviet war effort. It was incredible to me how many American employees of that firm had relatives in the manufacturing business to whom they could steer Soviet orders for material, meanwhile making themselves a neat profit on their purchases. The material was inferior and the prices they had to pay were completely exorbitant. Sometimes, after wading through one of these reports, I would feel actually nauseated.

"What's the use of people fighting and dying to destroy Fascism," I would ask Yasha, "when parasites like that are waxing fat and prosperous?"

He would shrug his shoulders. "That's why we need to build a new world where we can educate people to deal decently and honestly with each other. We can't do much with this sort of scum now except get them out of our organizations; when the Revolution comes we won't be able to rehabilitate them, so they'll just have to be liquidated."

By the early summer of 1943 I began to feel that I was chained to some inexorable treadmill that dragged me behind it as it mercilessly stepped up its tempo. Fatigue became a constant companion; I was so tired that I could fall asleep on buses, on trains, and even standing up. Each day I would say to myself: I can't go on any longer—I'll just lie down and never get up again. Yet each succeeding day found me doggedly battling on. With this physical fatigue went a mental weariness that made it difficult to concentrate on anything but the vital problems of the moment. It was an effort even to think back and remember what had gone on two weeks before. I could only hang on, moment by moment, hour by hour, and not think too much of the future.

I knew now that Yasha was a dying man and that the end might come at any moment—it was only by some miracle of will power he was still alive. Once, while talking to me on the interoffice telephone, he couldn't catch his breath. I slammed down the receiver and dashed across the street, knocking down people in my haste. That time I found him shaken and white-faced—but alive. I wondered what the next attack might bring.

From then on he spent many nights at my apartment, because I didn't want him to be alone. Although I had always been a very sound sleeper, I began to have frightful nightmares, from which I would awaken dripping with sweat. Then I would lie awake for the next hour, listening to the sound of his irregular breathing and wishing that I could hear the sound of his voice to reassure me.

Sometimes I was so edgy from tension that I would shout at him, "You can't keep on going like this. They have no right to ask you to destroy yourself!"

He would look at me listlessly and shake his head. "It's no use. Soon I shall be leaving you."

His very disinterestedness would only add to my alarm. I had never before known him to admit defeat; even though the odds were against him, he would battle on. Now he had ceased to care whether he lived or not.

"You must not worry about me," he would say gently. "There is no peace for a revolutionary except in the grave, and soon my troubles will be over."

Perhaps he is right, I said to myself; perhaps he will be fortunate to be able to escape from the pain and suffering of this world into a blessed nothingness.

"But you can't leave me," I would cry in agony. "What will I do without you?"

He would smile sadly and hold me close. "You will have to be very brave, and it will not be easy. Only, when I am gone, remember that we two found a perfect happiness that few in this world have ever known. Perhaps that memory will help you to bear the pain of parting."

With an effort I would steady myself and choke back the

tears; his days were few now, and I must not spoil them with any sadness. I would not think of the future.

Meanwhile, Mary Price had decided she wanted to give up her position with Walter Lippmann. Yasha and I tried to convince her that she should stay, but it became increasingly obvious that she was cracking up. Finally it was decided that she resign and go to Mexico for the summer to get her health back. We arranged to keep in touch with her through her sister Mildred (Mrs. Harold Coy), executive head of the pro-Communist China Aid Council. At first, Yasha and I regarded Mildred merely as an intermediary with Mary, but soon we discovered she would be a valuable adjunct to our apparatus in her own right. She was at that time, he told me, the organizer of the Communist unit which functioned in the Institute of Pacific Relations—a foundation for Far Eastern studies which had originally been set up by well-meaning philanthropists but which had long since fallen under the domination of the Communists. The organization, because of its respectable past and high-sounding title, had been able to enroll in its ranks a vast number of "innocents," among them professors and businessmen who were interested in Pacific affairs. Hence it had, he explained to me, become the center of all Communist activity in the Far Eastern field, offering a protective covering to a number of smaller, more obviously pro-Communist enterprises that clustered around it. Among these were the China Aid Council, of which Mildred was executive secretary, and the magazines *China Today* and *Amerasia*.

The Communist group in the Institute of Pacific Relations, which he told me was made up of every Party member in the Far Eastern field—regardless of what organization he was attached to—was set up in a very special way. Instead of being attached to a geographical section headquarters, as was the case with most units, it was handled directly by Frederick Vanderbilt Field, who in turn was responsible directly to Earl Browder. This arrangement was made necessary because the work that the cell was doing was so secret and so valuable that it had to be protected from any leaks. In actual fact, however, this set-up was pathetically inadequate to protect the activities of the group, as Yasha pointed out to me.

"It's a hang-over from the days when we didn't operate properly," he said disgustedly. "At that time all undercover work was routed via the Party. Now we know enough to have our agents directly in contact with the Russians."

"What are they doing?" I asked interestedly.

"Getting Party members and sympathizers into the United States government where they can be of use to us," he said. "They've already done pretty well along this line. They've placed several good solid people in jobs where they can effectively influence American policy on the Far East in a pro-Soviet direction, and I understand they are collecting good information that is being relayed to our friends via Browder. The only thing that bothers me is that they're operating so indiscreetly. It's an open secret that the Institute of Pacific Relations is red as the rose. Moreover, with that clumsy set-up, it will be a miracle if the F.B.I. doesn't trip over them sooner or later."

"Are we going to take them on?" I asked.

"Certainly not!" he answered. "I wouldn't touch them with a ten-foot pole. But they might be a valuable source of agents for us. We got Duncan Lee from the group and there may be others there that haven't yet been too tarred with the red brush. Keep in touch with Mildred and find out if she knows anyone in there that we could use."

I was still curious about the I.P.R. group. "But why, if it is operating in such a dangerous fashion, doesn't someone do something about the situation?"

He looked at me despondently. "I don't know. Sometimes I don't understand what is going on in Moscow. Things seem to have changed since my days. The old crowd no longer seems to be in charge, and the new ones are very different."

Thoughtfully I looked at him, realizing this was not the first time he had made these cryptic comments that seemed to indicate something was very drastically wrong. How many times in the past few months had he come back from his appointment with his Russian contact, a young man who had replaced Charlie, to say to me despairingly, "I don't understand what's happening. It's all so different from what it used to be." When I would anxiously ask him what was the matter, he would fall silent; and after a few minutes, he would turn on me savagely and say, "No matter what happens to me, keep on going." I remembered, too, how bitter he was at the Russians' inability to deliver the right amount of films in the proper condition.

"They're trying to sabotage my work," he would say fiercely. "They want to get rid of me."

What is going on, I would say to myself, feeling a queer sense of panic. Can it be that our own people would behave this way? Then I would steady myself. Undoubtedly, in Yasha's condition small incidents got magnified into unrecognizable phantasms. Yes, I would say to myself reassuringly, that must be the answer, and I would hold him very close, trying to make him feel the security of my love.

CHAPTER IX

By THE MIDDLE of September, Mary Price returned from Mexico and after some persuasion agreed to go on to Washington in the hope that she could obtain a position in the United States government. Unfortunately she had no luck. Although she seemed on the verge of getting a job in the Office of Strategic Services, she was turned down at the last minute. Later, through Duncan Lee, we found that the real reason for her turndown was "past Communist associations." Suspecting at the time, however, that it had been something of this nature, we began to realize that perhaps the United States government intelligence agencies had a dossier on her and that it would be impossible to push her into a productive position. We therefore encouraged her to place herself with one of the Washington newspapers so we could use her as an intermediary between some of our agents and ourselves. She agreed to this and meanwhile I made arrangements for her to meet J. Julius Joseph one evening.

Promptly at the appointed hour I brought Joe to her house, having previously told her to be sure to be alone. As she opened the door, I heard the sound of masculine voices in the living room. I opened my mouth to speak, but Mary put her finger on her lips. Hurriedly she led us out onto the back porch and then explained she was entertaining two men from the Office of War Information. To my horror I learned that one of them was a man I had known years before in my Communist unit at Columbia University, and this could be a very serious situation.

"Go back and get rid of them as soon as possible," I said in a whisper. "I'll talk to you later."

It was two hours before Mary's visitors departed. All that time Joe and I had huddled behind the stove, hoping desperately that no one would think to come out there. When we finally emerged from our hiding place, cramped and tired, I sent Joe on home and proceeded to give Mary a piece of my mind.

"What's the idea?" I demanded angrily. "Don't you know you're jeopardizing the whole apparatus with a performance like that?"

She began to weep. "I can't live like a hermit," she cried out. "I've got to have some companionship. They dropped in to see me and I couldn't get rid of them."

I eyed her severely. "Look, Mary, you are not supposed to have the kind of friends that visit you unexpectedly. It's too dangerous. Besides which, one of those men used to be a Party member."

"I don't care," she sobbed. "I can't take any more of this. I want to live like a human being."

I winced at her words. She was right, of course. None of us were living like human beings. We had become a pack of hunted animals. No, that wasn't correct; at least the animals lived normal lives except for brief intervals when hunters were on their trail. But for those of us who worked in the underground there was no respite, no rest, no relaxation. Why, I said to myself, do individuals have to be destroyed to build a new world? For a moment I looked at her sadly.

"All right, Mary," I said very gently. "Just take it easy. We'll see what we can do."

Back in New York, Yasha listened silently to my recital, his face expressionless. Then he finally spoke.

"Perhaps it is better this way," he said. "I'll try to get her back to the open Party where she can find friends, but I'm going to have some difficulty. The Russians want her for a special job."

"Job?" I asked, puzzled. "What job?"

He stared at the floor. "I didn't tell you before, but they've been putting the screws on me to hand Mary over to them. I've steadily refused because I know what they want her for and I don't approve." He stopped for a moment and then said bitterly, "They think she could be extremely useful to them. She's attractive and single, besides being intelligent and a trusted worker. They want to set her up in an apartment, buy her fancy clothes, and let her use her wiles on men who would be useful to the cause. I told them that they could hire prostitutes for that, but they said that I was a sentimentalist."

I stared at him speechless, trying to digest what he had said; I found myself struggling with a wave of disgust. It must be true if he said so, but I had never known before that the movement used women like this. Later on I was to be told that even in the open Party it was a common and effective tactic, used especially by waterfront "street" units interested in attracting sailors. Yet, up till then, due to the type of "shop" unit I had been in and to Yasha's desire to protect me, I had been entirely ignorant of such methods. He saw the expression on my face.

[198]

"I know," he said. "I don't like it either. But remember we are fighting a revolution and we sometimes have to do things that we don't like." Then he turned to me fiercely. "But this is going too far. I'm going to fight this thing to the end, no matter what the cost. If anything happens to me, take care of Mary. Don't under any circumstances let her be turned over to them."

Tired as I was that night, I lay awake for hours, thinking over what Yasha had told me. I remembered what Juliet had said about women giving not only their souls but even their bodies to the Revolution. I had discounted it then because she was a counterrevolutionary. Now I began to see some of the ugly and sordid aspects to the business of being a revolutionary. With increasing revulsion I wondered why we had to get down in the mud and wallow in it in order to build a new world. I found myself wishing passionately that I could get out of this undercover work and back into the open Party, where the air was clean and wholesome. Then I looked at Yasha lying beside me and knew that, loving him as I did, I could not abandon him when he needed me the most.

Mary was delighted when I told her she could leave. She packed her things and came up to New York to live with her sister while she looked for a job and an apartment. Meanwhile, Yasha had another agent, a girl of about Mary's age, who was going down to Washington to look for a job in the government. He asked Mary to hold onto her apartment until we could find some foolproof way of getting our new person in. This was necessary, because housing was so scarce down there that a newcomer stood little chance of finding even a small room, and for our purposes it was better to have a place where I could stay overnight.

Helen Tenney, the new girl, was a Communist of long standing, who had been very active in Spanish organizations during the Civil War. She had been introduced to Yasha by Grace Granich of the Intercontinent News Service when it appeared she would be useful to us. Previously, she had worked in New York for an organization set up by the Office of Strategic Services for the purpose of finding people of all nationalities who could be trained in sabotage and intelligence and then sent abroad to carry on undercover work. Helen had been quite valuable in that position. She had brought to Yasha the dossiers of all the prospective candidates so that we would know what type of people they were employing.

It was arranged that Mary would keep the apartment and the telephone under her own name, using the pretext that one day she meant to return to Washington. Then she was to put a small ad in the *New York Times* on a certain day, asking for someone to sublet from her. When Helen's letter came in, she was to accept her as the new tenant, disregarding any other offers that she received. This worked out very well. Helen got the apartment and we successfully avoided any tie-up between the two.

Helen had been told to go to the Office of Strategic Services and apply for a position doing research work—a field in which she was well qualified. We thought that, with her good family background and her previous work with an O.S.S. subsidiary, she would stand a good chance of getting in. Moreover, we alerted one of our contacts, Maurice Halperin, who was in their Latin-American branch, so that when her application was O.K.'d he could ask to have her placed in his division. Things turned out quite differently from what we had planned, but from our point of view

[200]

vastly better. Helen went through the screening successfully, but her knowledge of Spanish called her to the attention of the "hush-hush" Spanish division, which promptly hired her as a research worker. Thus she was able to collect highly confidential material, which she brought to Yasha every two weeks or so when she came up to New York to visit her mother.

Meanwhile, back in the summer of 1943 Yasha wanted to turn over to me a young Englishman who was then working for the British Intelligence Service. Cedric Belfrage had been a Party member in Britain and after coming to this country got in touch with V. J. Jerome, who in turn put Belfrage in contact with Yasha. For some time Cedric had been turning over to us extremely valuable information from the files of the B.I.S., most of which I saw before it was relayed on to the Russians. I remember one large volume of instructions to agents of British Intelligence which Yasha thought so good that we kept a copy of it in the safe at World Tourists, reading it occasionally for hints on undercover work. It was a most thorough manual: it gave minute directions on how to conduct a surveillance and how to avoid being tailed, and it even had a section on "breaking and entering" which had been "patriotically contributed by the burglars of Great Britain." As I looked through it, I realized why the British Intelligence Service had long been known as a very excellent one. Obviously they knew their business from A to Z. One thing that stuck in my mind was their evaluation of motivations in choosing an agent. The best person, they said, was one who was motivated by patriotism or idealism, although if he became disillusioned he might be very hard to handle. Adventurers they brushed aside as being unreliable, while they considered "bought" agents as being very risky, because someone else's intelligence service could always offer them more money.

Belfrage himself, Yasha told me, was an extremely odd character and rather difficult to deal with. Although passionately devoted to the cause, he still considered himself a patriotic Britisher, and hence he would give us no information that showed up England's mistakes or tended to make her a laughingstock. In addition, he was very nervous at what he was doing, and Yasha had all he could do to keep him in line. The prospect of taking over one more high-strung agent did not appeal to me, nor did I desire to tangle with the British Intelligence Service. I stalled the proposition off for a few weeks; then fortunately something happened that made any decision unnecessary.

In the early fall, Cedric brought Yasha some highly confidential information, cautioning him as usual to be very careful with it. Yasha, in line with his agreement, showed the material to Earl Browder, who incautiously gave it to *The Protestant*, one of the Communist-controlled publications. Immediately the data appeared in an article in such a form that the source could be readily identified by Cedric's superiors. It was a bad slip. Yasha, seething with rage, hotfooted it down to Party headquarters to give Earl a talking-to and then went off to see Belfrage. He returned to look at me hopelessly.

"Well, that's that," he said grimly. "We've just lost a good agent. Cedric is shivering with fright, and when I finished talking to him he bolted off in a panic, saying that he would never come back."

"But why did Earl do it?" I asked.

"Sheer stupidity," he said angrily. "He didn't think it

would do any harm. Wouldn't you think that after all his years as a revolutionary he would know better?" Then, very grimly, "But I can assure you he won't do anything like that again, not after what I said to him."

I could see now why Yasha was unwilling to have any part of the Institute of Pacific Relations. If even Earl was capable of committing such blunders, it was better for us to stay a long way off. Mildred had by then looked through the list of people she knew in the I.P.R. to see if there was anyone who could be useful to us. Her report was not hopeful.

"There's Philip Jaffe, of course," she said. "He edits *Amerasia*, you know. But I don't think he's safe to deal with, because he's too well known as a Red. Of course, he could get information for you through some of his contacts, but frankly I don't think it's worth the risk." She went rapidly through a list of other members, all of whom seemed unlikely to be of use because they were too red or too temperamental.

I took this information back to Yasha and he said he would take it up with his Russian superior. But his mind was evidently on other things, for he spoke almost absentmindedly.

"What's the matter?" I asked.

"The same old trouble," he said despairingly. "The Russians are making demands that I don't like. They are not only insisting that Mary Price be turned over to them at once, but they want the Silvermaster group, too."

I looked at him puzzled. "I can understand why you don't want to give Mary to them, in view of their plans for her, but why is it bad to put them in contact with Greg? After all, they won't hurt him, and since he knows he is working for the Russian Secret Police, there will be no difficulty in switching him over."

He stared out the window, without answering; then he finally said, "You don't understand. I've told you before that the Russians, having been steeled and toughened in a brutal war, do not know how to deal with Americans. They'll ruin Greg!"

None of this sounded reasonable to me, and so I thought Yasha was exaggerating the situation. Certainly Greg, with his background of Russian revolutionary activity, ought to be able to cope with the N.K.V.D. I started to tell him so. Then, as I looked at his face, I was struck with another idea.

"You haven't told me the whole story," I said.

"No, and I wasn't going to," he said despondently. "They also want to take you over as an intermediary between the Silvermaster group and their man."

Anger seethed through me. They couldn't take me away from Yasha. I wouldn't let them do it!

"Over my dead body!" I said violently, not realizing just how close to the truth I was.

Yasha looked at me very tenderly, then his mouth set in a grim line. "No, *golubishka*, that's one thing I won't let them do. No matter what happens, I won't let them take you away from me."

But the struggle over the fate of the Silvermaster group was a bitter one. Yasha would come home night after night, looking like a beaten man, and I would watch him with a growing rage in my heart. Once I forgot my caution and exploded in a burst of anger.

"They can't do that to you!" I said savagely. "Just let me at them and I'll tell them a thing or two."

"No," he said quietly, looking at me strangely. "I don't think that would be a wise thing to do."

"Oh, no?" I retorted. "Well, they may be able to kick other people around but they've never run into an American. Ordinarily we're peaceful people, but when we get mad, we can be plenty tough."

Yasha looked at me pityingly and seemed about to say something. Then he changed his mind and went over and turned on the radio. There was, I saw, no use in pursuing the subject, so I crawled wearily into bed and fell asleep.

Soon afterward Yasha won a partial victory. The Silvermaster group was to be turned over to a new Soviet contact but one who would not see it directly. I was to collect the material and turn it over to another courier, who in turn would give it to the new man. Also I was not to be taken away from Yasha, and I would be able to continue on helping him with the other agents in Washington. I greeted the news with a whoop of joy. Now things were going to be all right.

"You see," I said happily to Yasha, "you were imagining things. The Russians are intelligent people. Once you explained the situation, they fell in with your ideas. Obviously, they're only taking over the group to relieve the burden on you."

He smiled faintly but said nothing. Perhaps he felt that it would be no use to explain the situation to me; perhaps his loyalty to the organization sealed his lips. I was soon to learn that my first optimism was unfounded, for his relations with the Russians grew rapidly worse and worse. Day after day they steadily put the screws on him to turn over Mary, and wearily but doggedly he refused.

Often he would come home taut and grim faced after a

meeting with his Russian contact and would pace the floor silently, then throw himself on the couch and bury his head in his hands. Bewildered, I would sit beside him, unable to help, not knowing what was bothering him. I began to feel that I was in the midst of some hideous nightmare from which I couldn't shake myself awake. What was wrong? Why wouldn't he tell me anything? What could have happened to shake a strong man like Yasha, who was afraid of nothing? I would find myself shaking with terror. Something horrible was going on and I was helpless to fight it—indeed I didn't even know what it was.

Sometimes in the midst of his pacing Yasha would stop and stare at me savagely. Then in the tone of a man being tortured beyond his endurance, he would cry out, "If I turn traitor, turn me in!"

I would quickly look away, because the sight of that naked suffering was more than I could bear. Even today those words return to haunt me, and the pain of remembering is deeper because now I understand what they mean. Had I known the truth then as I know it now, I could have helped him—or could I? In that awful moment when all that a man has lived for crumbles into ashes and leaves him standing alone in the blackness of disillusionment, can anyone stretch out a helping hand?

It was much later on that I realized Yasha had been deliberately driving himself beyond his physical endurance because for him death was a merciful solution to his dilemma. The movement had been his entire life; he had given of himself unsparingly and without any thought of reward.

Even though he came from a well-off Jewish family in the Ukraine, Yasha had early seen the suffering and misery of others. At the age of eight he had helped to distribute

Communist literature, knowing the penalty for so doing was jail. Not long after this he was caught and thrown into prison. One day the guards dragged all the revolutionaries out into the courtyard and shot them down. But Yasha, by then wise in the ways of the underground, fell to the ground and played dead for two days, until the outraged citizens of Ekaterinoslav stormed the jail and demanded the bodies of their sons. Released as the result of popular pressure, Yasha resumed his undercover activities, only to be arrested two years later. This time he was sent to Siberia and I remember his vivid description of how he walked those many miles with chains on his hands and legs. Once there, he was left, as all prisoners then were, in a remote village where the authorities thought there was no chance of escape. He was given a room in a private house and the chance to earn what money he could. It had been bitter cold in Siberia, especially in the winter, but Yasha didn't seem to mind it. He used to tell me how he would sit in the house and listen to the sound of the howling wind playing weird symphonies on the telephone wires.

All this time he was planning his escape, and not long afterward he made his way through the almost-impassable mountains to China, thence to Japan, where he spent a year. By then he had received word through the underground that his family had moved to the United States, so he smuggled himself onto a ship and arrived safely on the West Coast. Through his parents he managed to obtain derivative citizenship, since he was still a minor, and went on with his schooling. At the time the United States entered World War I in the spring of 1917 he had completed his medical training but staunchly refused to participate in an "imperialist war" and hence never received his M.D. degree. I remember distinctly how the sinus specialist to whom I took him in the spring of 1941 when I was worried about his health looked at him thoughtfully and then shook his head.

"I'm sure I know you," he said. "You were in my graduating class at Columbia University Medical School, but I don't remember your name."

When the Russian Revolution broke out in 1919, Yasha worked valiantly in this country to get support for the new Bolshevik regime. In the twenties he returned to the Soviet Union and did whatever he could to help establish a new society. His jobs ranged all the way from being the foreman of a coal mine in the most deserted regions of Siberia to being a member of the G.P.U.'s internal police force that maintained order during a very confused period. He was a friend of Lenin's and worshiped him. I remember his telling me that he was warming himself in the railroad station of a remote village when the news of the Soviet leader's death arrived. For a moment he was stunned. Then he walked over to the one window and, breathing on it and wiping the frost off with the sleeve of his tattered coat, he looked at the stacks of frozen corpses lying half buried in the snow, waiting for the freight train to carry them away.

"Comrades," he said, half to himself, "we have lost our old friend Vladimir Iliyich, and that is a loss we can never replace. He has seen us through many a bad time and now he is gone. But you, too, comrades, have died that we might build a better world. I swear to you, in the name of the cause which we have all fought and died for, that I will never rest until we have reached our goal."

One day Yasha ran into a "ghost," as the N.K.V.D. called those former members who had left the Service but had not as yet gone over to the enemy. He seemed visibly shaken by the encounter and returned home to tell me about it.

"Poor devil!" he said compassionately. "He's been in hiding for some time, terrified of his life. Finally, he got to a point where he had no more money to live on, so he telephoned me and asked if I would buy his old Contax camera. I agreed and arranged to meet him on a street corner, but he was so nervous that he circled the block five or six times to be sure I hadn't brought anyone with me."

"Did you buy it?" I asked.

"Yes," he said. "Contaxes are scarce right now and we can use one. He literally grabbed the money out of my hand and dashed off, he was so terrified. He needn't have been so upset. I wasn't going to hurt him."

It was the middle of November and I decided to do my Christmas shopping early, so that I wouldn't find myself caught in the last-minute rush. This was a formidable job; not only did I have my personal purchases, plus gifts for the employees of both World Tourists and the U.S. Service & Shipping Corporation, but I had to purchase presents for all our agents, Yasha's as well as mine. For some strange reason, it was a tradition in the N.K.V.D. that at Christmas everyone who worked for them—no matter in what capacity—received a gift. None of our agents, of course, were paid salaries, nor were they given any money except cash to cover traveling expenses when they came up to New York to bring reports. As a matter of fact, it was they who were paying the Party, because they were assessed their Communist dues plus any special amounts solicited to help the international movement. Therefore, as a token of appreciation, we made it a point to give each of them a nice present at Christmas.

These varied in value and type according to the worth of the individual and his personal preferences. For example, Earl Browder always received several jars of Russian caviar and a bottle or two of scotch (all provided by the N.K.V.D.); Raïssa received bottles of imported cognac, and Earl's brother Bill several quarts of Canadian Club whiskey. The Silvermasters invariably received vodka and caviar, plus expensive personal gifts for each of them. Kazakevich was given a steamer basket of fruit and jams from the Hicks store, and Joe North a basket containing several bottles of rye. Most of our other agents received only personal gifts, ranging between five dollars and twenty dollars in value, although Mary Price, at the height of her usefulness, was given a magnificent lingerie set that must have cost thirty-five.

My first purchase was a personal one—a new wrist watch for Yasha, because his old one no longer kept good time and, in addition, was growing shabby. I remember wondering whether or not he would still be alive at Christmas time and thinking that perhaps I should give him his present right away so that at least he could have some pleasure out of it. Then I went on to get presents for my Washington agents, including some inexpensive toys for Maurice Halperin's children.

Laden with bundles, I staggered into World Tourists, to find Yasha in his office. I began opening the packages to show him what I had bought. When I came to the toys, he sat very quietly, staring at them with tears in his eyes. Then he pulled me down on his lap and put his cheek against mine.

"You know," he said wistfully, "one of the things I regret most is the fact that we never had any children."

By now the Russians had evidently reached the end of their patience with Yasha. This time they issued an ultimatum: either Yasha handed over Mary Price and agreed to carry out any future orders without quibbling or he would have to leave the Service and be considered a "traitor." He must give his answer three days later when he met his Russian contact. Yasha accepted this dictum listlessly. He was by now too beaten and tired to care very much.

What his decision would have been, I never knew. To this day I wonder over and over again whether he would have found the strength to break away. Sometimes I think his conscience would not have permitted him to do things of which he did not approve; sometimes I believe that the pull of the past would have been too great and that he would have given up in despair. But he was mercifully spared the ordeal of deciding. On Thanksgiving evening, the day before he was to meet his Russian superior, Yasha quietly died.

The night before, he was pensive and absent-minded. For the first time in his life he forgot to keep an appointment with a very important contact. The next morning he slept late and hardly seemed to have the strength to get out of bed. I, too, was exhausted and battling with a bad cold, and we thought briefly of staying home and cooking a simple meal. Then Yasha smiled at me wanly.

"No," he said finally. "Today's Thanksgiving and I'd like to go out and have a superspecial meal with all the trimmings."

We had a late afternoon dinner at a restaurant opposite London Terrace and went to the movies. Afterward Yasha thought he ought to go home to his hotel, because he wanted to change into a suit that was hanging in the closet there. I looked at him, and with a terrible feeling of panic I realized that the end was at most only a few days off. He couldn't be alone when that happened. I must be close to him. Hurriedly, I bundled him into a bus and we rode home.

When we reached the drugstore a block from my house, he began to worry about our work. He insisted that I go into a phone booth and call Mildred Price to find out what was going on currently in the I.P.R. I refused, knowing that he was in no condition to think about such things. I even resorted to strategy and told him I was much too tired to bother with our work that day. He looked at me sadly and said the first cruel words that had ever passed his lips.

"Why did I ever marry you?" he muttered bitterly. "I thought you would be a good, strong revolutionary and not a sissy."

I couldn't answer him; I think if I had I would have burst into tears. In silence we reached the front door of my apartment house and he slowly and painfully climbed the one short flight of stairs that led to my apartment. Once inside, he lay down on the couch and turned on the radio listlessly, selecting a station that had a symphonic program. I busied myself in the bathroom, washing out his socks and my stockings. Soon, however, the program shifted to a jazzy one, which I knew he hated, and I went back into the living room to see if he wanted it changed.

"Shall I find another station?" I asked.

He only shook his head and closed his eyes, drifting off

into sleep. I went back to the bathroom, changed into my pajamas, and set my hair in pin curls for the morrow. When I returned to the living room, he was sleeping peacefully. Completely exhausted myself, I stretched out beside him and must have dozed off for about an hour.

I awakened suddenly with the panicky sense that something was badly wrong. Then I realized that, although he still seemed to be sleeping peacefully, horrible choking sounds were coming from his throat. Frantically I shook him.

"Wake up, Yasha," I cried. "You're having a bad nightmare."

He did not respond but still lay inertly on the couch, the same choking sounds coming from his throat. Remembering my Red Cross training, I dashed into the kitchen, returning with a bottle of brandy. I tried to force some of it down his throat but he seemed unable to swallow. Then my mind flashed back fifteen years to my mother's last moments. This was a death rattle that I was hearing. No, he couldn't be dying! I wouldn't let him! I grabbed for the telephone and dialed the operator.

"Operator," I shouted hysterically, "get me an ambulance quick!"

"Just a moment," she said calmly. "I'll get you the Police Department."

Sickeningly, I realized that I couldn't afford to get involved with the police. It was too dangerous to the movement. But I didn't care then. My Yasha was very ill and I needed help. As I waited, the steady voice of the desk sergeant at the Charles Street police station came on the wire.

"What's the matter, ma'am?" he asked.

"A man has just had a heart attack," I said, trying to keep

[213]

my voice steady, "and he needs immediate medical attention. Can you help me?"

"Certainly," he said reassuringly. "I'll have an ambulance
there right away."

I slammed down the receiver and frantically tore off my
pajamas, meanwhile taking the bobby pins out of my hair.
Yasha still lay there unconscious, making those queer
sounds. As I threw my clothes on and tied my hair into a
severe knot at the back of my head, I kept crying out desperately to Yasha.

"Hold on, darling," I said in an agony of fear. "Just
hold on for a few minutes longer. There's help coming."

The buzzer downstairs rang and automatically I pushed
the release button. Then I walked over to Yasha and looked
down at him. He seemed to be still choking, but his eyes
had rolled upwards, giving him a fixed, glassy stare. Mechanically, without even thinking, I gently closed his eyelids. There was a knock at the door and I opened it to admit
two efficient-looking men in white from St. Vincent's Hospital.

"Which of you is the doctor?" I asked anxiously.

"Neither of us," said the stouter of them, cheerfully.
"There's a shortage of medics right now and we're not
sending out any internes on ambulance calls." Then, seeing
the look on my face, he added, "Don't worry, ma'am, we've
both had first-aid training and we can help you."

I looked at them horrified. Good God, I thought to myself, I've had the same course of training that you've had,
so what can you do that I can't? Then I realized that the
taller one had walked over to Yasha and was looking at
him thoughtfully. Carefully he lifted his eyelids and stared
at his eyes, then he listened to his heart. After a pause, he

looked at his partner significantly, then picked up the telephone and dialed a number.

"Hello," he said. "Yes, it's me. No, pal, it's too late. He's D.O.A. What'll we do now? Wait for the police? O.K., see you soon."

He hung up the receiver and nonchalantly lit a cigarette, without speaking to me. Quite suddenly my knees gave way and I sat down on the nearest chair. I knew that phrase; how many times had my doctor uncle used it! D.O.A.—that meant "Dead on Arrival!" The room swirled around me but with an effort I steadied myself. Yasha was dead, I said to myself numbly. Never again would I hear his voice —never again would I come home to find him waiting for me! I gripped the arms of the chair and fought back a rising hysteria. I wanted to give in to my feelings and sob my heart out. What did anything matter now that he was gone? Then I became aware that the two St. Vincent's men were arguing with each other.

"We've got to move the ambulance," one of them said. "It's parked in front of a fireplug."

"Oh, let's wait till the police come," said the other.

The police! That spelled danger. Yasha's pockets were full of vital material, including the coded telephone numbers of most of his agents. It must not be found. Why am I thinking like this, I wondered dully. The man I loved is dead and for me life is over. What does all the rest of it matter? But to him it did; he had given his life for what he believed in. And I had promised I would carry on for him. I couldn't let him down. Desperately, I forced myself to think clearly.

"Why don't you two go down and move the ambulance now?" I said, turning to the two men from St. Vincent's.

[215]

They shook their heads in unison. "We can't leave you alone with the body. We'll have to wait for the police."

Deliberately I pretended to misunderstand them. "Oh, please don't worry about me. I can manage to stay alone for a few minutes."

They looked at each other dubiously. Then, with a sigh of relief, they went out the door. Hurriedly I bolted the lock after them, then swiftly, systematically I went through all Yasha's pockets, abstracting the material and transferring it to my capacious pocketbook. Frantically I tried to roll Yasha over so that I could get at his back pockets, but he was too heavy for me.

Thinking fast, I realized there probably wasn't much there except small items like key case and handkerchief, so I decided to abandon the search. I put my pocketbook innocently back in the same place on the bureau, then I rushed to the door, unbolted it, and returned to sit on the same chair. I was none too soon, for immediately I heard the sound of their footsteps pounding up the stairs. When the hospital men saw that I was where they had left me, they showed their relief. It was later that I learned they were worried because they were not allowed to leave anyone with a corpse for fear he might steal valuables from the pockets.

It was then about nine-forty-five. A few minutes later the police in the person of two large, friendly Irishmen arrived. The ambulance men told them briefly what had happened and departed, muttering bitterly that they didn't see why people had to die on Thanksgiving evening. The policemen looked at me sympathetically.

"You look worn out, ma'am," one of them said. "If you

can just get in touch with his doctor, we can settle things up real fast."

At their awkward sympathy I found myself fighting back the tears. But I couldn't go to pieces now. His doctor —what was his name? I couldn't remember. Yasha's old one had gone into the Army a year or so before, but what was the name of the new one? A wave of dizziness swept over me and the room seemed to rock. One of the policemen, spying the brandy bottle on the mantelpiece, hurriedly poured some into a glass and handed it to me.

"Better drink this," he said brusquely. "You've had a shock."

I gulped it down and the warmth of it seemed to steady me. I thought furiously. Yes, now I remembered the name. I got unsteadily to my feet and dialed his number. His voice was irritated.

"There's no use in my coming down," he said crossly. "The man's dead, isn't he?"

I hung up in despair and stared at the policemen. What could I do now? There were no other physicians I could call except for Party men, whom it was unwise to drag into the proceedings.

"I don't know what to do," I said confusedly, trying to keep my mind clear and make up a plausible story. "He was a business associate of mine. He had a bad heart, and being in the neighborhood he came here when he began to feel ill."

"Do you know any of his friends?" they asked.

I thought frantically. I obviously couldn't call Earl Browder, even though I had his telephone number. Jack Reynolds, I knew, was now back home after having had a siege of virus pneumonia in a Bronx hospital. I would try him. There was no answer. In despair, I took a chance and telephoned Lem Harris in Chappaqua. No answer. Obviously on Thanksgiving evening no one was home.

"How about his relatives?" the policemen asked.

I knew little about his family, except for a brother-in-law who, I thought, lived in the Bronx. And at any rate, I didn't have his phone number. Yasha had it in his desk in the office. What should I do now? I seemed unable to make my mind function.

"Well," said the larger of the two policemen, "we'll just have to wait until the medical examiner comes so that we can get a death certificate. Then the body can be moved for burial."

Burial! Yes, Yasha would have to be buried. But there was no more Yasha, really. He had gone away somewhere and left me alone. That body lying there was not really he. I fought to keep from thinking about that while the minutes dragged on. Finally, a plain-clothes man from the Charles Street station wandered in and asked me questions. When I told him Yasha's hotel address, he sent some of his men over to the Hotel Madison to take charge of the effects. An hour later they called him; when he hung up the phone he looked at me suspiciously.

"Did you know that Golos wasn't his real name?"

Panic swept through me. I knew that his real name was Jacob Rasin but that some years before he had taken the name "Golos" (Russian for "voice") for use in his revolutionary activities and had continued to use it openly. He had, I remembered, written under that pseudonym in the *Novy Mir*, the Russian Communist paper published in the early thirties in New York; once he had said he intended to adopt it legally but somehow had never gotten around to filing the papers. Would it be wise for me to admit that I knew this much? An old piece of N.K.V.D. instructions filtered through my mind: when in doubt, deny everything.

"I'm sorry, lieutenant," I said, and tried to make my voice sound bewildered. "I know very little about him. We were officers in the same company but I had practically nothing to do with him outside of that. However, I wouldn't be surprised. I remember he once told me that he had been a writer and they often take pseudonyms, don't they?"

The plain-clothes man relaxed and nodded.

"It sounds logical," he admitted. "I asked because we found a draft registration card in his hotel room under the name Rasin. But you've a problem on your hands. Some relative has got to authorize the transfer of the body to an undertaker, even when we get the death certificate. Your company can't do it. Can you get in touch with his brother-in-law?"

"I can tomorrow," I said. "His address and telephone number are in the office. But I doubt if the building is open tonight."

"All right," he said, relieved. "After the medical examiner is through, go ahead and call an undertaker. Then, first thing in the morning, call me up and give me both the name of the mortician and the telephone number of his relative. I think that will work out all right. Obviously, you can't wait until tomorrow, and I don't think there is any necessity for taking him down to the morgue among the unclaimed bodies."

I felt a surge of relief. I didn't want Yasha's body carried off to a city morgue and put on a cold slab among strangers.

I wanted it taken care of by someone I knew and treated with friendly consideration. But what undertaker? At this point, the medical examiner sauntered in, clearly annoyed at being dragged away from a party.

"This is a hell of a time for anyone to die," he said with irritation. "Why didn't his own doctor bestir himself and come down here? It would have saved me a trip. What's his name?"

I fought back a sense of nausea. Yasha was lying there cold and still and helpless. I glared at the examiner and gave him the phone number. Just as he finished his call and started over to the couch where Yasha lay, the telephone rang again. This time it was Lem Harris. I explained the situation briefly to him without saying too much, and waited for his answer.

"Don't say anything on your end of the telephone," he said tersely. "Just listen to me. Golos was a long-time member of the International Workers Order. They'll make arrangements. Grace Hutchins, head of the Labor Research Bureau—a trusted comrade—lives around the corner from you. She'll call them, and then as soon as she can get dressed she'll be over. She comes from a good old American family so you needn't worry about the wrong sort of person coming in to spoil the set-up. And, by the way, don't bother the Reynoldses with all this. There are angles that they had better not know."

I thanked him and hung up. By then the medical examiner had filled out the certificate and was ready to depart, along with the police. As the door banged shut behind them, I realized it was now after one o'clock in the morning. The room was appallingly quiet. As I looked over at Yasha, lying huddled in a heap underneath a blanket that had been thrown over him, the whole impact of my grief suddenly hit me.

"He'll never speak to me again!" I cried out in my agony. "He's gone away from me—gone forever!"

Grimly I put my hands on the mantelpiece, gripping it tightly to control my emotion. Then the dikes seemed to give way and I put my head down and sobbed uncontrollably. Eventually, with an effort, I pulled myself together. Grace Hutchins would be coming soon and she mustn't find me like this. I walked over to the couch and, gently pulling down the blanket, I stared down at the face of Yasha. He seemed so unutterably peaceful, with all the lines of tension erased from his face. At long last he had escaped from this mad world into blessed nothingness. He would lie quietly under some tree, a part of the earth again, and I was left to go on alone.

A horrible sense of panic seized me. Now I must take his place and continue on without his wisdom and love to guide me. I was walking head-on into a ghastly nightmare and I had no way of knowing what lay ahead. I won't do it! I said to myself desperately. No one can expect me to. I don't know what's going on but something is very, very wrong— something that killed my Yasha. Whatever it is, I'm not going to be caught in it. I'll drop this undercover work and go back to the open Party immediately.

Yet Yasha had depended on me to carry on for him when he died. He would rest easy only if he knew that the work for which he had sacrificed himself would go on the way it should. Shame flooded over me. It was wrong of me to let myself be carried away by my own personal feelings when there were more important things at stake. No, I couldn't leave now. I must stick it out until the future of our agents was settled. Gently I bent down and kissed his cold forehead; this was my farewell.

"Goodbye, *golubchik*," I said. "Rest peacefully now that your labor is over. With you goes most of me, for without you I am nothing. I won't bother about elaborate ceremonies for you or expensive monuments, for you wouldn't have wanted that. My memorial to you will be to carry on your work the best I can in the spirit in which you yourself would have done it. You have left me a legacy and I will not fail you."

CHAPTER X

After the I.W.O. undertakers had carried Yasha away
in a canvas basket, I found myself standing in the midst of
an empty apartment whose silence seemed to press in on
me. Uncertainly I moved to the bathroom and looked at
Yasha's socks still hanging there; he would never wear them
again, I thought dully. Then I returned to the living room,
still moving as if in a dream, unable to decide what I should
do next. Perhaps I should go to bed and catch a few hours'
sleep; there would be much to do tomorrow. But, exhausted
as I was, I knew that I would only doze fitfully, waking in
the clutches of a hideous nightmare. Numbly I walked over
to a chair and sat down; the hands of the clock moved relentlessly forward.

With a start I realized it was five o'clock; hurriedly I
washed my face, brushed my hair, and put on my coat and
hat. When I walked into the World Tourists building the
sleepy elevator operator inquired why I was up so early. I
quickly replied that my alarm had gone off way ahead of
time and I had decided to get up anyway and pick up some
work to be taken over to my office. Once in the office, I
flew to the safe. Swiftly and methodically I stripped it of
all incriminating documents. Into a suitcase, left in the office for that specific purpose, I crammed all the papers and

[223]

about $1200 in cash; according to Yasha's instructions—to be carried out in the event of his death—the documents were to be destroyed and the money was to go to Earl Browder. Then I took a taxi home. Methodically, I tore up the papers into small pieces and burned them in the fireplace, poking the flaming mass occasionally to be sure that everything was consumed. Then, when the ashes were cold, I leaned back wearily in the chair. If I could only keep on going a little longer!

It was seven-thirty. I went to a nearby Childs restaurant and ordered a cup of coffee, then put through a call to Earl Browder in Yonkers. He answered the phone himself. Briefly I told him of Yasha's death.

"I must see you right away," I said desperately.

"Yes," he answered. "Come down to my office at ten o'clock; I'll leave orders for you to be admitted."

I went back to the table and drank my coffee half-heartedly, wondering whether I wasn't going to be violently ill. The waitress, who had known me for some time, hovered over me solicitously.

"What's the matter?" she asked. "Something wrong?"

"Nothing," I replied. "I'm just tired, that's all."

I dragged myself to my feet and went back to World Tourists; the worst task of all faced me—I must break the news of Yasha's death to his employees. As I sat in *his* chair behind *his* desk, I shrank from the task before me; they all loved him so much—indeed it had been perhaps only his personality that had held this office together during the war years when it was so hard to keep personnel.

The first employee in was a Russian girl who typed Soviet import licenses for us. She saw me sitting behind the desk and came toward me, her face white.

[224]

"Is something wrong, Miss Bentley?" she asked. "Where's Mr. Golos?"

"I'm sorry, Edith," I said gently. "I have bad news for you. Mr. Golos died last night; but don't feel badly, he didn't suffer."

She collapsed into the nearest chair and started to sob violently; as the others came in, I told them the news and they stared at me white-faced and unbelieving.

At ten o'clock I arrived at Earl's office on the ninth floor of Communist Party headquarters; the receptionist clicked the switch that released the gate, and I stepped in. Even dulled as I was by grief, I noticed that his greeting was theatrical; he advanced to meet me, both hands outstretched.

"Comrade Bentley," he said in a tone worthy of a speaker on a rostrum, "this is a great loss to the movement! Our old friend Golos is dead, but we shall continue to go forward!"

As he spoke he was leading me down a long corridor. At the very end we reached a neat, bare office with a desk, a few chairs, and three or four Revolutionary pictures on the wall.

"Is this your office?" I asked.

He nodded and then, as if remembering something, looked cautiously around and led me out into the corridor again.

"I think we'd better talk out here," he whispered. "Undoubtedly the F.B.I. has wired my office."

Briefly I told him what had happened. At the end, I handed him the $1200.

"Yasha wanted you to have this," I said.

He put it in his pocket absent-mindedly; then he turned to me.

"This thing's got to be handled with great care," he said

thoughtfully. "We can't let Golos be too closely tied up with the American Party—it'll wreck us. Leave the publicity to me; I'll talk to Budenz. You're taking Golos's place, aren't you?" he inquired anxiously.

I tried to pull myself together; emotional strain, plus lack of food and sleep, was beginning to tell on me. But I couldn't go to pieces now; there was too much at stake. What, actually, had been Yasha's job? Come to think of it, I didn't really know. Yet, now, I was in a tight spot; I had to answer. Suddenly one of the old Party maxims flashed through my mind: When in doubt, bluff—and keep on bluffing!

"Of course, Earl," I said, in what I hoped was a calm tone of voice.

He seemed relieved. "Good. Then you'll be taking care of all the Washington comrades. I'm glad of that; I think you'll be a good person to handle them. I don't like the thought of our Americans being turned over to Soviet contacts; I told Golos that over and over again."

The corridor blurred before me; with an effort I steadied myself and tried to think straight. This was the theme that had obsessed Yasha during the last few months of his life: don't hand the Americans over to the Russians. And now Earl, who seemed to be a fairly sane person, was saying the same thing. It couldn't have been the imagination of a dying man; there was something seriously wrong! Earl was an old friend of Yasha's; I could talk to him, and perhaps from him I could learn the truth. Then abruptly I checked myself; what had Yasha said about Earl?

"He's a good guy, *golubishka*, but he doesn't know all that's going on. Be very careful what you say to him."

With a sickening sense of fear, I realized there was no

one on this earth who could help me; Yasha, who knew what was going on, was dead and beyond any cry for assistance. And here I was in the midst of a spider web, holding all the threads in my hands and yet not knowing what pattern was being spun. Earl thought I knew all the answers; I couldn't tell him of my ignorance.

Yasha's voice once more seemed to come to me: "Easy, darling, easy! Just use your brains, as I taught you to."

My brains! What brains did I have without him! Then, quite suddenly, I found myself thinking coolly and unemotionally. I wasn't completely up on things, but it was a problem I had to solve alone, without help from anyone. I had inherited Yasha's job—with all its difficulties and twists —but without his experience to guide me. That didn't matter, though; in my hands lay the fate of all our Washington contacts who depended on me. I could not let them down. They were human beings; more than that, they were my friends. I must use every ounce of brain power I possessed to solve this problem. Ignorant as I was, still I must find out the answer and, having done so, make the correct decision. Earl was a part of the decision; so far, he seemed to be on the right side of the fence.

I eyed him appraisingly. "Will you back me up if I refuse to turn Mary Price over to the Russians?"

He hesitated, then he nodded agreement. "I don't think she should be turned over to them."

So far, so good. I turned to leave, but he stopped me.

"We must have some foolproof means of communication," he said. "You can't use your real name. Let's call you 'Nancy.' Hereafter, when you come to see me or telephone, I will be available—no matter whether I am in the most important of meetings."

Thoughtfully I walked down the corridor to the exit, thinking that Yasha must have been a very important person for Earl to be so subservient. Browder was the head of the American Communist Party and our leader; even though temporarily we were helping the Russians, we were still American comrades. It seemed odd to me that he was treating me not only as an equal but almost with a shade of deference. I shook my head and tried to make sense out of the whole situation, but I was too weary to fit things together. As I walked out the front gate, the receptionist waved cordially at me; I responded absent-mindedly, not realizing that such enthusiastic greetings were strictly reserved for the top people in the movement.

Back in the office of World Tourists, the day dragged interminably on. Several times Grace Hutchins telephoned, asking what had happened to the contents of Yasha's pockets; obviously she was worried about what the police had found. Warily, I answered that there were only the *usual* things that a man carried around, hoping to reassure her and yet not give any hint to a possible listener. The left-wing press arrived, one after the other—first Louis Budenz from the *Daily Worker*, who was careful to show no indication of knowing me; then a man from the Communist Jewish paper *Freiheit*; then a staff member from the Communist Russian paper *Russky Golos*, an old friend of Yasha's who was visibly moved by his death, and finally a representative of the *New Masses*.

On Sunday afternoon the services for Yasha were held at the Gramercy Park Funeral Parlors on Second Avenue; the small chapel was jammed with friends, relatives, and high-up Communist Party functionaries. I sat halfway down on the right-hand side, flanked by two of World

Tourists' employees; two rows ahead of me I noticed Kazakevich and his wife, but I was too drugged with grief to take much notice of anyone else.

It was the first revolutionary funeral I had ever attended; there was no mention of religion—it consisted mostly of speeches by comrades extolling the achievements of Comrade Golos. Finally, Alexander Trachtenberg arose and launched into what I later learned was one of his customary long-winded orations. On and on he droned, while I clutched the sides of my chair until my hands ached; I forced back the tears in my throat—I mustn't cry, I thought, I mustn't! Then, ironically, I remembered what Yasha had said about Trachtenberg.

"He's just a windbag and a coward," he had told me. "I kicked him out of my office and he hasn't dared come back since."

And this was the man who was standing up there, telling all of us how much he had loved Yasha! What a hypocrite, I said to myself. If Yasha could only hear, he would laugh over this.

Finally the services were over. The procession of cars wound its way out to a remote cemetery at the far end of Long Island. As we drove along, I kept thinking to myself how unreal all this was; I couldn't make myself realize that Yasha was dead. But there was the flower-decked hearse riding along peacefully up ahead of me. Tears came to my eyes as I remembered that Yasha had wanted to take his car out of storage and go for a long ride in the country just before he died. This, then, was his ride, and he wasn't here to enjoy it!

At the cemetery the burial service was mercifully brief. Someone said a few words, then each of us dropped a rose in the grave before it was sealed up. For a moment I looked at the vivid red of the flower in my hand, then let it fall gently onto the coffin. Out here he will be all alone and very cold, I thought; then I glanced at the name on the next tombstone—it was Misha Olgin, his old friend and comrade. Somehow I felt better; this was where he would have wanted to be. I turned and walked rapidly to the waiting car.

It's all over for you now, Yasha, I thought, wearily. You have at long last found peace. But for me, who knows what lies ahead? Had I but known what did lie ahead, I don't think I would ever have had the courage to keep on going. What faced me, I was to discover, surpassed my wildest nightmares.

However, I determined grimly that I would straighten out the matter of the Washington contacts and then I would leave the whole undercover business and return to the open Party. It shouldn't take too long to arrange for these Communists to be put in the proper hands; Earl seemed to have the same ideas that Yasha had had, and together we could convince the Russians that they must handle Americans in the right way.

In this frame of mind I went to World Tourists and set to work to see that the business was running properly. The girls were still stunned by the news of Yasha's death; they needed to feel that I was there to give them moral support. Around noon, Joe Brodsky—one of the members of the law firm that took care of World Tourists—came in to see me.

The situation, he explained, was extremely complicated as regarded World Tourists; the company was actually owned by the American Communist Party but it was registered under Yasha's name. Since he had left no will, the whole question of ownership would eventually end up in the courts, and that would leave the Party hanging out on a limb, since none of Yasha's relatives were members of the Communist movement and probably would claim the estate for themselves. I looked at him thoughtfully; this was an unexpected difficulty.

"What do we do now?" I inquired.

"Just sit tight," he replied. "You, as Secretary, can carry on the business, sign checks, and so forth, and meantime we will try to think out some angle on this matter."

He looked at the desk thoughtfully. "What's in there?" he asked.

"I don't know," I said. "Nothing much, probably. But the police have the keys and I can't get in to find out."

"Well," he said cheerfully, "I'm not an expert safe cracker, but I can always try. Get a screwdriver and we'll force it open."

After we had wrenched the lock open, we sat down and went methodically through the contents of the drawers. As I had thought, there was nothing but material having to do with the business. Joe looked through the safe and made a bundle of all the papers that related to the legal affairs of the business, putting it carefully in his briefcase.

"Don't worry," he said, as he took his hat and departed, "we'll take care of everything."

That evening at eight o'clock I had a prearranged appointment with my Soviet contact Catherine (who had replaced John) at the Newsreel Theater on 42nd Street, opposite Grand Central Station. I was sure that Catherine would not be alone; undoubtedly the Russians had heard of Yasha's death and would send some high-up man to discuss the situation with me.

Five minutes after I had arrived at the Newsreel Theater, Catherine silently slid into the seat beside me. For a few moments we watched the film without speaking; then she put her hand on my arm.

"Follow me out," she whispered. "We have an appointment to keep."

When we neared the corner of 51st Street, I saw her taut face brighten; I looked up the street to see a jaunty-looking man in his mid-thirties, his hat perched on the back of his head, approaching us. This, then, must be my new contact! As he walked up to us, Catherine greeted him with false gaiety.

"Hello, Bill," she said. "Helen, this is your new boss, Bill."

My new boss! I stared at him, noting his deep-set eyes like round brown shoe buttons, his high Slavic cheekbones, his straight dark hair that was only kept from falling over one eye by his hat. Certainly he must have spent plenty of money on that tailor-made suit and matching accessories. As I eyed him appraisingly, he slipped one hand under my arm and the other under Catherine's.

"You must be hungry, girls," he said, with a decided Russian accent. "Let's go get some food."

Once inside Janssen's, he insisted on ordering the most expensive items on the menu for himself and Catherine: caviar, oyster cocktails, broiled lobster. Although he pressed me to eat, I contented myself with a cup of coffee; I had already had a sandwich and besides, in the face of all this elegance, I could only think of poor Yasha who had scrimped and saved and eaten only in cheap cafeterias. I don't understand these people, I said to myself miserably, as I watched them eat their dinner with relish. Yasha told me that Communists should live simply and on a bare minimum, and he had certainly lived up to that precept; the only time we had gone to swank restaurants was when we were entertaining some of our contacts.

When Bill had finished his dinner he sat forward in his chair, the air of camaraderie gone, the brown eyes hard and calculating. Suddenly I realized I had underestimated the man; despite his superficial appearance of a boulevardier, he was a tough character.

"We want Mary and we want her immediately," he said, and there was an indefinable menace in his voice. "We've put up with enough nonsense on this subject."

I was stunned. I had come to him expecting to meet a comrade and instead I was being treated like an enemy. What was going on, I said to myself; why did he behave like that? I remembered my revolutionary training; with an effort I kept my face expressionless and my voice steady.

"I'm sorry," I said calmly, stalling for time. "Earl doesn't want her turned over."

He glared back at me. "Who the hell's Earl? You take your orders from us."

I fought for self-control, as my thoughts swirled around. Obviously, he was just a young whipper-snapper whom the organization, for lack of personnel, had had to use.

"I think you'll find that it's better to let the matter drop," I replied, hoping I was saying the right thing. "Mary's in a highly nervous state and she wouldn't be any good to you right now."

As I spoke, I glanced over at Catherine, perhaps half

hoping she would understand what I was trying to say; to my dismay her face was set and taut and there was enmity in her eyes. Startled, I looked back at Bill, to find that he was eyeing me savagely. With a sick feeling at the pit of my stomach, I realized that for some reason I couldn't understand, I was face to face with two bitter enemies.

Bill's voice cut like a whip. "Let's not argue the matter; we want Mary and we're going to get her. And you will be wise to play along with us!" The menace in his voice was now unmistakable. "We've spent months playing around with that traitor Golos and now we're going to settle this matter."

That did it! The bewilderment that had been clutching me disappeared; I was suddenly alive and alert. No one could say that Yasha had been a traitor; he had given his very life to the Revolution! Brother, I thought, I don't know what is going on but something is very, very wrong, and I'm going to find out the score. And when I do find out the truth, I will do whatever is necessary to straighten out things—regardless of the consequences to myself. You've left me a legacy, Yasha, I said to myself, and it's my job to carry on as you would have done. I checked the angry retort that I was about to make to Bill; from now on I would have to play this game the smart way, using every weapon I had at my command.

"Don't be so excited, Bill," I said soothingly. "It takes time to work these things out, but in the long run everything straightens out very nicely. Just give me time to work on Earl."

With a flash of triumph in his eyes, he nodded; he thinks he's scared me, I thought, but if he only knew! I said goodbye to Catherine and Bill, after having made arrangements to meet them at the end of the week; then I headed for home.

Exhausted, I fell into bed. As I was drifting off into sleep I seemed to hear Yasha's voice, as though from a long way off.

"Well done, *golubishka*," he seemed to be saying. "Just remember that the only thing that's important in this world is to do what's right, regardless of the consequences."

Tomorrow would be another day. It might be difficult, but somehow I would have to take care of it as things came along. I smiled to myself and rolled over and went to sleep.

On Thursday I went to Washington to see my contacts. I was barely able to catch the eight o'clock train in the evening, the affairs of World Tourists kept me so occupied.

It was after midnight when I arrived in Union Station and called the Silvermasters. Helen answered the phone, and the note of relief in her voice was obvious.

"Thank God you're here," Helen said. "We read the news in the paper and we've been worried ever since; we would have come up to New York tomorrow if we hadn't heard from you."

It was a sad group of people around the Silvermasters' kitchen table; as we sat sipping tea, we talked about what a wonderful person Yasha had been. Helen and Greg had known him for many years; for them it was a very personal loss. But even Lud Ullman, who had met him only twice, felt the weight of the tragedy; somehow, in that short time he had come to feel that Yasha was one of his best friends. In silence, I handed over Greg's instructions; he was too upset to make his usual protest. Lud carefully brought me the material to be taken back to New York; I took it and asked no questions.

[235]

The next two or three weeks were hectic ones. It was difficult enough to run two businesses alone and unassisted, but with the addition of the undercover work it was almost impossible. Moreover, during this period I was dashing around New York buying gifts for my contacts, racing madly against a deadline. I had been afraid I would meet opposition from Bill in this project; but strangely enough he seemed very happy about it.

"Don't spare the money," he said cheerfully. "Get them the nicest things you can and, of course, we'll foot the bill. Just keep the sales checks, hand them in to me, and I'll refund the money pronto."

I pondered his seeming change of attitude. Not only was he completely friendly, but he made no further demands for Mary. Moreover, this state of peace and quiet continued over the holidays; when I met him just before Christmas, he gaily presented me with a red-flowered silk scarf that he had bought for me at Saks Fifth Avenue.

"I hope you like it," he said happily. "I chose it myself."

Looking at his smiling face, I decided I must have misjudged him. At our first meeting we both had been under terrific tension: I, because I was nervously fatigued after the death of Yasha; and Bill, because his worries over the security of the organization had made him jumpy. This was understandable because he did not know how many incriminating documents in Yasha's possession had fallen into the hands of the New York City police. Besides, Bill, never having met me before, did not know how much he could rely upon me. But now everything seemed to be smoothed out; soon I could turn over to him all my underground contacts and return to the open Party.

On New Year's Eve all the grief and loneliness that I had

resolutely put aside came back to haunt me. I closed the office and started home, bitterly aware of all the merrymaking around me. Yasha and I had always had so much fun together on this evening; we had put aside our cares and laughed and enjoyed ourselves. I knew that I couldn't face going to a party so I went home, fixed myself some supper, and crawled into bed.

With the end of the holidays, I went back to my regular routine, hoping that I would soon be relieved of the burden of undercover work.

Returning from a trip to Washington, just after the New Year, I went down to see Earl and show him the material I had collected, before passing it on to Bill. He read it through thoughtfully, gave it back, then leaned forward in his chair and looked at me appraisingly.

"I've got another group to be turned over to our friends, but I want to be quite sure they're in good hands. Will you take them?"

"Our friends," I knew, meant the Russians; that was the way Earl always referred to them. His trust in me was very flattering, I thought, but right now I hoped to get out of the undercover business, not get more involved in it. He noticed my hesitation.

"I know you're overburdened already," he said, "and I wouldn't ask you if it weren't absolutely necessary. In the past, they were handled by John Abt and the material passed through me to Golos; now Abt is going to take over a fairly public position and it's too dangerous to continue on that way. They've got to have a new contact." He paused for a moment and then looked at me searchingly. "You know what the Russians are like; I can't give the group over to them. You've got to take them!"

I stared at him, wondering again what was in his mind. There was that same vague theme again: "you know what the Russians are like"; what did he mean by it? As far as I could see, they were no different from anyone else; certainly Bill and I were getting along nicely now. I started to tell him so; then a strange sixth sense warned me to stay silent. There was no use arguing with him; I might as well take on the group and then get rid of them with the others when I had made the proper arrangements with Bill.

"O.K.," I said. "I'll take them on."

But I was soon to learn that Earl had some cause for apprehension; that very evening, as I sat at dinner with Bill, he suddenly dropped his mask of spurious good fellowship and reverted to the cold brutality he had shown on our first meeting. With an undercurrent of menace in his voice, he demanded that I turn Mary Price over immediately; he had, he said, been patient long enough. When I tried to explain that she would be no good for the work, he cut me short abruptly; he lashed out at me vitriolically—demanding, threatening, even calling me a traitor. Bewildered and frightened, I dug my heels in and fought back; no one was going to force me to turn any contact over unless I thought it was the right thing to do. And from what I could see of him, he was certainly not the proper person to take care of anyone! The more I resisted, the more mercilessly he pounded at me, until I began to wonder just how much longer I could hold out under this treatment. When I left him that night, my legs were so weak I could hardly stand.

This was to be the pattern of our future meetings; night after night, after battling with him, I would crawl home to bed, sometimes too weary even to undress. Now I knew what Yasha had faced and what was worrying Earl; these, then, were the Russians! No, I said to myself, these can't be the real Soviet comrades. Bill, and for that matter Yasha's contact, must be the petty ones, carried away by a sense of their own power. Undoubtedly their own superiors didn't know how they were behaving; if I could only make contact with Moscow direct, I could get some action. But how to make contact? I didn't know.

Meanwhile, the only thing I could do was to stand firm and not allow any American Communists to be turned over to Bill, even though I was taking a fierce pounding in the process.

By the middle of March, Earl completed arrangements for me to take over the new Washington group, at John Abt's house on Central Park West. On a rainy afternoon I took the Eighth Avenue subway up to 103rd Street and walked to Abt's address. No sooner had I rung the bell than he appeared in the doorway of his apartment—tall, lean, intelligent looking.

"You're Helen?" he asked. "Come on in; the boys are here."

Seated around the living room were four men, Victor Perlo, Charlie Kramer, and two others.

Perlo, spokesman for the group, explained to me that his people had good jobs in the government where they could obtain valuable information. As we got down to cases, it transpired that Perlo himself was a statistician with access to aircraft production; he was with the W.P.B. Kramer was working for the Kilgore Committee and could give us what he called "Capitol Hill gossip." Of the other two, one worked also in the W.P.B. and could furnish data on planes, tanks, and guns. The second was headed for the Department of Commerce, but as he was not a well man, it was

[239]

doubtful whether he could be of great value. Besides these four, there were several others who worked variously in the research department of the O.S.S., the Treasury, the F.E.A., and with the U.N.R.R.A.

It seemed like an interesting group, and as I looked over the material they had brought, I recognized it as the same badly typed sheets of data that Yasha had been receiving from some source for several months. So this was where it had come from! Then I remembered who Perlo was; he was the bull in a china shop who had been worrying the Silvermaster group for a long time.

Somehow he had discovered that George Silverman was a Communist, and he had been trying to get information from him; unfortunately, his methods were, to say the least, lacking in tact. Every so often he would march up to George and say to him, "Have you got anything for Joe?" —obviously referring to Joe Stalin. At this, George would take to his heels and flee in panic. While I was musing over this, Perlo suddenly said to me anxiously, "Is Joe getting the stuff safely?"

A dead hush settled over the room; no one seemed to breathe. I glanced over at John Abt and saw the look of sardonic amusement on his face; then he stared intently at the floor. Carefully, I ignored Vic's question and went on to make arrangements for our future meetings.

In the meantime, the Silvermaster group was stepping up production and was giving us really valuable data. Lud Ullman had wormed his way into the good graces of high-up Air Corps officers in the Pentagon, and from them he was able to find out the date of D-day four days ahead of time; I remember his chuckling because he had been able to win a bet from a fellow worker. "The guy didn't have a chance," he said. "I knew the date and he didn't."

Around this time he also brought me samples of the marks the United States was preparing for use in the German occupation. The Russians were delighted, as they were planning to counterfeit them. However, due to a complicated ink process this proved impossible—until I was able through Harry Dexter White to arrange that the United States Treasury Department turn the actual printing plates over to the Russians!

Evidently these activities of the Silvermaster group interested the Russians very much, for by spring Bill had shifted his point of attack and, dropping the subject of Mary Price, launched into a stormy demand that Greg be turned over. I refused and, with Earl backing me up, continued to battle against any such idea. Bill, evidently unable to get any further in the matter, finally said he would settle for just one meeting with Greg; after that, he assured me, I could carry on as contact.

"After all," he said reasonably, "he's one of our most valuable people and I would like to have a look at him."

Dubiously, I consulted Earl. He thought the matter over and halfheartedly agreed.

The evening Greg and I met Bill for dinner at Longchamps restaurant at 34th Street and Fifth Avenue was an occasion I shall never forget. Bill was in his gayest mood and went out of his way to charm Greg. He insisted that he have the most expensive of meals, complete with wine; he flattered him on the work he was doing, implying that he was one of the pillars of the Soviet Union. I watched him cynically, thinking of the real Bill that lay beneath all this veneer of good fellowship.

[241]

After we had finished dinner, Bill insisted on taking us to a night club—Leon & Eddie's; I protested ineffectually. Yasha had told me over and over again not to take any contacts to such places; not only did it give them a taste of high living that might ruin their value as Communists but night spots were known to be watched by the F.B.I. Bill grasped Greg and me by the arm as he headed for a cab; he laughed derisively at my objections.

"Look at our little puritan," he said to Greg mockingly.

I bit my lip and said nothing; indeed I was silent the rest of the evening while Bill plied Greg with drinks and told him what a wonderful person he was. It was a nauseating performance, unworthy of a true revolutionary. How could the Russians send such men to the United States to work with our American comrades? Thank goodness, there was to be only one meeting; if Bill continued to see Greg, he would most certainly succeed in corrupting him.

For our next two meetings, Bill was unusually quiet and peaceful; he was undoubtedly up to something. I was soon to find out. One day, almost drooling with arrogance, he said, "Earl has agreed to turn Greg over to me."

I stared at him with a sinking feeling.

"I don't believe it!"

"Go and ask him," he replied, tauntingly. "You'll find out."

The next day, as I faced Earl across his desk, he refused to look me in the eye.

"I've told our friends that they can have Greg," he said.

"But why did you do it, Earl?" I cried out. "You know what the Russians are like. They'll ruin Greg."

He shrugged his shoulders and carefully looked at the wall.

"Don't be naïve," he said cynically. "You know that when the cards are down, I have to take my orders from them. I just hoped I could sidetrack them in this particular matter, but it didn't work out."

"But Greg's an old friend of yours," I said accusingly.

"So what?" he replied. "He's expendable."

Blindly I stumbled out of his office. Once in the street, I walked aimlessly, unaware even that it was a very hot day and that the sweat was dripping down me. I tried to comprehend what had happened. Why had Earl behaved like that? Why, knowing how ruthless Bill was, had he permitted his old friend Greg to be turned over to him? All along he had backed me up in my determination to protect our American comrades and now, suddenly, he didn't seem to care anymore—indeed, he was completely cynical about their fate.

My head began to ache from the heat; I walked into a nearby drugstore, sat down and tried to sort out my thoughts. What was it that Earl had said? Oh, yes—that he "had to take orders from the Russians." But that, of course, was absurd. Yasha had told me that every Communist Party in the world was autonomous and made its own decisions. So Earl, then, was lying to me. But why? Why should he have made such an abrupt about-face and then contrived such a fantastic tale to account for his actions?

Slowly I lit a cigarette and considered the matter. There could only be one logical answer. Earl wasn't the great idealist we had believed he was; he was indeed only a low conniving politician who was out for himself. Somehow, for reasons that I didn't know, he must have made a private "deal" with Bill to his own advantage. Revulsion swept over me. So this was Earl Browder—not the glorious leader of our American Party but a cheap, tawdry figure. He had put up such a wonderful front, hadn't he? He had given the impression of a true revolutionary—a brave, noble soul who would stand unswervingly for his own principles! I wished bitterly that all the American comrades could see him for what he really was.

I snubbed out my cigarette and sat for a moment staring into space. Earl was a disgrace to the American movement; I must report all this to someone on the Central Committee so that they could do something about the situation. But to whom could I go? There was, of course, William Weiner, the head of the Party's Finance Committee, with whom I had dealt in connection with the future reorganization of World Tourists. He was a short, fat man with scanty red hair, a deceptively peaceful face and shrewd eyes behind thick glasses. I had not been impressed by him; indeed, I had felt that he was pretty much of an opportunist and out for himself. And besides, what had Yasha said about him? "Look at Willy," he had said with contempt. "He's no revolutionary. I suffer from as bad heart trouble as he does, but I don't spend months in Florida in the winter. He says that he's saving himself for the cause, but he's preserving himself so well that he's no use to anyone."

Certainly, then, Weiner wasn't the person to approach. And of the rest? Rapidly I went through the list of names in my mind. Come to think of it, Yasha had been pretty contemptuous of them, too, although at the time I had dismissed his infrequently expressed feelings as purely professional jealousy. But now these half-forgotten and unexplained comments of his began to form an ominous pattern.

[244]

Just what had he said? It was important to remember, because it was all that I had to rely on now.

"I wouldn't give two cents for any of that bunch, *golubishka*," he had repeated savagely. "The only one that's worth anything at all is Earl and even with him I have to be careful."

So these barbed comments hadn't been due to professional jealousy, aggravated by ill health and overwork. He had, in these off-guard moments of his, told the real truth about the leadership of the American Communist Party, although I had been too blind to see it at the time. With sickening finality I felt the facts click into place. Yasha hadn't admired Earl as the best of a good group of revolutionaries; he had merely accepted him resignedly as the least unscrupulous of a bunch of weak-kneed opportunists. And that meant, in fact, that the leadership of our American Party was no good—that all my comrades were being betrayed.

Wearily I put my head on my hands, my initial rage giving way to a feeling of complete despair. Our American movement has been sold down the river, I thought desolately, and there isn't anything anyone can do about it. Certainly if Yasha, who had been a high-up Party official, had been helpless to remedy the situation, then there just wasn't any hope. Perhaps one day there would be a decent Communist movement in this country, but at the moment it didn't look like it. Well, I for one wasn't going to stay in the American Party any longer, knowing what I did about its leadership. I would stop paying my dues and get out. . . .

But what would I do about my Washington contacts? They had been entrusted to me by Yasha and I couldn't let them down. I would have to do something and do it fast. Bill had already succeeded in taking Greg Silvermaster over. How could I prevent him from taking over Mary Price and all the others, when and if he demanded them? Earl wouldn't stand by me—and certainly none of the rest of the top American leaders would either. I was really alone now and I had to fight on without help from any quarter.

I got to my feet. My mind was made up. I was mixed up in this business and it was my responsibility to straighten it out before I admitted defeat. I owed it to Yasha who had died fighting; I owed it to my contacts who relied on me. Somehow I would carry the matter to the top level of the N.K.V.D.; I would try to see the head of the Russian Secret Police in this country. He surely would be one of the old Soviet revolutionaries and a true Communist; after hearing the facts, he would most certainly take action. Meanwhile I would continue to see Bill, and await my chance to put this project into effect.

Not long afterward I met Bill for dinner at Schrafft's on Fifth Avenue near 46th Street, and later on we took a long walk down to South Ferry. On the way he suggested that I take a salary from the N.K.V.D., as he was doing. It would, he said, augment my income and enable me to live more comfortably.

"How about $50.00 a month?" he asked.

I stared at him in surprise. Why should he offer me a salary when my income was adequate for my needs? I shook my head but he persisted.

"Well," he said suavely, "if that's not enough, how about $100.00?"

When I again refused, he raised the offer to $200.00 and finally to $300.00 a month. Just what is going on, I wondered; could it be that they are trying to bribe me? I turned on Bill in a fury.

"What kind of a racket is this where they pay you for doing your duty?" I demanded.

For a moment he looked as if I had struck him in the face; then he looked away and said nothing. But this did not end the matter. After several long battles on the subject of my accepting a salary, Bill shifted his point of attack. He was, he said, in the fur business. He would like to present me with a Persian-lamb coat. When I turned him down on this, he came up with the idea that he wanted to get me an air-conditioning unit for my apartment. He was, he said, worried about my bad sinus trouble.

So they *are* trying to buy me off, I said to myself bitterly, and that means that not only is there something very wrong with the American Party but with the entire international Communist movement. But there can't be, I thought desperately. Yasha wouldn't have given his life for a shabby thing like this. And yet, all those horrible struggles he had gone through during the last days before his death. . . . Then, still not willing to believe the ugly truth, I turned to Bill.

"Bill," I asked, "is this your idea or were you told to do this?"

He looked away from me. "No, it wasn't my idea. I never do anything on my own." Then, very bitterly, "I'm only small fry; they can kick me around all they want to."

Maybe he's lying, I thought finally; perhaps it's his own mean little idea and he's passing the buck to his superior. But I must find out the real truth; I must get to the top man in the N.K.V.D. as soon as possible. Then I would know the answer.

The summer of 1944 dragged on; in my weariness and loneliness and growing disillusion, it seemed an endless procession of dreary days. I still missed Yasha terribly; even though I tried to put my mind on other things, he still was in my thoughts. Sometimes it was hard to believe he was dead; I would catch myself thinking, I must go home and tell Yasha about this, and then the realization would come that he was gone forever. Now and again something the Silvermasters would say brought back the same old grief; at other times, familiar scenes where Yasha and I had been so happy would catch at my throat. And always, at night, there was that empty apartment—with no Yasha waiting for me. I'm only half a person without him, I thought; how can I go on?

On the day of the 1944 hurricane I went down to Washington to collect the Silvermasters' material for the last time.

Our meeting was a very sad one; we ate our dinner almost in silence—no one seemed to be able to find anything to say. I went over their material briefly, then I reminded them that Bill would be expecting Greg in New York the following week. Silently we stared at one another, and in their eyes I read the same thought that was in my mind. This was the end of the good old days—the days when we worked together as good comrades. Now we were parting, I to go one way, they another—into an unknown and terrifying future. Even for them the life of their group would never be the same again; the Russians had decided for safety's sake to break it up and put each member in contact with a Soviet agent.

I got to my feet and said goodbye, trying hard not to

show my feelings. Then I stumbled to the door and walked out of the house.

Back in New York, I got their material together, adding to it the data from my other agents, and went to meet Bill. Wearily, I handed over the package and stood looking at him. He smiled and for the first time I saw what seemed like pity in his eyes.

"Goodbye and good luck," he said gently. "Remember you are to meet your new contact in two weeks."

In early October I went to meet this new contact in front of a drugstore on Park Avenue in the fifties. I was to carry a copy of *Life* magazine and wear a red flower. As I waited, I scanned the street both ways, but I couldn't see anyone headed my way. Suddenly from behind me a voice said, "Hello, Helen; Bill sends his greetings," and a hand grasped me by the elbow and propelled me down the street. I caught my breath and tried to steal a glance at him, but it was not until we reached the next corner and he stopped and faced me, that I was able to get a good look. Even then I had difficulty in assimilating his appearance so that I would know him when I saw him again. He was, I think, the most completely colorless and nondescript person I had ever seen; he could have faded into any crowd and never been noticed. His gray suit and hat were neither too shabby nor too new; there was nothing remarkable about his face except for the alert eyes—whose color I did not even notice—and the hint of strain at the mouth. This, I said to myself, is the most perfect undercover agent I have ever seen. He looked at me sharply. "Let's go up to Central Park and find a bench and sit and talk."

His English was as good as mine; there was even a touch

of Brooklyn about it. Could he be a Russian? I asked him if he spoke Russian; he smiled and said he didn't.

"You know," I said casually, "the Russians used to call me *umnitsa*."

He rocked with laughter and I smiled to myself; he certainly knew Russian; no one who didn't know the language could have got the implications of that word. Then abruptly he stopped and glared at me, realizing too late that I had trapped him.

"All right," he said grimly. "You caught me on that one; but I'm not a Russian—I'm a Lithuanian and proud of it."

Seated on a bench, he turned on me fiercely. "Now let's discuss what we're going to do with the rest of your contacts."

But I was ready for him. "I'm not going to discuss anything with you," I said, my jaw set. "You put me in touch with the head of the outfit and I'll talk to him."

He pounded at me mercilessly, using most of Bill's tactics and a few more besides, but I refused to budge. Finally he agreed to make arrangements for me to meet the "big boss."

"He's just been sent over to straighten out the organization," he said. "We are now getting modernized and on a more efficient basis."

I was, he explained, to continue seeing him every two weeks in order to deliver the material, but periodically I would consult with the new man, "Al," on policy matters. Next Wednesday night I would meet him in Washington at a drugstore on Wisconsin Avenue and N Street; I was again to wear a hat with a red flower and carry a copy of *Life* magazine.

As I rode down to Washington on the train that afternoon, I felt that at long last I was nearing my objective.

Now, finally, I was about to meet the top man in the Soviet Secret Police, and from him I would learn the answers to all the questions that had been torturing me for the past several months. What sort of person would he be, I wondered. Would he be a good old revolutionary like Yasha, or someone like Bill? For a moment the fears which I had carefully buried in my mind came back to haunt me. I began to wish desperately that I had never set out on this journey. Then I steadied myself. I'm being very silly, I thought; how do I know what kind of man I'm going to meet? He will probably turn out to be a very good person. After all, I had met other representatives of the Soviet Union in the past and had been tremendously impressed by them. I remembered back to the summer of 1936 when I had had a position as councillor in the camp set up for the children of Soviet nationals in this country. There, on parents' visiting days, I had met many of the old Russian revolutionaries and had liked them immensely. I had been convinced then that the future of humanity could be safely entrusted to people like these.

I lit a cigarette and stared out the window. You *are* being silly, I said to myself firmly. You've been judging the Russians by small people like Bill who tried to throw their weight around and show off. The real leaders of the Organization will be like Yasha and the other old revolutionaries you have known. Reassured, I settled down in my seat and began to read a magazine.

I waited for what seemed an interminable time on the appointed corner, but as the minutes dragged by, I began to be frightened again. Why hadn't he come? What was wrong? Just as I looked at my watch for the twentieth time, I heard a voice with a distinctly British accent say behind me, "I'm sorry that I'm late." I turned swiftly and found myself face to face with a short, fattish man in his mid-thirties, with blond hair brushed straight back and glasses that failed to mask a pair of shrewd, cold eyes. Dubiously I stared at him, noting his appearance of well-fed flabbiness, his well-tailored and expensive-looking clothes. Could this be the man I was to meet?

His sharp eyes never left my face. "I bring greetings from Moscow," he said expressionlessly. "And now I think we should have our dinner." He glanced at his watch and his voice became icy. "It is now exactly 8:31. Due to the stupidity of one of my subordinates, I went to the wrong place and hence both of us have had to go hungry for an unnecessary half hour. I am not used to such inefficiency; the man who committed this blunder shall be made to pay for this mistake."

My heart sank. This, then, *was* the man that I was supposed to meet. This was the head of the Soviet Secret Police in this country! I became uncomfortably aware that he was watching me intently with those steely, unwavering eyes. Did my disappointment show in my face, I wondered desperately, and forced myself to smile.

"Where would you like to eat?" I asked steadily.

"Anywhere that is not near the Soviet Embassy," he said. "After all, I *am* a high official there and I should not like to meet anyone I know." Then, as I hesitated, trying to think of a suitable place, "I do not understand why you did not arrange all this in advance; *I* cannot be expected to bother with such trifles."

My hands clenched at my sides and I fought for self-control. "We'll go to Naylor's on the waterfront; at this hour of the evening there won't be many people."

[252]

A cab was cruising on the other side of the street and, ignoring the heavy traffic, Al dashed over to hail it. When I joined him a few minutes later, he eyed me coldly.

"You have kept me waiting," he stated.

With an effort, I choked down the angry retort I was about to make; it would not be wise to antagonize him at this point.

"Look," I answered reasonably, "you can't go running in and out of Washington traffic like that. You'll get yourself killed."

His expression did not change. "No one can kill me," he asserted flatly. "I'm indestructible."

I started to laugh hysterically and then caught myself abruptly at the look on his face. He's not joking, I thought horrified; he really believes what he's saying. This man honestly thinks he is above the forces of nature!

Once seated at a table in Naylor's, Al summoned the waiter imperiously, brusquely gave our order, and then lit my cigarette and his with an expensive-looking gold lighter.

"I hope the food is good," he said thoughtfully. "Americans are such stupid people that even when it comes to a simple matter like cooking a meal, they do very badly." My face must have gone white, for he suddenly looked at me with the impersonal interest of a scientist viewing a germ under the microscope. "Ah, yes, I had forgotten for the moment that you, too, are an American. But then you are very different from the rest of your fellow countrymen— you, at least, have brains." He paused for a moment as the waiter placed a lobster cocktail in front of him. "And now, shall we concentrate on our meal? The business can come later."

Numbly I watched him pick up his fork and charge

wolfishly into his lobster. I wondered whether I would be able to get any food down me, and, if so, if it would stay there.

At the end of the meal, he threw his napkin on the table, lighted a cigarette, and looked at me thoughtfully.

"And now let us get down to business," he said. "I've known all about your work for the last two years." Then, as I looked puzzled, he explained: "I'm the man who sits behind the desk in Moscow and keeps track of the reports." He smiled suddenly but his eyes remained cold and watchful. "In fact, I've been sent over here especially to see you and tell you that we all think you've done splendidly and have a great future before you."

A shiver of fear ran up my spine. What was coming now?

To my astonishment, he drew himself up stiffly in his chair and looked at me seriously.

"You are very fortunate. A great honor has just been bestowed on you. The Supreme Presidium of the U.S.S.R. has just awarded you one of the highest medals of the Soviet Union—the Order of the Red Star."

I stared at him.

"The Red Star," I said dazedly.

"I don't blame you for being overwhelmed," he said. "It's an honor that few people receive." He pulled a clipping, in color, from his pocket. "This is a facsimile of the decoration," he said precisely. "The original will arrive very shortly. But you can take my word for it that this medal is one of the highest—reserved for all our best fighters."

I was thoroughly angry. Now I knew the score! The work that I had done for the cause had been small and unimportant and he, of all people, should know that fact.

And here he was offering me one of the highest medals of the Soviet Union! It wasn't just Bill, I said to myself; it's the Organization itself that's trying to buy me off. First, they tried money, then a fur coat, then an air-conditioning machine—and now this!

I fought down a hysterical desire to laugh. So, after all, it was only a dirty racket and not an idealistic movement. The Russian people were fighting and dying on the front, but they weren't getting any medals. No, these cherished little bits of tin were being used to bribe Americans like myself. I realized suddenly that Al was gazing at me fixedly.

"The Red Star entitles you to many special privileges," he was saying; "you could even ride on the street cars free." He stopped for a moment; then, seeming to sense that I was not too impressed by this, he went on: "Besides, you are a member of the most powerful organization in the Soviet Union; we are the ones who really rule the country. Just wait until you pay a visit to Moscow; you will be wined and dined and treated like a princess. We know how to reward our people for what they have done."

A wave of revulsion and nausea swept over me; I thought for a moment I was going to be violently ill. Hastily I pulled on my coat and got to my feet.

"I'd better leave now, Al," I said unsteadily. "I'm afraid I'll miss the last train."

As he handed me into a cab, Al took my hand and kissed it.

"Goodbye, darling," he said.

I didn't answer, for I think if I had I would have spit in his face. So this was what the top leaders of the Communist world movement were like! A slow rage crept into me; I knew then what I was dealing with. We have all been fooled, I said to myself; we thought we were fighting to build a better world, and instead we are just pawns in another game of power politics, run by men who are playing for keeps and don't care how they get where they're going. It was for this shabby thing that Yasha fought and gave his life—now I knew the answer to the awful struggle he had gone through the last days of his life. He had discovered what was really going on, but he was too broken then to want to live any longer. They had killed him, these people, killed one of the most decent people that had ever lived!

Blindly I paid off the cab driver and walked into Union Station; I didn't care now where I went or what I did. Indeed, I didn't seem to mind whether I lived or died; everything that I had fought for was a hoax and a sham.

Automatically I settled myself down for the night, but my mind kept ticking relentlessly on. There wasn't any hope for us American Communists. Not only was the international movement completely rotten but even if we were able to kick the cheap politicians like Earl Browder out of the American Party, we would not have achieved anything. After all, just what was our Party? Not an autonomous movement that had as its aim the bringing of Communism to the United States, but only a poor, puny little adjunct to Moscow. Earl hadn't been lying when he said that he "had" to take orders from the Russians. Al had made that completely clear. I remembered back to the conversation we had had about Juliet earlier that evening. When I told him how much I disliked her and then asked what had happened to her, he laughed humorlessly.

"She's six feet under," he said as calmly as if he had been asking for another glass of water. "That's what happens to all traitors."

But he had not finished. "You know," he went on thoughtfully, "your reaction to her is a very interesting one. It proves exactly what I have always maintained: that we must understand Americans better and handle them very carefully. In the old days, we did not realize that Americans are all sentimentalists and that we must sugar-coat the pill before giving it to them. Now we are doing better in our recruitment."

"Recruitment?" I asked, uncomprehending.

"Of course," he said impatiently. "The Soviet Union is in a bad position in regard to finding undercover agents; unlike the British Empire, which can call on any of its nationals abroad, we don't have many Russians who are sympathetic to the new regime. Of course, we can always buy people—and we do when necessary—but it is better to have people with the right ideology. That's the function of the American Communist Party; it's the reservoir from which we draw most of our agents."

This is the end of everything, I said to myself hopelessly, and felt a frightful sense of impotence take hold of me. I and all my good American comrades are caught in an ugly intrigue and there is no way out. What could I do?

CHAPTER XI

FINALLY I pulled myself together and tried to think of what to do next. The international Communist movement, I realized, was in the hands of the wrong people. My contacts and I were in a highly dangerous spot. There was only one thing to do: get as many people as I could out of the clutches of the Russians and then ease myself out.

Coldly I planned the first step in the project—I must rescue Mary Price, because she was in the greatest danger. The best way to do that would be through Earl Browder. So I told him that I thought Mary should be disconnected from the apparatus; she was, I said, too nervous and high-strung. He shook his head dubiously; all right, I thought to myself, I'll play rough if you want me to.

I glared at him menacingly. "Look, Earl. Mary is Mildred Price's sister and she knows all about your connections with the I.P.R. group and their information gathering. If she cracks up—and she will—you're going to get mixed up in it."

He seemed to shrivel in his chair; then he shrugged his shoulders despairingly.

"O.K.," he said in a tone of defeat.

So far, so good. Who else? Bill Remington, fortunately, had gone into the Navy in the spring and he was safely out of it. Two others I had dropped on orders from the Russians: Harold Sloan, because he was about to see a psychiatrist, and Louis Budenz, because they thought he was too close to the American Communist Party for safety. Who was left?

Well, there was the Perlo group, which under my directives was flourishing and producing more and more material. Although some of them were scared and refused to cooperate much, others were really going to town. Vic, himself, was bringing us complete and up-to-date information on aircraft—production, distribution by countries and theaters of action.

Then there was Duncan Lee, my prime headache for the last several months, who was exceedingly nervous and jumpy. Indeed, by that time his hush-hush work at the O.S.S. had made him so hypercautious that he had taken to crawling around the floor of his apartment on hands and knees examining the telephone wires to see if they had been tampered with. I remember one evening he had begged me to see him, and when I met him he was white and trembling and the sweat stood out on his forehead.

"What's the matter, Duncan?" I said.

He peered around him nervously, as if he thought someone was listening; then he told me the situation. It seemed he had found out that his boss, General Donovan, had conceived the idea of exchanging intelligence missions with the Russians; the N.K.V.D. was to send about ten or twelve men to this country and the O.S.S. would ship an equal number over there. The matter had been threshed out in a top-policy meeting of the United States government; most of the people present had not opposed the suggestion, with the exception of Admiral Leahy of the Navy, who had said flatly "no." A representative of President Roosevelt had suggested tentatively that perhaps it wasn't such a good idea during an election year; however, if the N.K.V.D. came in plain clothes and without any fanfare, the idea might work out. J. Edgar Hoover, alone, sat back and looked amused, and his words, as Duncan reported them, have stuck in my mind.

"I don't see what difference it makes," Hoover said. "Ever since the Amtorg Trading Corporation moved into this country, the N.K.V.D. have been wandering around the United States. It probably would make it a lot simpler for us if they came already labeled."

Duncan wasn't sure whether the exchange would go through, but the mere idea of it upset him. He had turned to me desperately.

"I'm finished," he said. "They'll come to call on me, and when I let them in, they'll shake my hand and say, 'Well done, comrade.' "

The situation was so ludicrous that I almost laughed; then I realized he was serious about it. What will I do with him, I wondered; he's too panicky to tell the truth to, and surely the Russians will fight to the death to keep such a valuable contact.

Helen Tenney, too, presented a problem; she was doing excellent work in the O.S.S., bringing us stacks of ditto-machined confidential O.S.S. reports from their undercover operatives in places as far away as Persia and Kurdistan.

Yet, even if Helen lost her job, she would still be very useful. Like Mary Price, she was young, attractive, and not married; perhaps they would want her, also, to lure men. Nausea swept over me; how could I prevent them from taking her?

That left only three more important ones in Washington: Maurice Halperin, Robert Miller, and Joseph Gregg. No, I was wrong; there was also J. Julius Joseph. All of these, with the exception of Bob Miller—who was still terrified and not producing much—were valuable contacts; undoubtedly the Russians would want them.

For the next month I continued to go down to Washington and collect material from my agents, meanwhile trying desperately to think of some plan. Each time I looked at them it was a fresh reminder that I was responsible for keeping them in this ugly affair. Nights I couldn't sleep; I would pace the floor or go out and walk around the Village until three o'clock in the morning trying to figure a way out of the situation. I began to look thin and pale and tired; it was an effort to walk even two blocks.

After putting out tentative feelers, I was convinced that all my Communist contacts—however loath they might be to do undercover work—were so completely saturated by Communist ideology that it would be useless to take the chance of telling them the truth. They would only go up to Communist headquarters and denounce me as a traitor. I decided on strategy: I would slant the information I had on them to such a degree that they would look like poor risks to the Russian Secret Police, who perhaps would drop them. This path I followed.

Where they were nervous and high-strung, as in the case of Duncan Lee, I reported them on the verge of cracking up; where they had had too much open Party work in the past, as in the case of Joseph Gregg—who had been in the Spanish Civil War—I overemphasized the fact; where they were in too close contact with dangerous elements—J. Julius Joseph had formed a friendship with an Army counterintelligence agent—I warned that the whole organization might be in peril if they were kept on.

At the same time I tried to carry on a campaign of counterpropaganda among my Communist contacts, using highly indirect methods. I knew that Helen Tenney was tired and lonesome and beginning to feel the nervous strain; I subtly insinuated that this was no life for her, that it got worse the longer one stayed in it and it was a pity she wasn't out of it and back in New York with her old friends. Perhaps, I thought, she'll take the hint and give up her job in Washington; then she will be of no further use to the Russians.

With people like Victor Perlo, who were Communists of long standing and unlikely to be scared off, I used a different tack. I treated him as Bill had me at our first meeting, using the same brutality and the same savagery; I demanded, I threatened, I almost beat him into submission. It doesn't matter what he thinks about me, I decided, just so long as I save him. Let him learn what the N.K.V.D. is really like, I thought; let him get a taste of their methods firsthand. Perhaps it will act like a dash of cold water in his face and wake him up; if it doesn't, then there isn't any hope for him anyway.

By now it was getting on toward the holiday season and mechanically I began to buy the usual Christmas presents for my people. This year was more difficult, because I had more gifts to purchase; it seemed like an endless problem. I finally settled on scarves and wallets for the members of the Perlo group and disposed of them in one fell swoop; then I bought for the others. Jack, meanwhile, was demurring at caviar for Earl Browder; he didn't see why the guy merited it, he said. They don't like Earl, I thought to myself; this is only one of many indications I have had. Obviously, the Russians don't like the fact that he's getting too independent; they have had their knife into him ever since he tried to hold out on them by protecting Mary and the Silvermasters. Moreover, they distinctly resented his building up his own position and prestige by meeting with Sumner Welles of the State Department; Earl himself had told me that it was his own idea, which he had engineered through Lauchlin Currie. He's getting too big for his boots, I thought, and pretty soon they'll cut him down to size.

Laden with three suitcases of presents, I went down to Washington the week before Christmas; I was to deliver them to my contacts, collect their information, then meet Jack for breakfast the third morning at the Hotel Statler. Everything went very well; all the people were pleased with their presents and gay with the holiday spirit. Duncan Lee, who with his O.S.S. training fancied himself somewhat of a sleuth, eyed his leather writing case and his wife's red-leather compact thoughtfully; then he uttered a whoop of joy.

"I've discovered where you work," he said happily. "Last year you also gave us leather goods; you must be in the wholesale leather business."

Amused, I moved on to my next contact—Maurice Halperin, who lived out in Takoma Park. As I rode out on the bus, I began to worry about him; of all the people I had, he was the one I had been unable to tell the N.K.V.D. would be a bad risk. He was such a well-balanced, stable person, with a wife, two lovely children, and a happy home life; I don't believe there was a nerve in his body. Moreover, he had never been openly associated with the Communists, and although the Security Division of the O.S.S. knew he was pro-Communist, they had done nothing to dislodge him from his job.

It was simply amazing, I thought, how careless the O.S.S. was, in keeping on people who were extremely dangerous; Maurice, after all, was not the only one. I remembered how, a few months before, we had asked Duncan to find out why Mary Price had been turned down in the fall of 1943; he had promptly produced the information that the reason was because she had been associating with known Communists. When we discovered he had access to the security files, we had asked him to bring us information that might be of value. Thereupon, he had given me a slip of paper on which he had written down the names of people that the O.S.S. considered dangerous risks, divided into three categories—"known Soviet agents," "known Communists," and "Communist sympathizers." In the first group were three names—none of whom I knew; in the second, was an active member of the Perlo group, and in the third, Maurice Halperin. We had quite promptly alerted Maurice and told him to be careful; the other, since he was more reckless, we had "put on ice" and told to abstain from any activities for a six-month period. That had been some time before; yet, in spite of our forebodings, both of them were still holding their jobs.

Obviously Maurice was in no danger of losing his; moreover, he would be an extremely valuable person to the Russians. By now, he not only had access to the O.S.S. secret cable room and the reports from their undercover men abroad, but because of an exchange agreement he was also able to secure confidential State Department cables and reports. These were of great interest to the N.K.V.D.; I remember how amused they were by Harriman's confidential report on what he thought of the Russians and how he was trying to handle them. I wondered how the American Ambassador to Moscow would have felt if he could have known that the Russians knew not only every move he made but even his inmost thoughts. Certainly he wouldn't have wanted them to know just how much he disliked them.

My mind drifted back over the months I had known Maurice. I remembered with some amusement that it had been Maurice who caused me one of the worst frights I had had. It had been arranged that I pick him up at his garage out on Florida Avenue. It was a bitterly cold morning; I arrived bundled up, with my knitting bag full of microfilms and documents, and waited in front of a garage on the corner he had specified. As time went on and he did not appear, I grew colder and colder; finally I decided to go inside and see if he wasn't waiting there. I opened the door and stepped in; it was filled with shelves of documents that reached to the ceiling, and I found myself surrounded by three menacing-looking men in uniform with revolvers. Ye gods, I thought, in a panic; this must be a storehouse for secret documents for the O.S.S. or some other similar agency. What should I do now? If they arrested me, they would find material in my possession that would give the whole apparatus away. My knees shook but I managed to keep my head.

"I'm sorry," I said in a bewildered tone, "but I seem to be in the wrong place. I'm part of a car pool and I was supposed to pick up the rest of the people in a garage on this corner. But this can't be the place."

For a moment that seemed years they stared at me; then they nodded comprehendingly.

"It's easy to make that mistake, Miss," one of them said

finally, "especially if you don't know the neighborhood and the queer intersection we have here. The garage you want is just around the corner."

I had quite literally tottered out of the garage, wondering if my face showed what a fright I had had; around the corner I found Maurice patiently waiting.

I finished with all my contacts by the end of the second day. I spent that night with Helen Tenney and set off the following morning to have breakfast with Jack at the Statler. After I had passed over the material to him, I handed him the Christmas present I had bought for him—a rather good-looking leather wallet. I was surprised at his reaction; probably I had expected that he would take it and say "thank you" quite casually. He took it in his hands and smoothed it lovingly; then he looked at me as if I had given him something really rare and precious.

"I've never owned anything as expensive and beautiful before," he said to me wistfully. Then, with great reluctance, he put it away. I thought of his reaction the following night when I gave Al his present, an imported wool scarf and some leather gloves; he looked them over very critically, fingering the material and holding it up to the light.

"The scarf is all right," he said precisely, "but the gloves are not well made."

With difficulty I suppressed a hysterical laugh as I watched him charge into his food and rapidly dispose of it; even though I had had no dinner, I simply couldn't eat with those tight knots of tension in my stomach. The meal ended, he settled back in his chair and leisurely lit a cigarette, looking at me appraisingly. Here it comes, I thought, bracing myself for the worst.

"Well," he said, dragging in a mouthful of smoke and

exhaling it with sensuous pleasure, "we have at last decided what to do about all the contacts that Golos handled. You cannot, obviously, continue to handle them; the set-up is too full of holes and therefore too dangerous. I'm afraid our friend Golos was not too cautious a man, and there is the risk that you, because of your connection with him, may endanger the apparatus. You will therefore turn them over to us; we will look into their backgrounds thoroughly and decide which ones we will keep." He paused for a moment, while I stared at him with the fascinated gaze that a bird gives a snake about to devour it; then he continued: "This shift-over must be made immediately, so you will stay on as long as necessary to make the arrangements."

My brain seemed paralyzed; I didn't seem able to think clearly. Frantically I stalled for time.

"But I can't, Al," I protested. "It will be impossible for me to get hold of all my contacts at such short notice, and besides, I can't be away from the office that long."

After some argument, he agreed to my proposal; I was to return to New York the next morning, settle any urgent business, return to Washington, and prepare my contacts for the transfer. This, however, was not all he had to say to me; he had also made plans for my future. I was, he said, an excellent agent; he would like me to continue with the N.K.V.D. In this case, I was to sever all connections with the U.S. Service and be put "on ice" for a period of six months until they had determined the F.B.I. had lost interest in me, and then I would be set up in a new "cover" business in Washington, Baltimore, or Philadelphia. "We only operate out of large cities," he explained. At that time I would be given a new group of government contacts to take care of, probably more important ones than I had already had. In the event that I insisted on remaining with U.S. Service—an eventuality which he hoped would not happen—I would be permitted to drop out of active undercover work, although I must be ready to help them at any time.

"I hope you will choose to remain with us," he said suavely. "You have an excellent record in the Service and you can be of inestimable value to us in the future. You are one of those rare people—an American with brains." This last was said with a note of profound contempt; then, looking me up and down appraisingly, like a trader about to decide whether to buy a horse, he added: "Besides, I like you personally; I think we could work very well together."

Fear, nausea, and rage churned inside of me; I couldn't decide whether I wanted most to spit in his face or take to my heels and run as far away as possible. But I wanted to know one more thing before I left; I kept my voice steady.

"And if I leave U.S. Service," I asked, "what happens to John H. Reynolds? Will he be left there as before?"

Al assured me that they didn't want Reynolds, that he would be too difficult a person to handle; they would replace him with someone else, buying out his interest and retiring him from the firm. I nodded thoughtfully and left him.

On the train back to New York I tried hopelessly to think of some way out, but the more I pondered the matter the more I realized I had now reached the dead end. I couldn't hope to save the Washington contacts; if the organizations couldn't get them through me, they could go around me and force Earl Browder to turn them over. The contacts were doomed now, and there was nothing I could do to change the situation. I could only hope that either the Russians would take some of my recommendations seriously and drop a few of them or that the contacts themselves, under the influence of my propaganda, would fight their own way out. But there was one person I could save, if I made the right decision—John H. Reynolds. He and his wife had by now become good friends of mine; I didn't want to see them any further involved in all this mess. If I remained with U.S. Service he would only be dragged deeper into the racket. Obviously, Al intended to use the business for some purpose, in spite of his protestations. If, on the contrary, I left the U.S. Service, the Russians would buy out Reynolds and he would be safely out of their clutches.

Moreover, that would mean that I had been able to burn one more bridge behind me.

I made a sudden decision: I would leave the corporation, thus rescuing the Reynolds family; then I would go "on ice" as Al had suggested. Little by little I would impress on the Russians that I was worn out from too much undercover work—if necessary, I would put on an act and pretend that I, too, was cracking up. They wouldn't want to take any chances that I might fall apart and talk too much; they would probably drop me in a hurry.

By the early part of January all of my contacts had been turned over and I found myself completely tired, mentally and physically, from the strain of leaving them. It hadn't been easy; even though there had been no choice, I was still haunted by the thought that I might somehow have been able to save them. In spite of the fact that they were part of a job I had had to do, I had regarded them as my friends —an attitude that the Communist Party frowned upon. I hated to feel that I had let them down. Yet, in the long run,

[269]

I thought, probably the shock treatment is the best; they would never have believed anything I told them. Their only chance was to learn at first hand, as I had done.

Not long afterward the Russians decided it was dangerous for me to remain in the apartment where Yasha had died; they felt sure it must be under F.B.I. surveillance. I was told to find another place at once and move as quickly as possible. I was too weary to argue the matter, even though I knew that with the housing shortage it would be well-nigh impossible. Finally, after searching days on end, I decided to take a room in the Hotel St. George in Brooklyn Heights; it would be more expensive but there was no other way to solve the problem. In the early part of February I put what few pieces of furniture I owned into storage; then I gathered together my personal belongings and prepared to move out.

As I packed, it seemed to me that I was cutting my last link with Yasha and setting out all alone into a strange new existence. Despite the growing ugliness of the outside world, I had always felt at peace when I entered my front door; the apartment was full of memories of happy times we had spent together. Somehow, here I had always felt very near to him; I could close my eyes and imagine him sitting in his favorite armchair and smiling encouragement to me. Especially in the last few months, in the midst of my increasing disillusionment, I had thought about him constantly; he, too, had gone through that same terrible awakening, only in his case it had killed him. If he had lived, would he have found the strength to break away, I wondered; I thought he would have, and that feeling was giving me the courage to go on myself. As I packed up the last of his clothes to be given to the Russian War Relief, as he had wished, I thought to myself: if he was able to face death unafraid, then I shall find the courage to go out and walk into the unknown alone.

The N.K.V.D. had evidently been right about the F.B.I.'s interest in my apartment; a few days before I left, the landlady told me that a strange man had been to see her, asking for someone with a name like mine. I recognized the tactics; it must be a man from the Bureau. On the heels of this occurrence, my front-door bell rang one evening, and when I answered it, I found a tall, dark, athletic-looking young man standing in the entrance. Oh, oh, I said to myself, here we go again! He was, he explained, looking for someone who was supposed to live where I did; he spent five minutes carefully telling me about his nonexistent friend, while he stared at me intently and seemed to be memorizing every detail of my appearance.

When he reluctantly departed, I closed the door and sat down thoughtfully on the couch. What an odd predicament to be in, I thought to myself, suppressing a hysterical desire to laugh; here I am running away from the Russians and now I'm being pursued by the F.B.I., too. On one side of me stands the merciless Russian machine and on the other the equally tyrannical American government; I am caught in the midst of this fray in a strange little no-man's land all my own. I found myself thinking about the F.B.I. agent that had just called; he was the first one I had gotten a good look at. He looked very nice—just like any other clean-cut young American; his eyes, too, interested me—they held none of the ugly hate and fear that so characterized the N.K.V.D. agents. What a pity that such a seemingly decent person was mixed up in such a sordid business!

It was during this period that, returning from seeing Earl

Browder, I ran into Berny Shuster, then organizational secretary of the New York District of the Communist Party. He was an old friend of Yasha's, had constantly visited him at World Tourists, and I knew he had turned contacts for espionage over to us. I tried to avoid him, but he rushed up to me; he looked tired and not too well.

"Wait a minute," he said urgently. "I want to talk to you."

As we stood in the middle of East 13th Street, he told me what was on his mind; he was worried about the people he had turned over to Yasha and myself. In his excitement, he forgot all caution; he gripped my arm nervously and began to tell me that we were ruining the American Communists he had given us.

"I won't give you any more," he kept crying out. "They come back to us smashed up and we have to send them to our psychiatrists. They're no good to us any more; they're nervous wrecks!"

I looked at him thoughtfully; what was there that I could say? He couldn't feel any worse about the situation than I did, but what could I do? I didn't even dare to confide in him. Listlessly, I shrugged my shoulders and moved on. Yet all the way home his words haunted me; when I arrived at my apartment, I moved over to the mirror, and what I saw frightened me. My face was thin, tense, haunted looking—the eyes were wary and filled with mistrust. I turned away in sudden disgust; this, then, I said wearily, is what has happened to me. I once started out with high, idealistic hopes and now I look like someone who is not even human. What has happened to us all, I cried out passionately; what has happened to all of us who started out so gallantly to build a new world, where men would live like human be-

[272]

ings and not like animals? We had been corrupted and smashed by a machine more merciless than anything the world had ever seen, and there was no hope left for any of us. This was the end to all our dreams, all our futile strugglings to build a world where there would be justice and mercy. The only way out of this blind, senseless world was a merciful death. "Not that they die, but that they die like sheep," I quoted to myself, and I knew that now I understood what Louis Untermeyer had meant. We were the sheep and we had, with the best of intentions, been led astray; now we had gone too far ever to turn back. And what could we go back to? A world that had no meaning and no sense, where people lived and died like animals and had nothing to look forward to? No, it was better to keep on fighting, fighting for one's own personal integrity, even though it was a losing battle. I would keep going, as Yasha had, and perhaps one day I would find release in eternal nothingness; perhaps one day I, too, would lie quietly under a tree and go back to the earth whence I had come.

At my next meeting with Jack, he told me that he would have to leave me. From then on I would be in contact only with Al. I was sorry to see him go, for of all the agents I had met since Yasha's death, he was the most decent. He even dresses as a revolutionary should, I thought, noting that he had on the usual worn gray suit, the thin, inadequate trench coat, and scuffed shoes with one sole coming off. Moreover, under all the merciless N.K.V.D. discipline he seemed to be a very human person; although, unlike Al, he didn't help me off with my coat or light my cigarette, he was kind in small ways.

Jack looked at me wistfully.

"I'm sorry to have to say goodbye," he said. "You've always brought me good luck. Twice since I've known you I've had promotions in the Service, and once a medal." He stopped for a moment and then added: "But that's as far as I'll go; they say that sooner or later water reaches its own level and I've reached mine. There isn't any further to go."

I looked puzzled. "I don't understand what you mean."

He laughed bitterly. "I know our work in the United States better than anyone else, including all the big shots like Al that they send over from Moscow. I guess I'm too good; they'll probably send me down to Latin America next."

So that was it! The Organization didn't like people like Jack getting to be too powerful; when they became too efficient, they were shifted somewhere else. For all his years of service and his good work, he was in a more precarious position than I was.

"Look here, Mary," he said abruptly, calling me by the code name he used for me, "if they want to send you to Moscow, don't go there. You wouldn't like it, not after you've lived in the United States."

He paused, and his mind seemed to be miles and years away. "You know, Mary, I sometimes wonder how I came to be mixed up in this. It all started when I was a kid in my teens in Lithuania during the Civil War; I started out doing odd jobs for the Bolsheviks, because I thought their new regime would be better for my country than that of the Czar, and then somehow I just kept on going." He paused for a moment and went on: "It's funny, even now I remember the day my brother discovered what they were really like. We were literally starving to death; we used to sleep all we could to conserve our strength. Then somehow he got hold of a small cheese and proudly set out on the road

[274]

to bring it home to the family. Halfway there, he was stopped by two ragged and hungry Red Army men; they demanded the cheese, and even though they threatened him, he refused to give it up. Finally, rather than hand it over, he ground it into the dusty road with his bare heel; he wasn't going to let them have it."

Startled, I stared at him; he smiled grimly, his mind still in the past.

"You know, Mary," he said sadly. "We had had so much of the Czarist men that we thought these people would be different. But they weren't! They kicked us around just like the others."

I could think of nothing to say; I wanted to ask him why he was still working for them, but I didn't dare. Then he pulled himself together.

"Forget what I told you," he said roughly. "Just take my advice."

I had thought myself incapable of any more feeling, but Jack's words hurt with a pain that cut through all my numbness. Must I stand helplessly by and see decent human beings mangled by the Soviet machine? Could I slide out of this ugly mess and watch in silence while other young idealists, with high hopes of building a new and better world, were sucked into this intrigue and systematically corrupted and smashed? I found quite suddenly I didn't want to run away any more—I wanted to dig my heels in and fight back. But how? I couldn't do it alone; I had tried that and failed. If only there were some group of decent people—no matter how few—who would band together and do something about the situation, I would take my chances and join them. But where would I find such an organization?

What was it Jack had said? Yes—I wouldn't like Moscow

—not after the United States. But that meant that he, who had lived in both places, thought that my country was by far the better. Could it be that I had been wrong about the United States? I suddenly remembered a conversation I had had not long before with Mr. Rosowsky, head of the American Federation for Lithuanian Jews, when he had come into World Tourists to ship some parcels to the Soviet Union. He had been unusually quiet that day, and when I asked him what was the trouble, he looked over at me with eyes full of pain.

"I am an old man," he said sadly, "and I have nothing further to live for. When the Nazis invaded Lithuania, they decimated the Jewish population; most of my relatives were killed off. When that happened, I lived only to see the Red Army come in and liberate my country; they, I was sure, spelled hope for the future. But I was very wrong; bad as the Nazis were, the Soviet Army was far worse—I cannot tell you what atrocities they committed on my people." He sighed and went on. "Perhaps I shouldn't tell you this; probably you, too, are impressed by their clever propaganda, as are so many Americans. It is easy to believe these glowing reports of a new world, for each of us in his heart wants to think there is some place on this earth where there is no oppression and injustice."

I had sat quite still in my chair, finding nothing to say. He shifted his position slightly in his seat and smiled.

"Forgive an old man for taking up your time," he said, "but I have no one to talk to. I wish now that I had been able to bring my relatives over to this fine, beautiful country of yours where they could have built a happy life for themselves. You look surprised? Ah, you are like so many Americans who see only the ugliness of your own country

[276]

and not its good points; you do not realize that compared to anything that my country has known—or is knowing now—it is a paradise. You Americans at least have the right to earn your own living as you choose, you have adequate food and shelter, you can even say what you want—even to criticizing your President—and no one can stop you from that. Yes, I know there is misery and suffering and injustice; I see a lot of that in my business. But it is nothing, I tell you —nothing compared to what I have seen over there."

I forgot my caution and asked him a question. "But how can this be such a good country if it is controlled by greedy interests and crooked politicians?"

He smiled very gently. "Those you have everywhere; it is, perhaps, a part of human nature and we must accept it. But here, at least, such people are not in complete control, as over there. There is a chance for you Americans to change things that you do not like; it may take a long time, but it will come. I am more and more learning that we cannot build our Utopias overnight by wildly throwing over an oppressive regime and starting a new one. We have all been, perhaps, too impatient; we have not realized that it may take centuries to achieve our goal."

At the time, his words had impressed me profoundly but I had resolutely put them out of my mind. Now they returned to haunt me with renewed intensity. Perhaps he and Jack were right; certainly they of all people should know. Perhaps in comparison with the other countries of the world, the United States did offer a maximum of freedom and justice; perhaps here, more than anywhere, the individual was treated like a human being. It was true that the Fascist elements in the government were strong and well organized; yet in spite of that they had made no serious inroads into the basic freedoms of the country. Could the United States maintain this state of affairs and even improve it? I didn't know. There were seemingly grave weaknesses in the American system; it depended entirely on the voters of the country to keep it going. A good many people, I had found, were unwilling to take the time or the trouble to carry out their duties as citizens; they sat back and let others take the initiative. That meant that possibly a small, well-organized clique could take over power, provided they moved slowly and with sufficient cleverness.

Yet, frail though this system was, it was at the present time the one bulwark against the growing power of Communism. Undoubtedly it was not perfect and certainly it was ineffectual but it was all there was. I brought myself up short; if I had found something decent that was worth fighting for—and it seemed that I had—then, regardless of the odds against its ultimate victory, I belonged in there fighting. I could no longer slide out of the mess I was in and stand by watching; I must pitch in and help. I had seen at first hand how efficiently organized the Soviet machine was, how successfully it had been able to penetrate into even the highest places in the United States government. Somehow it must be stopped, and I was in a position to contribute my little bit.

The conclusion was inescapable: I must go to the F.B.I. and tell them what I knew about Soviet undercover work in the United States so that they could break it up. Horror stricken, I shrank back from the idea; no, I couldn't do that. They were my enemies; they would beat me up, they would put me in jail, they might even kill me. And the Russian Secret Police! If I just slid out quietly and did nothing, they would leave me alone; but if I talked to the American authorities, they would certainly take drastic action—action that wouldn't be pleasant. They would start a smear campaign against me, as they had with all previous Communists who had broken and talked; they might even resort to physical reprisals and put me, too, six feet under. I shivered with a sudden uncontrollable fear; I didn't have the courage to undergo all that. Then I thought of Yasha and pulled myself together; if he had felt the way I did, he would have the stamina to do what was right. It doesn't matter what happens to me, I said to myself firmly; perhaps, after all, I'm only living on borrowed time. What is important is that the F.B.I. gets the necessary information.

Then the weight of the past crowded in on me; though I was gradually emerging from the grip of the Communist ideology, I found myself being pulled almost inexorably toward my past associations. Ten years before, I had burned all my bridges behind me and in the interval had built up a new and happy life for myself, all centered on the Communist Party. As I sat there thinking, I realized that those had been the best years of my life; there I had found peace, security, and a sense of doing something constructive. My mind wandered back again into the past; I felt once more the warmth of comradeship, the close bond of experiences shared, the sense of satisfaction that comes from an ideal believed in and fought for. Could I leave all that behind me and go out into a strange, cold world all alone? Did I have the strength to pull myself up by the roots and transplant myself to some new soil?

And what would I face if I did? There would be no welcoming arms to receive me; my fellow Americans would regard me with suspicion and distaste. They would be unable to understand just why I had ever gotten into such

[279]

an ugly business; they would turn away from me in disgust and shun me as a leper. I would have no friends. But that would not be all. It would be difficult to find a job to support myself; the Communists would put every barrier in my way and I would have no help from anyone else. How would I eat?

And even if I could do all this, what about my comrades, with whom I had worked in Washington? I would, of course, have to turn them in; there was no other way to smash the Soviet machine. But I couldn't do that; they were my friends, my comrades—together, through bad times and good, we had fought to build a better world. I tried to put aside my emotions and think logically. They're not my friends any more, I said to myself firmly; if they knew that I no longer believed in the Communist ideology, they would denounce me as a "traitor." We're in opposite camps, now, I thought sadly; when the Revolution comes, we shall have to shoot each other down. I shut my eyes against this prospect; even if I hadn't recruited them into the Party, I had helped to keep them good Communists. It was I who was responsible for the plight they were now in; they had sensed that I honestly believed in the revolutionary movement, and that reliance on my sincerity had kept them believing in the Communist doctrine, even when they, themselves, had been assailed by doubts. I had let them down badly once, when—knowing what the Russian Secret Police were like—I had permitted them to be turned over; now I was thinking of betraying them in an even worse fashion. I can't sell my past friends down the river, I cried out desperately; it doesn't matter what happens to me—I, at least, am expendable. Expendable . . . Perhaps, in the long run, all of us were expendable; somewhere along the line, with the best of motives, we had taken a wrong turning and we had to answer for it. Now it was a question of our small lives or the lives of the vast majority of decent people in the world; perhaps all of us would have to be sacrificed to save the values that humanity held dear. What did the fate of a few individuals matter, stacked up against the fate of the world?

Now you're thinking like the Russian Secret Police, I thought bitterly; you're treating human beings as if they were little more than pawns on a chessboard. These are people, not automatons; if life has any meaning, each one of them has a worth as an individual. Yet all these old friends of mine had become, in the hands of the Communist movement, no longer individuals but robots; they were chained in an intellectual and moral slavery that was far worse than any prison.

With a swift flash of clarity, I saw that what happened to a man himself—his honesty, his integrity—was far more important than what happened to him physically. We who had become Communists had done so honestly, but over the long years of indoctrination we had become so warped that we were no longer true even to ourselves. I, somehow, had found my way out of this perverted thinking, but the others were gradually being dragged deeper and deeper into a hell from which there was no possibility of escape. If I turned them over to the authorities, they would no longer be useful to the Soviet machine and would therefore be free of any further entanglements. Back in a normal life again, perhaps they, too, could find their way back to that integrity which they had lost, while believing that they still had it. But could I do it? I didn't know.

Somehow I seemed unable to find the strength to take any

action. As the weeks rolled by and I wrestled with my conscience, I vacillated back and forth; one day I would determine that I would go to the F.B.I., the next I would decide that under no circumstances could I do it. Night after night I would walk the streets, unable to sleep; when I would finally doze off in the early hours of the morning, I would awake an hour or two later, dripping with sweat and in the grip of a dreadful nightmare. Always it was the same one and always, no matter how thoroughly I waked myself out of it, I went back to it again. I was watching an execution: the firing squad, with their rifles leveled, were facing the prisoner who, with his eyes blindfolded, stood against a brick wall. The victim was always different—sometimes it was Mary Price, sometimes it was Greg Silvermaster—yet, every time, I had the strange sensation that it was I, myself, who was about to die. As I stood there, rooted to the spot with horror, the victim would suddenly wheel around and point his finger at me. "Traitor," he would cry out. "It is you who have killed me!" A volley of shots would ring out and it would seem as if all of them had entered my own body.

I became thinner and paler and more tired; yet I could come to no decision. Sometimes I wished desperately that someone would force me to take drastic action; although I was tearing myself apart, I could not make up my mind. If only the F.B.I. would arrest me, I thought; perhaps then I would be forced to do something. At last one day I pulled myself together. There's only one thing for me to do, I said to myself; I must go out to the country—away from this problem—and get enough rest so that I can think clearly. I packed my bags and set out for Old Lyme, a small Connecticut town on Long Island Sound.

When I reached my destination, I felt that at last I had found a refuge—a place where, far from my old Communist associations, I could rest and think things out. Quite suddenly the full weight of the past years' fatigue seemed to pile up on me; I wanted only to vegetate and not try to grapple with any problems. At first I did little but eat and sleep and lie on the beach in the sun; even swimming a few strokes seemed to exhaust me. I avoided as much as possible talking to people; I didn't feel up to the effort of making conversation.

Then, bit by bit, my strength came back; I started to take walks and explore the town. It was, I discovered, very much like my home town New Milford; there were the same old houses with their well-kept lawns and fine old trees, the same white Congregational church with its tall spire, the same small stores. Even the people seemed the same—they are sturdy and independent and solid, I thought. They have an innate sense of the worth of an individual. To them, it would be important what happened to their neighbor; they would feel a loss of self-respect if they let him down in his need. If only the whole country were based on values like these, there would be no fear for the future. In this changing situation, could the old values continue to hold? I didn't know. Once before, as I was growing up, I had faced this same problem; reluctantly I had come to the conclusion that the world I had been born into was crumbling under the impact of a new mechanistic civilization. We had needed a new faith that reaffirmed the brotherhood of man and the worth of the individual, I had thought, and in my groping, I found a seeming answer in Communism. Yet that, too, had failed me; far from answering the problem of suffering and injustice, it had only intensified it.

[283]

Sometimes in the evening I would start out by myself and, passing the creek with its nostalgic smell of the sea, I would take the winding road to the top of the hill, where I could look out over the town. Here I would stand and, as I watched the last rays of the sun gleam on the white spire of the church, a strange sense of contentment would seep into me. Somehow, alone up there, I would feel that the past ten years had only been a bad dream; I was a new person in an old-new world.

As I descended the hill again, my problem would come back to haunt me in full force. My faith in my old Communist ideals was gone now; even the embers were growing cold. And yet, I thought wistfully, I shall never feel like that again—never again will I be able to think and feel and live with such intensity and passion. Part of me has been left behind in those ten years; I shall never again be a whole person.

But I can't believe that the world is empty and meaningless; as long as there are decent, solid people like these, there must be values that transcend mere expediency. And since there are, I belong in there fighting for them. I must go to the F.B.I., I thought; but how could I find the courage to do it? I'm only one person—just another insignificant individual—and I'm frightened. If only there was someone bigger than I am, someone to give me the strength to do what I have to do!

I was passing the Congregational church; almost without knowing what I was doing, I opened the door and walked in. It was quiet and peaceful inside; I sat down in a back pew, wondering just why I had come in. Then, suddenly, without any volition on my part, I found myself trying to pray—calling out for help to Someone whom all these years

I had denied. Oh, God, I cried out desperately; help me to find the strength!

As if in answer, the old familiar words of the Twenty-third Psalm came throbbing into my mind: "Yea, though thou walk in the valley of the shadow of death, thou shalt fear no evil; for I am with thee." I caught my breath and held onto the back of the pew ahead of me; somehow a strange sense of peace came over me. And then, in the empty church, the voice of my conscience seemed to ring out loudly: You have no right here—yet. You know now that the way of life you have followed these last ten years was wrong; you have come back to where you belong. But first you must make amends!

Slowly I got to my feet and walked out into the bright sunshine; dazedly I sat down on the steps and tried to think. I must go to the F.B.I., but how? There was still the practical problem of contacting them without the knowledge of the N.K.V.D. who, for all I knew, might be close on my heels. None of their agents were completely trusted—especially when they were Americans—and often there were counteragents keeping tabs on their own workers. Quite probably they were inconspicuously watching me; how could I throw them off the trail? And even if I got to the F.B.I., how did I know that I would reach the right person? How did I know that my old friends hadn't infiltrated there—as they had in every other government agency—and that it wouldn't be my luck to run into a member of the Russian Secret Police?

I was suddenly cold with terror; even on this warm summer day I found myself shivering. Then I pulled myself together; I would have to take a chance on running into a Communist in the F.B.I.; the main problem was to get to the Bureau. But that, I thought, presented grave difficulties. I couldn't, obviously, telephone them; that would be very unwise. And the Washington office, I remembered, was located in a very conspicuous place; no one could sneak in there. What about the New York office? I didn't know, but I decided that when I kept an appointment with Al a few days hence, I would look over the situation on my way through New York.

Although I waited almost two hours, Al did not show up; unaware that with his usual absent-mindedness he had been in the wrong place, I found myself in the grip of terror. I haven't been too clever in concealing my feelings, I thought in a panic; he knows what is going on in my mind. My time is running out, I said to myself desperately; the N.K.V.D. suspects me and it won't be long before I, too, am six feet under. There is no human agency that can save me; they always get their man. Then I realized that I had a job to do before I died; I must get this information to the F.B.I.

In New York I looked up the F.B.I. office in the telephone book; it was located in the United States Courthouse building. That didn't look too good; I could never get in there unobserved. Then I remembered hearing the Bureau had a field office in New Haven, Connecticut. I will go there and see where it is located, I thought.

To my joy, it turned out to be located in an ordinary business building where the danger of detection was at a minimum; here is where I will go, I decided.

On a hot August afternoon I stood in the hallway, just outside the office of the F.B.I.; one step more and I would be inside. I wondered nervously if I were being followed; I had taken the elevator three floors above and sneaked down the fire stairs, but still I was worried. If the Russian Secret Police knew what I was about to do . . . I steadied myself and glanced up and down the corridor; there was no one in sight. Taking a deep breath, I opened the door and went in.

The small office was clean and bare; there were only a few chairs and a long wooden bench. Halfway down, a receptionist sat behind a waist-high wooden partition, engrossed in some papers; beyond her stretched what seemed to be private offices, although the glassed-in part was so high that I couldn't see in. At the click of the closing door, she looked up inquiringly; this is it, I said grimly, and with shaking knees I walked over to her.

"I'd like to see the agent in charge," I said in a voice that I hoped was steady.

"Just a moment." She smiled at me. "I'll see if he's in. Won't you have a seat?"

Slowly I walked over to the bench that faced the doorway, and sat down; I braced my feet against the floor so that my legs wouldn't tremble. What would I say to him, now that I was here, I wondered. Just how did one start out with a story like this? I began to feel panicky; I suppressed a wild desire to bolt out the door and never come back. No, I said to myself firmly, you've got to stick this out; if you go away now, you'll never come back. Desperately, I fought for self-control; then into my mind flashed an old maxim of my revolutionary days: when you're in a tight spot and want to keep calm, think of a group of words —it doesn't matter whether they make sense or not—and repeat them over and over to yourself until you have drowned out everything else. My glance fell on the inscription over the doorway—Federal Bureau of Investigation; doggedly I concentrated on that group of words, repeating them over and over to myself like a litany.

The sounds of traffic outside seemed to die down, and the office was very still. Gradually, under the rhythm of the repeated words, I felt the tension ebbing out of me. The gate clicked open. "Won't you come in?" the secretary said.

CHAPTER XII

THE SMALL, DARK F.B.I. man sat across the desk from me, his face neither hostile, I decided, nor friendly. He picked up a pack of cigarettes, offered me one, lit it, and settled back in his chair. I was somewhat disconcerted. Instinctively I had expected that he, like the Russian Secret Police, would immediately pounce on me, asking questions, demanding answers. Certainly the F.B.I., having taken the trouble to follow me around, must know who I was. There must be something very wrong. But what?

Desperately I gathered up courage and told him the highlights of my story. He sat smoking quietly, his eyes narrowed, and when I had finished he snubbed out his cigarette in the ashtray.

"Thank you for coming in," he said. "We'll get in touch with you."

As I walked out into the bright sunshine, I felt a great tide of relief. Now, at last, I had done what had to be done. Then, as I began to analyze the interview, I found myself shivering with an odd fear. Why hadn't the agent asked me any questions? Why had he been so noncommittal? Could it be that the United States government wasn't interested in Soviet undercover work? Or, and my heart jumped into my throat at the idea, could it be that the Communists had infiltrated into even the F.B.I.?

[289]

Steady, I said to myself; there's no reason to get into a panic. Perhaps this particular agent doesn't know anything about the situation, and that's why he's being so cagey. Undoubtedly, he would get in touch with headquarters and someone who was an expert on the subject would contact me. Yes, that must be it, and, reassured, I took the train back to Old Lyme.

I had had no way of knowing, of course, that the F.B.I. was also in a predicament—one that rivaled mine. Far from being unconcerned, they had been somewhat startled by my sudden appearance in their offices. They knew, naturally, who I was, but, because of this knowledge, they suspected it might be a trap that was set by the Russian Secret Police. Hence they decided to move cautiously.

Back in New York three weeks later, I learned to my horror that Al had double-crossed me. Instead of buying John H. Reynolds out of the U.S. Service & Shipping Corporation and putting someone else in his place, he had persuaded Reynolds to stay on in the business. This, I knew, could only mean one thing: the corporation was to be used as a "cover" for the Soviet Secret Police. And Reynolds, of course, was being kept because he would be a perfect "front" man.

What am I going to do, I wondered hopelessly. Far from bailing Reynolds out of the conspiracy, I had on the contrary only dragged him in deeper. I buried my head in my hands. Somehow this matter had to be straightened out. But how? The F.B.I. evidently wasn't interested, for they hadn't as yet gotten in touch with me. That left it squarely up to me.

Well, at least I can die fighting, I thought to myself grimly. I'll disobey Al's orders, go back to the U.S. Service

& Shipping Corporation (John Reynolds had been begging me to return for some time), and be in a position effectively to block the plans of the Soviet Secret Police. The Russians are going to learn that here is one American they can't scare.

Repercussions were not long in coming. A few days later, I received a message that Al was coming to New York to see me—an unprecedented move on his part since he had always demanded that his contacts come to Washington. I had planted myself squarely in his way and he was obviously worried. As I hung up the telephone, I smiled. Well, the battle was on now and at least my opponent was somewhat off balance.

Yet there was another reason for my increasing optimism. The day after I had returned to the U.S. Service & Shipping Corporation as vice president, I had finally heard from the F.B.I., and after my lengthy conversation with the agent in the New York office, I felt very much relieved. Now, at last, I was no longer battling alone against the Soviet Secret Police; I was working side by side with the American government.

When I met Al that night in front of Bickford's restaurant on 23rd Street, he greeted me with a cordiality that was patently false. Here we go! I said to myself, praying silently that I would be able to keep up the proper pose. Forcing a smile, I advanced to meet him, my hand outstretched.

"Hello, Al," I said in what I hoped was a cheerful tone of voice. "It's good to see you."

Al, as usual, was hungry and steered me into the Cornish Arms Hotel across the street to have some supper. Then he suggested we stroll around a bit. He headed toward Ninth Avenue, and as we walked along, he started to tell me what a mistake I had made and how useful I was to the organization. When we reached the dock area of the Hudson River, I turned to go back, but Al stopped me.

"Let's walk along here," he said. "It's nice and private."

As I matched my steps to his, I found myself shivering in the grip of an almost uncontrollable terror. It was by then quite dark and the empty docks loomed up blackly, unbroken by a single light. The street, too, seemed deserted. In the oppressive silence our footsteps rang out. Could he know that I was working with the F.B.I., I wondered desperately. I hoped that the agents were somewhere close behind me, but I didn't dare look for fear I might tip off Al. I must have drawn an audible breath, for he looked at me curiously.

"What's the matter?" he asked. "You're shivering."

"Nothing," I answered hastily, "only it's so deserted down here. We could easily be attacked by thugs."

"Don't worry about that," he replied soothingly, "I'm an expert at jujitsu."

Far from reassuring me, this remark only made me more nervous.

At last we headed away from the river, and I drew a breath of relief. Then I realized Al was talking about the old problem of my being paid as an agent. Insistently he demanded that I take my back pay, which he said was piling up in Moscow. Just as firmly as I had in the past, I informed him I didn't want any salary and had no intention of taking any. We argued all the way to Fourth and Tenth Streets in the Village, until suddenly he stopped and turned to me, his face grim and set.

"Let's have no more nonsense about this," he said in a menacing voice. "I have $2,000 right here in my pocket.

[292]

It's part of your salary. You're going to take it now! If you don't, I shall be forced to the inescapable conclusion that you are a traitor!"

I started to refuse, then stopped myself. I had been told not to arouse Al's suspicions, and I must hold to that line. This is a showdown, I thought. If I don't accept the money, he will know that something is wrong. Much as it went against the grain to let the Russians think I could be bought, I must give that impression. I forced myself to smile lightly.

"Don't be silly, Al," I said, "of course I'm not a traitor. Come to think of it, I could use a little extra money. As a matter of fact, I must confess that I went back to the U.S. Service & Shipping Corporation because I needed cash. After all, it's time I began to think about myself."

His face relaxed and he looked at me with the gloating expression of a cat that has found the mouse walking into his grasp.

"Now you're being sensible. Why didn't you tell me before that you needed money? I would have given you all you asked for. You didn't have to ball things up and go back to your old job. It could have been handled very nicely, if I'd only known." He stopped and looked at me thoughtfully, then went on, "Oh, I understand—it's your stupid American pride. Well, forget it. Here's the money. Give me a receipt and we'll be square."

Out of his pocket he drew a long white envelope which contained $2,000 in the usual $20 bills. I tore off one corner, on which I wrote, "Received $2,000," added the date and my name, and handed the scrap of paper back to him. The envelope I tucked away carefully in my pocketbook.

Al, meanwhile, was regarding me with a satisfied expression. His face seemed to say: well, it's taken a long time to bring her to terms, but at last I've succeeded. I could see him rushing back to the Soviet Embassy in Washington and sending a jubilant cable to Moscow. Undoubtedly he thinks he will get a medal or an increase in rank for this achievement. Well, this time he is wrong—this time he is going to find out that it isn't wise to play around with Americans. The thought cheered me considerably. I was even able to shake hands with him cordially as we parted.

As quickly as possible I turned over the money to the F.B.I. The two agents with whom I was in contact counted and recounted the bills, then put them into a fresh envelope and initialed it. As one of them stowed it away in his pocket, he whistled softly.

"It's a lot of money," he said. "They must have plenty of it over there to spend."

As the fall wore on, I spent more and more time with the F.B.I., going over the information I had in my possession. There were many threads in my hands which, by themselves, might make no sense but, combined with other data, could weave a pattern. I had no idea what the F.B.I. men thought about me personally, nor did I know what my own fate was to be. I never asked them and they never volunteered the information. Oh well, I thought, that is really irrelevant. What is important is that I help smash the Soviet espionage machine.

In spite of this strange relationship, I liked the F.B.I. men. They were so very different from what I had expected. I remembered I had been quite sure they would beat me up and throw me into a dungeon. That, of course, was the notion every Communist had of the F.B.I. The Party propaganda had continually stressed the idea that it was

[294]

a merciless and inhuman organization. Instead, they were unfailingly courteous and considerate.

This pattern of behavior persisted during all our relationship. I discovered, too, that in other ways they were quite different from the Russians, and I began to be more and more impressed. The eyes of the Soviet Secret Police agents had always betrayed a terrible fear; despite their superficial arrogance, they had cringed like whipped dogs. Yet the faces of the F.B.I. agents, although they showed the strain of fatigue and tension, had none of this terror. Instead, they behaved like free men who were proud of the organization they worked for. The Russians, moreover, never seemed to work as a team. Under the merciless discipline and the inhuman competition, each agent had been out for himself; and, trying to claw his way up the ladder, he would disparage the efforts of his fellow workers, even going so far as to pass on vicious pieces of gossip about them. This was lacking in the F.B.I. To my great surprise I found that one agent would go out of his way to praise the efforts of another. I had been completely wrong about my own country. Here in the United States even government agents are very decent people.

One day the agent to whom I was talking left the room and soon returned, looking serious.

"Well, Elizabeth," he had said, sitting down in a chair, "now we come to the $64 question. Would you be willing to keep on going as you are now? It's important to us that you stay in the U.S. Service to keep it from falling into Soviet hands. With you in there, we can keep tabs on what is going on. Then, too, it's vital to keep in contact with the Russian Secret Police and also with the people you know

[295]

in the American Communist Party. Also, you should pick up Earl Browder again. Even though he's technically out of the Party, he's certainly not changed his ideas and we'd like to know what he's up to."

I looked back at him thoughtfully. I did want to get out of all this mess, but I couldn't leave with a clear conscience until every last tag end had been tied up.

"Of course," I agreed.

And so I continued outwardly to lead the same life as I had before, although I was working in close cooperation with the F.B.I. It was a difficult procedure, for I was continually on edge for fear my foot would slip and I would betray the whole scheme. Moreover, it was a complicated, fence-straddling position, dealing with three groups of Communists, plus the F.B.I. The American Communist Party officials must not know I was in contact with the Russians. Even more urgent was the fact that under no circumstances should they find out that I was dealing with Browder. Earl had been expelled from the Party back in June and it was *verboten* for any Communist to see him. If they discovered my connection with him, they would immediately denounce me as a traitor and the fat would be in the fire.

At first, I had thought future meetings with the F.B.I. would be difficult, but with a bit of maneuvering it worked out all right. For safety's sake, we generally met outside their office—or sometimes in a room in the Prince George Hotel, just around the corner from my office. Sometimes they picked me up in one of their cars and we rode around and talked. When it was necessary for me to go down to headquarters, they carefully sneaked me in the back door. Luckily, too, I had in the past accustomed my office to the fact that during the day I wandered out for appointments.

Now they found nothing extraordinary in my behavior, even though I took off half days, or even days, to work with the F.B.I.

On November 20 I had an appointment with Al in front of Bickford's cafeteria. Escorted by a contingent of F.B.I. men, I arrived late in the afternoon. Would he come, I wondered, as I had before, or by now has he been tipped off that all is not well? The minutes clicked by. I watched the F.B.I. men across the street changing positions. Then, twenty minutes later, I saw Al rushing kitty-corner across the street. I carefully advanced to meet him, my hand out.

"I'm sorry to be late," he said, trying to catch his breath. "I knew that one of the avenues in New York had been changed to the Avenue of the Americas, but I thought it was Eighth Avenue instead of Sixth. I waited in front of Bickford's on 23rd Street and Sixth Avenue for fifteen minutes, until suddenly I had the bright idea that possibly I was in the wrong place."

I glanced across the street. The F.B.I. agents were still there. I smiled happily at Al.

"I'm glad you got here," I said. "I was almost ready to leave."

Cavanagh's being only a half block away, I suggested we go there for coffee and talk. I asked him why the Russians had failed to pay the American Communist Party the $12,000 they had promised as the purchase price for U.S. Service. Lem Harris and Willie Weiner, I said, had been haunting me, demanding the cash. They, I added, had even insinuated that I had walked off with the money. Al looked cynically amused.

"We're not going to give them any cash. Moscow has decided it's an unnecessary expenditure. Why should we

[297]

spend any money on the business when we can get the American Party to carry the load?"

"Why don't you tell them so, then?" I asked.

He shrugged. "What's the use? They'll only raise a fuss and we'll have a lot of unnecessary trouble. Let it ride as it is."

The full cleverness of this scheme dawned on me. The Russian Secret Police wanted the business—but without paying for it. They didn't want difficulties with the American Communist Party, so they were going to say nothing and let it appear that I was at fault. So I was to be the goat!

"What's the idea of leaving me in the middle?" I demanded irately.

He looked at me as if he were savoring a very special joke.

"You're not. Just tell the Finance Committee that Earl Browder received the money from us before he was kicked out of the Party. That will settle the matter nicely."

"What a lovely mind you have, Al!" I said ironically.

Out on the street again, Al paused to light his cigarette with a gold lighter. After a moment, he held it out to me.

"Why don't you take this as a gift from me?" he inquired. "I notice that you don't have one of your own."

I shook my head. Cigarette lighters, I told him, didn't appeal to me—they were never in working order when you needed them. Then with half-hysterical amusement I noticed a few feet away from us was parked an F.B.I. car, with two agents inside. Luckily, Al had his back turned and couldn't see, and I hoped my face revealed nothing.

As we walked down Eighth Avenue, he discussed my future. I should stay with the firm temporarily, he said, yet it was quite possible that very soon he would need me back in undercover work. I didn't know whether to be glad or sorry at this pronouncement. Undoubtedly I could be of great help to the F.B.I. if I went back in, but on the other hand everything in me revolted at the idea. Al shook hands ceremoniously on parting.

"Nothing much is going to happen for the next two months, I think," he said. "So I won't see you again until January 20. In the meantime, if I need to see you, I'll call your office—pretend that I'm a Mr. Alberg who is interested in sending packages to Sweden. That will mean we will meet the same day at Bickford's at the usual time."

Walking home, I wondered just what Al's position was in this country. All I knew at that time was that he was a high-up official in the Soviet Embassy. I had identified his picture in the F.B.I. photo gallery but the agents, although undoubtedly sensing my interest, had not offered to tell me anything. It was, indeed, some time later on—in the spring of 1947—that I finally learned who he was. With amusement I found that he was indeed a high-up Soviet official—he was Anatol Gromov, the First Secretary of the Russian Embassy! Today he is the head of the Russian Trade Mission in Japan.

As Christmas time drew near, I wondered what to do about Earl Browder. If I was to keep up the pretense that I was still working for the Russians, I must produce a present. Unfortunately, I could not ask Al about it, for he was, and must remain, unaware that I had any connection with Earl. I took my predicament to the F.B.I.

"I think I'll go out and buy him a bottle of Scotch whiskey, and Raïssa a bottle of imported cognac. The only thing is that they're very hard to find. There seems to be a shortage," I said.

The agents looked at me and laughed.

"Don't bother, Elizabeth," they said. "We'll provide the liquor. This Christmas Earl Browder will have a present from the United States government!"

Armed with the package, I went up to Earl's office. As before, he sat disconsolately in a chair, halfheartedly leafing through some papers. I walked over to him and held out my bundle.

"Merry Christmas, Earl," I said quietly.

His face lighted up for a moment and he looked pathetically grateful. He thought the Russian Secret Police had sent that present. More than the value involved, it spelled the fact that perhaps he was not completely in the doghouse. It was too bad I had to fool him like this, but after all he was my enemy. Much as I pitied him, I knew that Earl Browder was too hardened a revolutionary to desert Moscow. Some of the old life came back into his face as he looked up at me.

"I'll get back up there some day. This position I'm in is only temporary. Moscow will need me again. I'll be useful to them." He paused for a moment and then went on savagely, "Anyway, it's all the fault of my old enemy Foster. Ever since I displaced him, he's been waiting for a chance to stick a knife in me. And look at him—what is he? Just a half-crazy old fool who has spent most of his life in and out of mental institutions. He hasn't the brains to run the Party!"

"If Foster doesn't run the Party, who does?" I asked.

"Gene Dennis, of course," he said venomously. "He's the brains behind Foster and the rest of them. He's a smart guy —he's just using Foster for his own purposes."

Then I remembered how, every time I had gone to Communist headquarters to visit Earl, I had had to pass Dennis's office, which was just across the hall—in an excellent position to watch what was going on. His door was always open; he would sit there motionless with all the savage intentness of a cat watching a mouse hole, and his expression as he stared at Earl's office seemed to say: "Some day, brother, you'll be out and I'll be in there."

On January 20 I went over to Bickford's to keep my appointment with Al, but although I waited for almost three quarters of an hour, he didn't show up. I wondered what had happened to him. Could it be that by now he was suspicious of me? It didn't seem likely. I had been very careful, and certainly his previous actions hadn't indicated any alarm. What I didn't then know was that Al was no longer in the country but had been sent back home earlier that month. His departure, as it later turned out, was the result of the now-famous Canadian spy case, which made sensational headlines during 1946.

By now I knew the F.B.I. believed my story. And they trusted my motives completely. One agent finally told me that every detail of the information they had been able to check had turned out to be absolutely accurate. This, as also the fact that we were working together so closely, increased my good relations with them and we were in constant telephonic communication. Fortunately Jack Reynolds had a private wire in his office, and since he was still with the Army, I was able to use it and not go through the company switchboard. Besides this, I saw them several times a week—checking on information and sometimes even going on surveillances to identify people I had known. These tailing jobs were rugged affairs and I would reach home at night completely worn out. The agents, themselves haggard with fatigue, would look at me sympathetically. One of them remarked that on a two-week detail like this he had lost ten pounds.

Once I remember that, in the process of trying to identify one of my old contacts, Margaret, we were parked in a car on a street in the nineties, around the corner from Riverside Drive. Suddenly two agents, who had been stationed in front of her house, dashed madly up to us with the news that she had just taken a cab for Grand Central Station. In a flash they jumped into the back seat, one on each side of me, the driver stepped on the gas, and away we went. It was one of those wild rides that you see only in the movies. Had I not been wedged firmly between the two agents, I most certainly would have landed on the floor. Through Central Park we flew, rounding corners on two wheels, and arrived at Grand Central Station a good five minutes or so before our quarry.

In midspring, Earl Browder suddenly announced to me that he was going to Moscow. Undoubtedly, he said, they wanted him over there, because they had given him a visa and made arrangements for him to cross the border. Jack Reynolds, on hearing of this, wanted to see Earl. Intourist had again decided that they would not give us an exclusive contract the following fall, and he thought that Earl could intervene to persuade them. Although I knew that Intourist would not yield unless the Soviet Secret Police intervened, which they would not do unless they had plans for the business, I decided to let Jack carry out his idea. In this way, I would be able to check up and find out what the Soviet Secret Police were up to. Earl, when approached, was delighted with the idea. Although his trip to Moscow was being financed by his old friend A. A. Heller, who had not

only left the Party together with him but had been support-
ing him ever since, Earl could always use more cash and he
hoped that Jack would give him a handout.

When Earl finally returned from Moscow, he looked
jaunty and self-assured. Doubtless he had made his peace
with the powers that be, because the old look of fear had
been replaced by an almost arrogant expression. Happily he
showed me a copy of a signed contract that appointed him
sole agent for the sale of Soviet publications in the United
States. Now, he said, he wouldn't have to go back to writing his "old newsletter."

"Then you'll have to return the subscribers' money," I
said.

He shook his head and said he didn't think that that could
be managed. What a racket, I thought. His subscribers pay
the immense sum of $100 for a year's subscription and then
only get a few issues. Nor did I see how he could eke out a
living under the terms of the new contract, which paid him
only a small commission on books actually sold, since the
market for Soviet publications was not a large one. He
shrugged his shoulders.

"I know it's going to be tough. I can only make something if they send over another best seller like *Quiet Flows
the Don*."

Meanwhile, the F.B.I. asked if I would get in touch with
one or two of my old Communist contacts in Washington
and see what was going on in the apparatus. It was, I knew,
a somewhat risky procedure—like sticking my head into
the lion's mouth—but I agreed to try. So, on my next business trip to Washington, I telephoned Helen Tenney. To
my surprise, her voice was friendly, even relieved, and she
agreed to have cocktails with me the following evening.

I approached Pierre's, where I was to meet her, with a sinking feeling in my heart. How did I know I wasn't walking into a trap? Casually I entered, found a table, then sat down, wondering if, when she arrived, my knees would have stopped shaking. Just as I had almost given up hope that she would show up, Helen came through the door and, after looking furtively around her, sat down opposite me. She looked thinner and more tired, and in her eyes was that old look of fear I had known so well.

"I didn't know whether or not I should come," she said in a low voice. "You see, the F.B.I. are after me."

I stiffened in my chair and stared at her. Across the room two personable young agents were sipping cocktails and seemingly paying no attention to us. Could she have discovered them, I wondered. But she was rushing on, glad to get the worry off her chest.

"I haven't seen any of them behind me," she said earnestly, "but they came to my house in New York and made inquiries of our chauffeur. Of course, he told Mother and she told me." She paused for a moment and looked at me with a pathetic eagerness. "I'm so glad you've come. After I lost my contact a few months back, I've been sitting and worrying, thinking that something must be wrong."

A sick sense of revulsion swept over me. She was coming to me in the expectation of finding a friend, and instead I was her enemy. I can't go on with this, I thought desperately. She and I were comrades together, and I can't fool her this way. Then I steadied myself. It had to be done, and perhaps in the process I could get her out of the mess she was in.

"You'll be in contact with me from now on, won't you?" she asked anxiously.

That would be best, I decided. She had been dropped by the N.K.V.D., it was true, but from what she said, she was in a most confidential government position and they might easily try to pick her up again.

"I'll take care of you from now on, Helen," I said. "But don't do anything about bringing me information for a while. It wouldn't be wise, with the F.B.I. after you. Try and forget all about that now."

I continued to see Helen until she lost her position in Washington and returned to New York. Thank God, I thought, now she's out of the government and probably no longer useful to the Russians.

By the fall of 1946 I was sure the Soviet Secret Police would not renew our exclusive contract with Intourist. Not only had Earl Browder made this point abundantly clear, but Intourist itself confirmed this impression. Moreover, from Browder I learned that they wanted Reynolds to go in person to Moscow. Apparently I had succeeded in influencing him too much for their purposes. Once in Moscow, wined and dined, he would be theirs without interference.

Reynolds, who had left the Army in June, was uncertain what he wanted to do about the matter. Definitely the business was flourishing, and he was unwilling to abandon it under such circumstances, yet he didn't particularly care to go over to Moscow. Back and forth he vacillated, while the F.B.I. and I held our breaths. One day he was sure that under no circumstances would he budge out of the United States, the next he was all set to start out, taking his wife and me along.

"What shall I do?" I asked my F.B.I. contact despairingly.

"Try and dissuade him from going," he replied. "If he gets in the hands of those people over there, heaven knows what will happen. And obviously you can't go along. It's not safe." And then half seriously, half amusedly, "With your penchant for getting into the middle of things, you'd probably start World War III."

While all this was going on, Jack and Grace Reynolds and I went down to Washington to see Ernest C. Ropes, the head of the United States Commerce Department's Russian division—a kindly old gentleman who was sincerely interested in bettering trade relations between the United States and the Soviet Union.

"I hope you'll continue on with your operations," he said to Jack and me that morning in his office, "and in the event that you do, you should be very sure that you are complying with the rules and regulations of the United States government. You've never registered as Agents of a Foreign Principal, but I think you'd better check up on that ruling while you're down here. I'll ring up a friend of mine in the Foreign Agents' Registration Division of the Department of Justice and you can go over and see him."

This was an unexpected development and a highly dangerous one. Obviously the Department of Justice shouldn't give a clean bill of health to the U.S. Service & Shipping Corporation. If its officials knew the true facts, they most assuredly wouldn't, yet I didn't know if they had been tipped off by the F.B.I. or not.

Hearing Mr. Ropes make the appointment for early that afternoon, I wondered frantically how to get out and make a telephone call.

"You go to lunch, Jack," I said; "I have an errand to do."

He looked surprised but said nothing as I hastily left. My knees were shaking as I dialed long distance. It seemed like years, but finally I heard the voice of the agent in charge. Rapidly I told him what had happened, whereupon his voice came reassuringly.

"Don't worry," he said. "We'll get word through to Washington. We've got two hours on it."

The two men across the conference table from us that afternoon were, I was sure, not F.B.I. men. The tenor of their conversation, too, made me wonder whether or not the message had gone through. The minutes clicked by and I began to get more nervous. Then the door opened and a third man walked in and casually sat down. I took a good, hard look at him and then relaxed. It was all right now!

From then on the conversation took a more constructive trend. Although nothing was said that would tip Jack off, he squirmed uneasily under some of the searching questions. At the end the Department of Justice men were noncommittal. We would have to file papers and then they would see.

"Why didn't you come to my assistance when they were badgering me so?" Jack asked, as we were riding back in a taxi.

"You were doing all right," I replied.

But I felt heartsick. I had tried to detach him and as many comrades as I could. There was no more that I could do. I sensed that the Department of Justice would soon take action, and though I longed to warn him I knew, aside from the fact I was under orders not to, it would be unsafe for me to do so.

Before the year was out I was summoned before a special

federal grand jury in New York. I spent two weeks testifying. Then agonizing months passed, during which I was called back repeatedly to clean up various points.

By late winter I became definitely alarmed. The situation had reached an acute stage. The Communists had by now learned that I had talked. Either they had put two and two together from the leaks that were coming out in the press, or some of the witnesses called by the grand jury had compared notes and decided I was the only one who knew that particular combination of facts. I began to receive mysterious telephone calls at all hours of day and night and threatening letters. I began to wonder just how much longer I could hold out under this terrible strain without any friends to confide in.

But then, bewilderingly, things happened in rapid fire. The grand jury brought in indictments against the eleven Communists who composed the so-called Politburo of the American Communist Party. The following day the New York *World-Telegram* commenced to publish the substance of my story. Two days later the telephone rang. An investigator for the Committee on Un-American Activities wanted to have dinner with me. William Rogers of the Senate Investigating Committee landed on my doorstep with a subpoena. It seemed he was investigating William Remington.

Four days later, when the reporters got hold of my name, pandemonium broke loose. The story was splashed over the front pages of the newspapers in the most lurid terms. Reporters, unable to find me, haunted my hotel in Brooklyn, called my friends and relatives, even visited my office. Disgustedly I read the newspapers and added them to the stack on the floor and wished I had never gone to the F.B.I.

[308]

I hadn't realized the story would make such a stir. From now on I would be a notorious person—the "Red Spy Queen." Would there ever be any peace for me from now on?

Then followed days of testifying, with flash bulbs popping, newsreel cameras grinding, and television! I resented it all and even the guards that suddenly appeared. But after days of strain I became grateful for them. At least I had someone to talk to.

I had expected that, soon after my revelations became public, the Communist Party would start a campaign of smears and slander. And I was not wrong. The *Daily Worker* itself didn't dare touch the story beyond such indirect comments as: "They call her the blonde spy queen, but her hair's really a dirty brown." But the Communist Party, via its transmission belt of fellow travelers and misguided "liberals," promptly sent out a barrage, including a story that I had spent some time in a mental institution. One day, I remember, Robert Stripling, chief investigator of the Committee on Un-American Activities, looked up from the phone with a frown on his face.

"That's the A.P.," he said worriedly. "They want to know if you were ever in an insane asylum."

"When do they say I was in it?" I asked and, given the approximate dates, I started to laugh. "That's the time when I was spending most of my hours with the F.B.I. That's certainly an institution, and if they want to call it mental, it's their privilege."

But it really wasn't funny. And as time went on, it got less so. The San Francisco police found on the Golden Gate Bridge a woman's clothes, her handbag, and a letter addressed to "E.T.B.," the initials which I always used on my interoffice correspondence. The letter started "Dear Elizabeth" and was obviously intended for me. It was a long, incoherent epistle, stating in substance that because I had betrayed her, she had taken her baby girl and jumped off the bridge. I didn't know anyone in California—let alone a woman with a child—and I told the wire services so. Not long afterward the San Francisco police found it was all a hoax.

But the worst ordeal of all was sitting in the Committee hearing room and watching my old comrades as they testified. Those who were obviously still convinced Communists stood firmly on their constitutional grounds and refused to talk. Not only were they silent when they were asked about Communist Party membership and espionage activities, but they would not answer such simple questions as: "Were you ever in Union Station?" or "Have you ever played tennis?" for fear they might be trapped. It was, of course, a dead giveaway, for honest men do not behave that way. Others, who I believed were now out of the Party, evidently couldn't bring themselves to admit their guilt. Their pride seemed to hold them back from admitting they had ever done any wrong. They slid and slithered around the questions, trying to exculpate themselves, meanwhile insinuating that I was a "neurotic" and "drank too much."

As I listened to person after person, I felt sick. There's Lud Ullman, I thought; he's my age, yet he looks like an old man, burned out and hollow eyed. Over there is Greg Silvermaster, a shell of a man. As my eyes wandered over all of them, I felt a terrible sadness.

And then pictures more poignant came to me, pictures of other comrades who had been smashed by the Soviet machine. There was Helen Tenney. "She tried to commit suicide," said my F.B.I. man gently, "but it didn't work. She's in Psycho—at New York Hospital. She clammed up on the psychiatrist, but you may be able to help, because her only response has been to someone mentioning 'Russian Bank,' which sent her into hysterics." When I finally saw her, she looked pathetically grateful and kept repeating proudly, "I never talked. I never talked!"

And Caroline Klein. A life-long worker in the Russian wing of the American party, she had known Yasha for a number of years, and when he died, she and I had become great friends. When Caroline discovered she had developed cancer of the liver and had, at most, four months to live, the Party decided she was of no further use to them. Her telephone calls to erstwhile comrades were left unanswered. Alone in her four-flight walk-up apartment, she lay in agony without friends. At that time I was working with the F.B.I., but I could not bear to see her suffer alone like that. Every few days I would go up to see her—bringing small gifts of fruit and flowers and hoping some of her old comrades would come. But they never did. Bewildered, disillusioned, cursing the Party, yet still held in the iron grip of Communist ideology, she died.

Then I no longer felt sad. I was angry with a great cleansing anger.

And now I looked again at these people before me in the Committee Room. They are spiritually dead, I thought with sudden and final release. But I am alive and I can speak for them, for all those whom I have left behind—those lost ghosts that have died for an illusion. Telling their story and mine, I will let the decent people of the world know what a monstrous thing Communism is.

[311]